I0153146

CAN YOU PRAY?

We Are All Here To Seek The Way

By

Ruth Lee, Scribe

ISBN: 978-1-934509-95-1

Love Your Life

Love Your Life Publishing
Wilmington, DE

Contents

Reviews:

Ruth Lee has channeled a wealth of information for the transformation of those on the planet at this time. Can You Pray? is the spiritual alchemist's bible, offering formulas for self-revelation and personal transmutation. The Teachers who speak through Ms. Lee are sometimes witty, other times stern in their advice to the Group, but the wisdom they bring is an undeniable resource in the scope of our changing times.

Carole J. Obley, author and teacher of Spiritual Development seminars, and a Certified Medium and graduate of Delphi University.

~~~~~

Inspirational!

In this book, many soul-searching questions are brought to the surface, such as, Why am I here? Where will I go when I die? Teachers from other dimensions come to Earth to deliver wisdom and enlightenment to the human race.

Freddie Cecchini, The Business Minister, Creating Soul In Your Business, Making Life Easier, Certified by Deepak Chopra in Primordial Sound Meditation.

~~~~~

Published in the Spring of 2003, this is the printed version of a series of channeled sessions that occurred in 1997. Pittsburgh native Ruth Lee, sat with a physical group of individuals as she conversed with a Spirit group of teachers, some who have lived on Earth before, some from far-flung planets and some who refused to give up any personal information lest more attention be given to the messenger than the message. This ethereal group provided a blueprint for exploration into the deeper questions of life, and at the same time asking, "What if we had the ability to create our own reality?"

Ruth spoke and typed at the same time. When finished, the physical group were given the computer files and were asked to collectively produce the book, a task in which they were put to the test of implementing the knowledge of Truth presented in the book to create the book—an interesting way to prove the validity of it's teachings and of their integration into the consciousness of those who witnessed their acquisition.

This is a book rich in eternal truths and presented in an "old world" style of language that does much to communicate the rich wisdom expressed during channeled sessions.

Point Of Light Magazine

Acknowledgements:

The Lee Way Publishers would like to express our love and gratitude to everyone who participated with us in this unusual experience. Every person whose name appears in the book was present in the room with us at some point if only for a brief moment in time. They experienced the same flow of energy as those who were there to see the assignment through to completion. We want to thank all of them for their love and continued support of the work.

More Books By Ruth Lee

Other Books of Wisdom From
The Teachers of the Higher Planes

The Work Begins
The Art of Life - Living Together in Harmony
Now is The Time
The World of Tomorrow
Bliss is It!

The Word of The Maya
The Making of a Scribe ~ How to Achieve a Life
You Can Write About

Novels by Ruth Lee

Angel of The Maya
Within The Veil: An Adventure In Time
Writing In Spirit ~ Jeanne's Story
Writing In Spirit Workbook
Writing In Spirit Notebook
A Timeless Life ~ Maddie's Story

Prelude to the Work

Spiritual Teachers arrived from another dimension and worked through spiritual channel, Ruth Lee, Scribe. These entities known as The Teachers of the Higher Planes made it clear that they had never lived on Earth themselves, but had been sent here to help humans prepare to ascend at the end of their lives. They and other spiritual teachers and a small group of human volunteers assembled during a series of sessions in which these transmissions were delivered through Ruth Lee as she worked in trance.

Some teachers who had previously lived on Earth were known to the group as saints, some were individuals whom we did not recognize by name, and others who refused to identify themselves because they felt it was egotistical to seek recognition or fame by being named.

These transmissions are the basis for the book 'Can You Pray'.

When the manuscript was completed, Ruth Lee released it to the group and offered her editing services, if needed. She retained the right to veto and prevent it from being printed should she disagree with the way this spiritual work was produced. She remains steadfast in her refusal to accept any benefit from the sale of the manuscript.

This is an overview of what happened in 1997

A group of volunteers sat with Ruth Lee and closely observed her as she rapidly typed and simultaneously read aloud messages being channeled from another realm. As she did this work, a dimension far beyond anything we had ever experienced before opened to us each time we met with her. We were given a rare opportunity to listen and learn about life as taught by spiritual beings way beyond our comprehension.

For most sessions, we sat silently in a balanced grouping so as to maintain a grid of electromagnetic energy needed by The Scribe to do this work. The volunteers had one prerequisite to meet: each had to be able to sit silently, at peace, in deep meditation for at least an hour. If not, they could not participate since Ms. Lee usually typed rapidly and read aloud for at least that length of time. Without a group, she would not have been able to ' pull in ' the diverse groups of teachers sent to help humans ascend at the end of their life plan. We truly sat at the feet of Masters.

The group experienced some problems remaining totally still as Ms. Lee united the energies of The Teachers of the Higher Planes with teachers who once lived and continue to teach on Earth today. Each member of the group sat directly opposite another person, paying no attention to anyone else in the room. Silence was easily maintained because of the awe felt by each person and the power of this inter-dimensional communication.

We watched Ruth's fingers fly across the keys as she took dictation from unseen beings, her voice changing as each entity arrived in our time. Energy moved through the room and we each felt it differently. Some felt heat circling in front of their faces and others felt temperature changes in the room, while some smelled roses and other perfumes.

When the manuscript was complete, Ruth Lee turned it over to the group to produce. The first test for us was to use the wisdom we gained from the book while preparing it for publication. Did we understand the wisdom well enough to apply it to our own lives? Would we be able to teach and preach the words? If we could not, the book would revert back to Ruth Lee to be produced by someone other than this group.

While editing and studying the wisdom within the pages, we succumbed to ego and flights of fancy and we began to see flaws within ourselves. It became even more apparent as we worked in a not so cooperative group to see the project through. We just didn't get it! We gave into all kinds of power struggling craziness within the group such as you see in everyday life. We thought we knew better, but within a few years, the group fell apart and never did revive as they once were.

One member of the group refused to let this amazing work die on the vine and took it into production with the help of Ruth Lee.

The Group:

This group came together, seemingly by a random turn of events. We thought we met quite by accident, but found, we had worked together in other lifetimes and were back to give it another try. Did we succeed? We think we did. We are a group of people from many walks of life, some in business, some employed and some who are neither. Who we are is not important. However, we are a reflection of you and the world we live in now.

Note to Reader:

Ruth Lee works as a scribe and channel who receives messages from the realm she calls the Holy Spirit. The text, "Can You Pray?" as she received it, has a certain 'old world' flair to the language used by those who came through to her during these extraordinary sessions. In the interest of retaining the uniqueness of this particular experience and to allow the work to flow as it was given, the Lee Way editors have not altered in any significant way the text witnessed being channeled directly to print by Ms. Lee.

The manuscript was given to the group assembled at Ruth's home and later formed the Lee Way Publishers to produce it in book form. All were warned before this work began not to rearrange sentences, paragraphs, and words in an egotistical attempt to satisfy what was personally believed to be the standards of modern English. As it was given—it remains. The following is an example of the prose.

> "When the lines of a page are all the same, are you able to see inside the work you have to do? You do not see things easily if we line up the words vertically, so we horizontally work with you."
>
> "What can we be teaching if we cannot use a word correctly, or are we deliberately trying to make you analyze what you see"?

CAN YOU PRAY?

We Are All Here
To Seek The Way

An inter-dimensional dialogue that communicates fundamental information about life, and living successfully on Earth at this time. The Teachers of the Higher Planes, saints, and others join a group of human individuals to explore a new way of teaching and sharing wisdom from a world beyond what we know now.

Scribed by
Ruth Lee

CHAPTER 1

There Is No More To Life Than This, But You May Believe Whatever You Wish.

Today is the day and any other day is just a wish. You will begin this day to see that there is a way to be, and that day is exactly like this: You feel like you are. You do what you like.

You do not decide enough now what to do with life, so you let life take you and leave you out. You will not do that now. You will aspire no longer. You will decide. You will ignite or sputter out.

The candle of life is brief and not sweet if you never use the heat, so be sure to do what you need and want to believe and then proceed. If you hesitate for long, the path is closed and may never open in this life. You are who decides what to widen and what to leave, so move forward and let the path close behind you so that the pressure will explode and make you move forward at a faster rate than you would otherwise move.

Yes, this is a book about the time and why many who have lived and moved on would come back for you and try to help you. You will notice that there are many who speak as one, but there are three who will be remembered as the main speakers. You will know them by name and reputation from the time when they were upon this plane, but the actual teaching remains in the same vein. The Teachers of the Higher Planes remain and will be in the work, but so will Francis Assisi, Francis Xavier and Sister Theresa of the fame of never going long to school. You will know all of them by name, but you will not judge the work they do. You are why they strive to remove the boundaries of being in another higher plane and yet remain among you.

Many work daily with each of the three Saints and they strive to teach all who call upon them now, but there is only so much time. You all are gathered into the time line and asked to regain the value of your own mind, but if you cannot, you will not have to go or remain. It is your own mind game. Decide and then go or remain.

Within the week from the time you begin to work with these three and the Teachers of the Higher Planes, you will either grow or remain the same behind the scenes. It is your right to never proceed. It is also your denial of life that causes you pain. Death is not to be grieved and life is not a procession of tasks that have no meaning. You are who sets the pace and commits the acts that lead you to onerous tasks, and if you believe otherwise, you are not wise.

Think of the work of who you are. Are you wise or are you just another pair of legs, arms and eyes? You may not have all three of these pairs working today in the usual way, but in some sense you are alive and can use them. You will know why, but now it is time to supervise the work of the group who are here to help you. Why? We need a level field of energy in which to meet. If there were a grid on Earth large enough to support others, we would meet in the middle of Chichen Itza with Ruth and find the work that the world is to do, but there is no such group and one will not be available until there is, so we meet like this with such a fragile mood of women and men who are not yet able to comprehend the delicacy of this room and why they are here to work with Ruth or should we say, work for Ruth?

You may not know Ruth Lee, but she is not here for history. She is a teacher of renown in this plane and is known in many towns, but now she is the Scribe and alive to the need to be as good as she can be. We have helped to develop Ruth Lee from another who was once unable to do this, but her needs were few and her character strong and able to be made elastic enough to conduct electricity of such a high intensity that she is able to now withstand the entrance of three who were once on Earth, plus the emergence of four teachers who never were on Earth.

You will find that Francis Xavier is the most diplomatic of the group and the four who have never emerged into the Earth plane are less and less tolerant of the blame humans love to use to focus on others rather than on their own blame in the pain they suffer. You will find that Theresa is a polite and gentle flame who is never so dominant as she is patient and kind and withstands the impatience of the others who are more educated in ways, but less understanding of human pain.

Francis Assisi is the most developed Saint ever because he left God and returned and delivered his mind and body like no other sinner, but he is not the only one who is in this work. There is another who refuses to commit to the work and work within the framework with the others. He is a saint by name and a disciple by fame, but chooses that no one know his name. He is a very large saint and will not be blamed for choosing to remove the pride that he believes others have in being named by penitents and petitioners over and over. You will know his name, but Peter is not the one who is going to work with you. He is another fisherman and his crew was not as stable as the church that Peter built. He never denied his Lord or any other, but he is not going to remain silent when he is able to gain energy enough to fill out the group.

The three, plus one who will float through, will join the group of improbable, but wondrous teachers who come from beyond you in outer space. You will look to the Pleiades, but the Pleiades is not quite that way. When the sky is open to you, look through the Pleiades and see beyond that place into deep space. You will be able to sense then the probabilities of one.

The possibility that you are more than one is not a proposition for superstitious ones, but it is usually adopted by those who are not happy as they are. You will find more and more are able to open to the belief that there is life in other provinces other than Earth, but most still cannot believe in a second or third birth. You will. We promise.

This is the beginning of the first chapter and you will all know who is going to write and who is going to ignite the work, but begin by breathing in your own oxygen and breathing for everyone. Yes, you can read and breathe, so let us all join now in a celebration of life!

When the world is open, and that happens so seldom that we cannot come to you, we work on opening the few who zoom through. You will know when it happens to you. You can zoom into the stratosphere and wait there or you can go beyond and work for the old you to catch the next wave and carry you through to the bigger part of what you are to do—meet You and work to do what YOU tells you to do.

The simplistic way of today and the simple past are some of the ways you talk to you about facts that do not seem to be true, but you will learn what to do—regardless of the work you came to do.

Think of the work of Ruth. Think. Are you able to type and write and not be upset about that which is not what you always thought were true? Are you able to just write and not erase what you do not like? You are not a scribe if you do. You may be a writer and able to do much, but only a scribe would be entrusted with the work of prophets and others who are not here to make a profit. You are, but none of these is here to please or make money from you or others in an effort to advise you on what you already know to be—thee.

Thee is a name we will use from time to time to define the sublime you and what you came here to do. Do you feel that you have time? Do you wonder who is ahead of you? Are you worried that you might not be able to float and fly away when the end of time comes to you? Why not try to ascend long before the end? You can attempt it and do your tests and be ready for the end. You will not actually ascend until the time comes to you and ends, but you can be ready for it and not anxiously regret that you did not live.

When you work for the ascension of man, you are not ascending again and again? Why not? You work on the work you are and what you grew within you, but others are also able to do whatever you do. You may be 'gifted' and thus able to do more than another may do, but your gift will be revoked if you never use it for the purpose given to you—to help you ascend.

The fixture you are and the moveable machine that may be are still not useable until you add the will. If you never do use your own free will, what is to become of you? You will return to use it over and over until you do know what to do with it. Is this the age or the time of your life? You will find that it is if you are willfully pursuing You and doing what YOU told you to do—be you and fulfill all the assignments you came to Earth to do.

You will know forever that this is a clever bunch of images and you are not the only computers who have no brains to use when the time to emerge from Earth is there for you and you arrange to ascend and leave your brain behind. Your mind never is there at the end, so you need not be so upset that some of you leave it behind long before you are ready to leave the world. You are only pretending to be there. You are still scared about floating away from Mother Earth. If you can advance your life one stair at a time, you will be there, but some of you try to stop time and that is not going to work.

You will form a line? Why? Who cares who arrives? We are all there!

The time and lines are all fixations of the mind. There is no such thing as a line or time in the higher acts of work that you must prepare to complete at this time, so let us all forget them now.

The reason we write on a computer is because it is faster and the waves of light let us all ignite and write with less energy than if the pen or quill were used at this time. The speech you admire in some is so cumbersome that the words are over long and not able to express the entire essence of the meaning of time and loneliness and what you do that is not good for you or others, but when you are able, we will continue.

There is a break in the line in order to accept that some of you will leave to do mundane chores from time to time, and we want you to conclude that there is a time to move away and a time to stay with us all the way.

If you break up a room by leaving when the speaker is about to announce an important meeting, some never know what you did for them by breaking up the sound and others are unable to remember it for days. Please do not leave this book lying around.

Read and seek and then proceed? No, you will read and, indeed, work inside to do all the things that are not in your head. When the head is unable to face the work, it usually will break down and not work, but the spirit is going to work.

You will know when you are un-spirited. It is a hopeless feeling that comes when you forget that you are descended from the God of All and believe you need a friend on Earth. You will proceed. Now, go to the next page.

Please refrain from being upset over anyone, but those who choose to remain are not here to linger or to give pain. You will not upset the group, but the teachers are not going to remain. You have to do more if you want to be represented in this domain.

Thank you all for your patience and understanding and that is all. We will call up and find out if the hall is a problem at all. You will move up if it is, but otherwise the group can sit as is.

The time and energy are so much a part of this work that if you feel that you cannot work with us, that is okay to do, but do not be upset. You cannot do anything by yourself if you are a member of a group, and this is a group and that is why we are here with you. We do not wish to work with only Ruth if we can pursue more work with you as a group, but if it is hard and you cannot do it for you, please do not fret. It is not easy to do. There is a person who is now able to heal. We will help you to place your spine in a line and it will be just fine.

You are all here to do more and more for your own line of ascent and we want you to not disappear at the end of the evening, but if you have to leave, please agree that it is with the permission of the group when you do leave.

You have to see that there is harmony and not a degree that is required of thee. If you cannot combine energy within you at this time, no one else is going to be able to harmonize as well within them, too. You are all now combining into a single "line" or two, which you will find combines all of you over time. There is not a problem. There is a situation where a mind is confused, and that is okay, too.

You will find that the soul is okay, but the mind does not wish to be confined today. She is okay. You will send a list of things that you will be able to do now, but it is not okay to speak today. You will all sit and do whatever you wish, but do nothing to stop the work. Now, the way is open. The way is clean.

We will announce the disappearance of the air that was so in despair and we will now create a life that is not in existence anywhere. The life of a group that is about to unite and work with a group who are already able to talk and educate the group, but not willing to unless there are more of you willing to work within you.

You have to see that some are not progressing by degree but are very well endowed naturally and only now beginning to see. You will all be expected to open your own life and inspect it over and over and over, week after week if you are to be here. You will not be allowed to hurt your own fate by being late and not able to work in this room all the time you are here with Ruth. We will begin soon. The room is not ready yet.

The room is now stable and there is a bit of labor to it, but that is going to help you. Please refrain from sitting and staring and not doing whatever you wish inside your own brain. You can work or sit or do nothing, but if you can meditate and work it so that the meditation flows, you can ignite all that is inside of you. Why not use this night to work on your inner life? Now, let us proceed.

This is a class and not a classic case history. You will find that several men and women at this time are alive to the work inside and we will bend and work with them and for you who are not able to believe, this is okay today, but you will leave. You will not fight in any way the work you do today. Let us proceed to the end of the lesson today.

What did you learn? You learned patience and honesty. You learned not to look down on your own energy so much by seeing the lack of discipline and the loss of energy when one is unable to do what she truly would love to do. You, too, can do more, but your own body is not able to use any excuse. But, you do. You constantly confuse others with what you think of you.

You will not advise any one else tonight on what to do, so you amaze you. You truly do think that counseling others means you tell them what to do. We are shocked, but that is what two people we watched try to do. What do you think of you to be able to tell someone else what to do? Your will power is not the same as your life, but your life is full of will and power and very much going to help you now to learn what to do when another comes to you with a problem and asks you to solve it for her now.

You do not have any power to seek out the other. You are not able to say a word today, so you could suggest that you pray or you could say that you do not know what they should do, but that is not what your ego would love to do.

The ego wants to say and do whatever it can today to tell others what to do and how to live and when to give up on a person in some way. You cannot know. You do not even forgive your own body today, so you cannot know what is in another who is unable to walk in your path today. You will not know why you are so unique and yet the same as all others are on Earth today.

You will find that if your mind is unearthed in an urn someday, it will burn. It is liquid and oxygen and not very much else, but the mind is not able to last until the end of the time. Your mind is here to remind you what to do to stay on your own line of ascent and to be on time if you really do mind being in a group that does not work unless the room is full and able to do more with you.

You will find that this writing is flawed a bit and it is caused by some not being able to fit, but as the group fits into one and moves beyond the thought of anyone, the room fits and the work begins and you know why you are here within it.

You are to be full of energy and able to fit into your own work, but you cannot commit. You seek others and then you reject them if they do not like you. Is that a pain for them? It is for you, so stop and look and be sure before you commit. You are who is going to be hurt if you do not.

If you commit your life to work, you work for it and keep it and do not submit to others who never work at all, but if you do not care to work, you can leave it and never feel that you lost much by doing it.

When the unique and weird and zany and scary come near you in a crowd or on the street and you can move, you generally will duck behind someone who is larger than you. Why? You do not know? You realize that there are others who are stronger and armed and able to take care of anyone who is alarming to you. Don't you?

You feel better being told that angels come flying to rescue you, but do you know for sure? Are you able to know who you are, too?

You know, but you do not seem to be upset that the inner you is not always aligned within you to what you know and you often are unable to show what you know, so you often feel proud of you when you are not doing anything at all for you, and upset when you are being blessed by you. What is wrong?

You. You have to upset you to grow or so it would appear to most who observe you. Are you aware that if you scare you enough and do enough to others to make them stay away from you that you can be bare of soul and not be able to care so much? Are you aware of that now? No, but when you are done with the lesson we have begun, you will be able to have fun and not be so upset with anyone. We want you to do more and more to raise the energy of everyone!!! If you were given such a work assignment, what would you do?

First, you would take a deep breath and ignite you and suggest what you might like to do. If no voice or fear or instinct or intuitive flash overcomes you, then you will do what you think that day or moment is best to do. If it turns out that you are doing great and everyone is going straight and everyone is having a great day, you are perfect and did the best that way, but what if no one listens to you? You, personally, had a great day anyway. So, why not start out today and say, "Hey everybody, let's go to lunch and see who else cares enough to try to warm up a cold or bleak or cloudy day that way." You might think that at 9 o'clock in the morning is a funny time to meet for lunch, but so what? You might find a new time to be with someone. You can meet and eat and stop and rest whenever you please, but most today are regimented to such a high degree that they cannot be anywhere unless it is scheduled and it is arranged to happen that day.

What will happen to you when you no longer have any work to do? You will find you are not organized to do anything else good for you.

You and others and simple folks are going to now know the way to have it all today. You will all just meditate upon the Earth and the work you do today. You will not even say why you wish some of it to go away, but it will float and you will never gloat that your work is better than others because you know the way.

You will find that pride in your spiritual work is the worst way to proceed on any day, but if you are overcome by ego and it begins to look like that to you in some small way, pray. Ask what you have to do to remain in the humble way, and we will all tell you.

The area of expertise and the area of interest is not the same today, but you will pray and find out what way you need to improve you today. Sit now and do nothing.

What did you do? You thought. You thought about it and said, "I can't do it." I have to do something or I will not be able to pay my own way. Why?

You are who enlarges your own view of you and needs so many things to do. You are who says to you, I have to attend so many meetings again. You do not. You do not have to do anything you truly do not wish to do. Stop and see and then agree, what I do is what I wish to be. I attend meetings and see friends because in the future I will want them to help me to do something. I will be a friend because in the end I wish to sit with them and not have to sit alone under a tree. But, you will see that when the final outcome is in, you are not going to have a friend. You will end and you will ascend if you did all the work you came to be.

Yes, you are your work and you are not going to end until your work is done or you are totally unable to pursue what you came to do.

Now, Francis and the others are in the room and we are teachers, too, but we teach the subjects from a totally different way of being than they, so here, here are your friends from others beliefs from what you had today. Now, let us pray.

There is a lot of work and a lot of missionaries are praying today that the work of the world is not going to stay as bad as it is today. What is wrong? Are you all able to work today and do whatever you wish to do with you, too? Are you?

Well there is so much that I wish to bring to you, but this is a simple prayer that I feel is good for you. Pray every day that your soul is going to have time to play and you will be fine and all will dine in the most excellent way. I feel that fear is not the way to be and why would you like to fear anyone today?

The fear of life is such that when a wife cannot see her own life as her own, she is a slave that life, so let's free all who are not happy. What? Yes, let's free the minds of all who are not having a great time. You are? Well then be happy. If you are smiling and never upset with anyone at all, you are the exception in any crowd now.

You might think that being angry is a masculine way to be today, but women have so much more intense feelings when they are mad, the entire Earth shakes in some way that men will never ever be able to say it does not sway them in some way.

You are here and we have so much to say, so let us begin to pray as we play with you again. What kind of work would be done if the spirit was playing and not working and doing what was begun?

Fun and games and fun in serious ones are the same, but for me fun is when the spirit is free. I love everyone. I truly do believe that if you are having fun and doing what comes naturally to everyone, you will be fine until the end of your line.

That is so sweet and you are definitely the only one in this group who is able to compete with the sweet of the roses that lie at your feet, but today this is a day to begin to work and pray and never say to anyone again, I am not able to do whatever because of someone. You are free. You will believe that you can come and go and leave a job or a brother or a mother or a child if that is to be. You cannot leave the child homeless, but you must be able to leave home if the child is not able to have food on its own and you need to work in another town. You would go, but you might not return. That is the problem today with so many families and the situation is not good, but what to do?

The job is not a savior of man, but a pursuit of passion and energy and whatever is good to do, but today the job is a change of plans in every way. You are not of Earth for pay, but to pray and work and do whatever comes to you to do. If a church asks you to work, do you? You are asked to do things all day, but do you? Are you able to do anything you wish? Yes, and to believe otherwise is to be a lie and have no truth. You ask for your life and you aspire to strife in order to be able to not pray and ask God to provide all this life. Your ego is what believes that you must provide all that you need in this life.

Look at the anger that flows in the tide. What anger? The tide flows and goes and never sees the sea in any way but calm. The air is where the anger resides. The air is where the breeze becomes a huge energy system and dares to attack the sea. You can let the air attack you; but do you have to attack back? You might if there were no others there and no air, but you have enough oxygen to live on Earth—at least now, but when you leave and you might be here only a few more hours at most, so what do you think the Earth and other folks need?

Oxygen. You all are here and the water supply is low. You all talk a lot and even say you will do much today, but no one cares enough to even work on a project long enough to clean up the total atmosphere. What do you all do with your time on Earth if you cannot clean up after you?

You are all going to find that if your mind is made up to be a martyr or worse, you will not enjoy anything at this time on Earth and not agree to clean it up, so we want no more martyrs, you see. We want you to be happy enough that you have energy enough to clean up the water.

You will find that energy is not going to leave Earth, but the water shortage is going to cause others to overflow into a neighbors place and take much. You can have as much water today as you like, but air conditioners and others who use the water to sprinkle their lawns and such are inconsiderate of those who have no water to wash their clothes. You are not going to be able to pay enough to have slaves drag water casks to you everyday. None of you has money that earns half as much as a laborer made in a single day a few centuries away.

You all have too many material possessions. You all want things that take you away from where you were yesterday by degrees and you want to be happier than ever, but never try much. You will find that money is not a matter of time, but energy spent and used or not abused. If you spend more than you have, you are in debt, but that simple equation seems to escape many today.

You think big. You think in ego states and then you relax and begin to spiritually work within, but that is in the wrong way. Begin in the spiritual state and do your work in the ego state and you will do fine. You can. You are permitted to prosper and work and explore the Earth, but do not take more than you work for.

You might see homes and families that look so prosperous now that you wish you could be more and more with their kind and not with those whom you wish to leave behind, but more of what?

Greed is not good. Greed is not going to help you conceive a brilliant career at all. It can end your life and all that you provide you and a family, too. You have to see that if you proceed to be anything less than you are, you are not using all you have, but to seem to grasp way beyond what you have just to have, is greed. You are not going to be happy enough to pay back all the bills and such, so leave them and go beyond them and see why you are upset today and need so much. You will then pray.

If you are still in debt after two months of actually trying not to buy much, you are deeper than you can get out of in a year or two, so sit down with a trusted advisor or supervise your own life in a fairly jaundiced eye and look at what you like too much. Are you able to judge you?

You are? If you can fairly evaluate you and do, and then work things all the way through, you can teach others much. You will also be able to counsel them if they ask you to help them, too, but all others; you must not counsel anyone who is better than you.

You will find that finances today are a measure of the mindset you are in. If you have to have a lot of cash or you have no cash with you at any time, you are on obsolete works of time and you will meet in the middle sooner than you expect to and it will end with a complete change of medium of exchange soon. You will all be using less money, so you might as well begin.

You see work disappear, but then someone else begins a new line of work and it is great and lasts a long time. Why? That person has prayed and asked for work to be there for them. The work appears and then it goes inside them and if they follow to the end of the work, the work disappears on them and becomes a piece of them. You are your work.

Yes, this is all true. You do have a lot of work inside you, but on Earth the part that gets disturbed is the part where a person is unable to work because a few take too much of it for themselves to do.

If you all do all you have to do for you, you have few possessions around you, but you have so much you wish to do and so many things you wish to pursue, that you do work so much that you never have time to be you.

Yes, and there is no time like the present to give yourself a present now. I would never work so hard that I forgot the man or woman who helped me learn to be, but so many families do now.

I see nurses caring for parents and children not caring at all. Is it any wonder there is crime in the young? Are you afraid to do more for family today?

When I was in China and there was a problem and the family was involved, all members were there to see what was wrong. Who cares today?

No one seems to be there to stand there and take up the plea of anyone who is not able to see they are wrong and have to pay back or do over or replace or repair what they did wrong. Are you just a lot of egos? Are you so selfish that others cannot be seen as deserving the respect of the young for the old?

We watch teenage girls talk as though they are able to work and provide as a man did for them all their lives, but who else talks like that? The wife obviously or the child would never be allowed. You have to see why there is strife in life if you want to be free of it permanently. You can free you and not incur a bit of disharmony. You can.

Yes, and there is a time and a source of harmony today that is not used by many. I prefer the church to many, but a quiet stream with a lot of honey is so much better than some churches seem to be. What is wrong with our lives in this time?

We are all out of harmony.

While you are there in your own chair and able to stare into the air, can you see Francis of Assisi? You can. You just have to prepare. I am there. I will be there to help you to feed the Earth and the birds and the bees and anyone else who cares to eat with me. I live. I subscribe to the belief system that if you live and thrive, you have an obligation to help others breathe pure air. I feel despised never, but you might think that others despised me in my life, but never. I was respected. I was clever? No. I was just myself to a totally acceptable degree. You are all so afraid of being angry and saying that people are sinners and you accept them and what they do to the streams as if a fisherman or an activist are not the same.

Well, there seems to be a flame in Francis again. I feel that so much is revealed by all of you and so I came. I was sure that the part in the preamble about my not revealing my name would be accepted and not spoken, but here I remain as a name. I am not as well received by others because I want no title or fame.

You fear that someone is not going to realize now that you are here to help them, but we all remain adamant at this time that there will be a lot of air when all of you are done. We will help you to do whatever it takes to humiliate those who make such tragic mistakes in the elements.

Your life is your life. Congratulate no one ever again who is smoking in front of you and exaggerates how miserable is their life because others are not helping them ruin their lungs. Why are you so sure that they have the right to ruin your life?

When you feel concern and you must if you are loved and not able to confess everyday and every night what you have and do and feel within you, but some of the humanness is there and will be all this life. You will be miserable and do things that are not good to do. You will make mistakes, too, but why not try to remove more of them than you do?

Well, let's see, you all attacked the readers of this world and you all attacked the writers who are not writing about the terrible conditions of the Earth, and you will know now the machinery is shouting to be heard at this time.

You will find that when a machine is out of line, the reader knows immediately, but if a speaker is out of line, who knows?

You will find that for you and all mankind, the Earth is not going to heal itself this time. It did not do this. It is a planet and is huge, but you did too much to it to survive with the usual ways of cleansing it. A tide is not high enough to shake back the houses and shacks at high tide that block the crustaceans from living in the flats. You are all too tired of being alive and you confuse your contrition with being mad at others who do such things to the tide as being upset with them when most of you envy them.

You could restrict the tidal flats, but who is going to pay them for relocation away from them?

When you feel that there is nothing real, please look within. I tried everyday to say something nice to everyone who was near enough to think of then, but now I work inside men and women and help them mend their own lives. I work. I do not sit among them, but I pray with them and help them to understand that God is in them.

Your work is going well, my friend. You are a help to many fine women and some men, but you do not see them. You are so into your own freedom that you cannot conceive of them not being good. You think all men and women are fine and if given enough time will be able to ascend, but my friend, you will find that many of them will just end. That is a flat denial of the way that God works in the world today.

I refuse to take anything back, but today is another time. You will find that from this time forward, there is a rush to move back to God everyday.

Yes, and we see it happening in degrees. The work is blending and bending in so many different places today, but what do they say about the congregations? You are the expert among us, so Francis, what is wrong with the church today?

I am not an expert in any way. I traveled and I fought and I taught the experts in various days of their own ways, but on Earth, there is a state of mind that consumes time and there is nothing that anyone can say at this time.

If your mind is made up to see all as black and some are white, are you able to say there is a difference?

You make it sound as though we are not prepared to see things as perfect if they could be.

You paint a bleak and despairing picture of Earth today. I see people and you see degrees of bleakness and no pretty pictures.

We are here to teach. We are not pupils. If we were, we would be able to sit and do nothing and just complain later in the game that they did not do enough. I would, for one, sit and have a lot of fun and never work on the work that my teacher had begun. I would just fool around. Isn't that what they do today?

The world is not as pretty today, but it is a place where beauty does stay. There are hills and trees and streams almost brand new today. Why? Some people have pulled up their own human energy forms and used them to help others move along more.

The saints of Earth are always there, but today no one believes or cares that they are there. We see no one congratulate anyone too much today.

The times to be upset and to teach are not on the same day. I am not a teacher in the usual way, but I feel that if people would just move and do more in the usual way and not try to be like others so much inside that today would be beautiful for all.

This is a small way to repay all who came here today, but the fall of another is about to occur far away and we will stop her from falling. She is going to be okay.

A miracle not witnessed is not a miracle to many today, but it is a miracle anyway. You will find that there is no more time. The time you have today or any day winds down about this time in your mind, so let us depart and you can play or pray, but do not depart in the usual hasty way. Sit and do your own business with you. Sit and review what you love to do. Sit and feel that whatever you do is real and exists inside you and will be great if you just do it for you. When the day is over and you have a time to be you, are you?

The beginning of this lesson was in the next view of you and now we have returned you to the beginning of this view of you. You now either have the lesson in you or you are not committed to being inside you long enough to change you. We will help all of you, but the saints are no different from you.

You are saints when you live a different life and it is great to be alive within you, but if you shirk your own life in order to be a man's wife or a daughter and a man who is unable to live his own life, we cannot do anything for you. You have decided not to live this life.

The chapter and verse are not important as long as you rehearse where you are now. You may not feel that you have aged, but you are always moving in some way and it is usually in a progressive way, so age and let the years go. You will feel the age of the mind is a blessing in time. You will be relieved of the ego and the work of pride if you just let the body be healthy and not so upset about the way it looks on the outside. If you are able to let the body be healthy and you well in your mind, what else can you do for God on this side?

Things will be doing you no harm, but you might do it and not realize you are. Why? Personality traits, limited resources, lack of intelligence, good looks that make you prone to conceit, and a lot of individual woes that we will not repeat, but you know. You do not have to save for a rainy day, but today is sunny and wherever you are the work is going straight, so go fast. You will know when you have to go slow—it will snow or the ice will form in your eyes and you will not be able to grow. The way to age is to go inside and let the flow know you are happy in your old age. It will arrive any day, so be ready to enjoy the flow and know you deserve to slow in your old age—if you did your work all of your younger days.

We will work now to cleanse the work of others. How? Let us all now work together. You may be working on this book or just rereading a few lines, but work now. Get your mind to leave the brain and go into the arteries and clean up the residue left behind from other areas.

Work in a way that you can remove plaque everyday in every way and it will not mount up and decay. Here is the way:

Look at your middle eye or third eye or the center of your forehead. See inside what the eye is doing now.

Open the eye as wide as you can and peer inside the mind. It takes experience and practice if you never visualize, but you can be as good as you wish to be. Take the time to learn it now. It will be a tool to save you time and enlarge this life, but mostly it will save you your own work for better things and better ways to be.

Now that you can see your own mind, look at why it intends to harm you. Do you do anything now that is not good for the body? Do you look like you are having a good time? Are you able to move the bowels and have a smile upon the face as it moves the waste? Yes, the waste is the most important work you have to do everyday. Erase all traces of toxic poisons at once. Food that does not agree and whatever else that comes into contact with the mouth and is not good must be urged to proceed to the gullet and out the anus in time to be on the next day's work. Please use sense and proceed.

You will cleanse the bowel and the bowel will care for the engine of the human body—the heart. If you do not have a heart, you may proceed to not listen and read, but if you still use the pump God of All created for you, then read and proceed.

You have to exercise inside. You do not have to run, but oxygen is not enough if you do not pump up the lungs. Pump them up by placing your mind at a fast pace? Not the mind! Rush the lungs full of oxygen in gulps and get the pump to fill up and surge and empty the lungs in a rush. That is all you need. If you rush the pump and proceed to empty it once and then twice and three times every few minutes or so, you will never need to have an attack to know what it means to be without a life. You will also be able to eat what you like.

If your lungs pump and the bowels are an endless run, you can do whatever you like the rest of your life, provided the liver is able to function and do what it likes—make a new life.

If the liver dies, you die with it. Do not drink so much that the liver has no means to cleanse itself and the body is awash in alcoholic beverages that do nothing for you. If the mind is so messed up that it cannot tolerate pain or sorrow or whatever all others can, you will be unable to move up, so you might as well drink, but if you want to move beyond hell—stop any abuse to the liver. It will make the life you do have a compulsive way to give up. You need to deliver a cleansing tonic to the liver once or twice a week to make sure it is well and can go on forever, but if not, you can eat not cheese or saturated fats for a week and let it all cleanse by itself. The liver is the best friend God presented to you. Treat it well.

If you cleanse the outer body once or twice a day, you remove too much. You have no time to restore the natural products that are in the body to reproduce the skin and hair and nails over time for you. You cannot buy a product to make up for abuse, but if you choose style and fashion over sense, you will not be able to complain if you die in pain with skin that is cancerous and hair that is not there or nails that are so thick that you cannot feel tension in them. You decide why you have a hide, but it is not there to hide behind. It is there to protect you and the body from abuse of the elements around you.

When your life is cleansed of meanness and those who are not friends, you will thrive and live and be happy just to be alive, but that is the hard thing about now. You all want to be loved by others, and we do not think you can change that about you. We would not be able to make you love you, but you could revolutionize your day and start each day by embracing you and saying that you do love you. Why not do that every day?

When you are cleansed of all that the world has induced, your spirit is free to be you only if you do cleanse the spirit of the abuse the mind heaps upon you. You must not let the mind take off and abuse you all the way through life, but if you do, you suffer enough. At the end you will normally not have to come and do it again, but why have such a hard life when it was never intended to be that way?

Life is enough. Live it and get on with it. You can ascend. Be there at the end. Do the work you came to do and be over it by the end you are in queue, but we will help you. You do not have to be rescued? You do. We know the work you do. We know how few of you truly do know what to do.

Work. Look. Seize this moment and do what you are best at doing all the way through. If you never follow up on a belief, it may not be with you. Seize you and believe that you can be anything you believe. It is the truth.

CHAPTER 2

The Beginning

In a few moments you will begin and you will be able to live forever? No, you live and will be forever and ever and ever and ever, so how can you die and not be alive?

This is a time to delve into the work of the beginning of time and how to develop a sense of being and what you need to know about you in order to be the human being God created to live inside the soul that is a part of the universe and remotely controlled by the other souls who also move and do not collide over the wide expanse of what is to be euphemistically called "the man" and will not refer to the sex of anyone again.

You will not be bothered by the order or the sorting of your own birth, but you will learn to control the ego that sorts and orders all of you according to birth. You are on Earth. You live. You will be. That is enough to know and work with.

Your life is an extreme. You are not a being sent to Earth to live and then be used up and given nothing else to be, but a being who is here to learn what it is Earth can bring to your soul and what you can do to help the soul move further into the evolving state of being. You will be. That is the fate.

The fact that you believe in fate is a long convoluted practice of others and not what you yourself knew when you arrived on Earth, so first let us all remove the artificial ingredients and begin to see things for ourselves.

We all are here and going to help you disappear. You will find if you can align the spine in an identical line to everyone on Earth, you could all disappear at the same time. Is that true? You must believe it or it would not be allowed to be here, but it is not true.

You cannot believe everything you see or hear, but the truth does appear. It can arrive in your life at any time, but you have to be able to know if you believe and what you think and how you are to proceed if the truth is to be able to set your mind free. You have to publish your own beliefs more and more as you grow older or accept what others say about you.

If you do not believe in the facts that surround you, what is there to believe? You. You are the entire sense of direction and acceptance of what you are and believe. If you are healthy and happy and not wealthy, you do not like to concentrate so much on that sort of work that would necessarily bring you money, but you might like to do it if you were given it to do at birth. You can arrive at the right time to do little and be able to thrive, but usually you have to work for everything you do. You will believe in you, too, better if you do, but we will not preach to you.

You have to see that to teach is a practice anyone can do, but you only believe a few who try to teach you. You do not let anyone who is not a friend of your own being teach you. You could send someone on ahead to help you, but most of you expect that someone older will protect you. Do you now? Do you believe that the elders will provide a stage for you to go forward, and you do not have to work as hard as they did for you?

You are not ready then to go into the work of your own being if you look forward to another leaving and giving you more. You are immature and very boring. You cannot know that more is not enough to give you credit or understanding of the blessings you get; but if you suffer loss and depression, you might realize you have much that you never knew you had before the episode taught you a lesson. The lesson? You are you, and if you are sad, you alone can get you to learn why you are and what to do.

If you never learn to leave anyone, you have never left the crib; but if you leave too soon, you never wander around enough to do more and more as you grow older. You have to learn to lean on no one ever; but if needed, you can use a crutch and clutch at someone until the matter is solid and you can leap forward again. You will know nothing if you never wish to grow older.

You will know now that the elders of Earth are wiser because of the time they have spent working on their own lives and not helping you or others, but the older ones who constantly use themselves to wipe up after everyone will not die young—but not very wise at all. You cannot pretend to be wise and not fill up others' lives with what is not very good for them to do. You must admit if you do not know. It is a sin to pretend what you do not do—or say you are wise when you do not even open one eye.

The work of the wise is to help the unsure. All are wise, but some do not like to take a risk or do what others do, so you have to do more and more to help them explore their own lives and see why they did anything at all unwise. Many do not miss an opportunity to miss. Why? They believe that life is not easy or life is not going to be a breeze from God to Earth, but we all do.

You are of the Earth, we were once on Earth, too, but now we can work with channels all over the Earth, we do not have to incarnate and go through birth. You can find the wisdom you derive from channeled work never collides with what you truly hold within you. Your mind may not like the idea of another being able to listen and hear and speak what you do not see or feel within you, but only a fool says it is not real. Are you a fool or a wise person unrevealed?

You will find channels differ from one to another and there are a few who are not real, but most of them can do whatever is necessary to get into the reel of the Earth work and unreel it one frame at a time and discover what you love and need to uncover in order to love the work of Earth. Read a lot of the channeled work and you will see that the texts of the Bible, the Koran, and whatever are all channeled by man, but the words are not the same as what an author would write in a novel.

You will find this is a novel way to channel today, but in the past, two overused it. It was the way of the church to only let one or two channel and be paid to do it, but today you will find a channel such as Ruth is not paid to do anything at all like this for you. You will find she even pays you to listen to the tape or the work of others as they go forward into the time of her own life. Are you dedicated enough to do that, too? Are you?

If you can channel now, please look up and see inside and abide in that time and let the new you come forward and do not sit in a slump or let others think of you as a lump. Stop speaking from the ego of you and channel what is there inside you. We will not be able to say much about you if your work is never the same as what you say you do, but you will learn in several years you cannot fake whatever you do. It comes to you—as is, the way it is and the way you said you would not be if you were unable to live.

Think deeply on this and think of your own commitment to live: Are you able to do anything at all that is not good for you?

You live in a fog and you believe as others, but is that right to be so dependent upon another? You do not see love and romance as a deep lasting thing, but it is. You cannot pretend to love someone and then treat them badly. It will make you end your life in a sad reflection of what you have done. But if you love, you will end with the only wisdom you need have—love is from God and you have it inside you and have loved someone and done things you might not have done otherwise. You lived. You were loved or you took it for granted, but you loved and lived and had a reason for being. That is a very wise thing to do.

You may not live in a hostile environment now, but all of you are going to have time to reflect on what you might have done to preserve Earth a lot longer than you do have now to live upon the Earth. You all preserve your money, and the Earth does not have a purse. You all have time to see that some will be able to live a lot longer than others because of adopting healthier attitudes shortly after birth, but some of you lived a long time in non-adaptive habits that have ravaged the lungs so much you might not be able to live much beyond the turn of the century of your own birth. If you could live to turn 100 years of age, would you do it gladly?

If you were able to live? Is that a statement or a demand or a command? None of these. You are not going to reside all the time on Earth, but you will live. You will be and exist. You will not reside in this time, but you will not collide with anyone who is not going to be able to go forward at all after this time.

You need to do more and more for the work of the world? You are the world and whatever you do is going to help the world if it is good for you. If you do anything unwise, it is going to negatively impact upon others who are not going to realize you are not doing what is good to do. Others will simply avoid you. You cannot be unwise and build a large life with others. They will all simply know you and not wish to be like you and, therefore, not go around with you—unless you threaten them with whatever and do what you think they will hate to do for themselves, and then they will surely shun you. But the world will forgive you if you learn to listen, assume responsibility, and do what you truly believe is good to do. Try.

If your mind is deprived of rest and has not exercise, you think in riddles to exercise and you do not reason well among others if there is not rest for you. These are some of the prices you pay for not taking good care of you. What you should, would and could do, do not matter when it comes to being you. It is what you actually do that counts the most. If you do nothing, you will return to Earth.

You must have done a few things or you would not be this far along in your evolution as a man of the Earth, but if you did nothing at all, you would not be able to smile long in this world.

The world remembers only those who perform with a love of what is inside—the rest are gone over night.

What you will do now is rest.
Think of the time.
Go inside now and think of nothing inside that is not going to help you and help the rest of the people who are close to you.
If your mind is not connected to you, where is it?
If your mind is floating inside, what do you do to connect inside with the work you know you have to do?
What if you knew the answer to every question? You do.

You know the answer to every single question, but you do not have the patience to reveal that answer to you. You ask rather than listen to the voice of others inside you revealing to you what it is you need to do.

Your own spirituality is not a source of news to you if you have worked on you, but if you never do? Wow! Are we neat or what? You will repeat such nonsensical points of view of you, but others already knew. Does that make you a fool? No. You found you while still on Earth, so you have done what you came to do. Some are wise at birth and never spoil that view of what is inside or they do not hide their lives, but many do. You may be one of them, too, but be you—that will take you to the top of the heap in which you grew.

If your work is not going well and you can see others do less and end up with more, what does that mean?

Are you doing exactly what you mean? Are you being mean to you? Think of all that you do and why. Scheme to be you. Try anything that will get you to get back into the beam of light that is you. Try. Be alive to anything that will help you do that now.

Scheme? You are who makes a word negative inside. You are who plots all the time, but if reminded try to say it is not plotting but trying to make things happen. That is saying you are pushing others and wanting them to do things they would not like to do. You cannot scheme and plot against others, but you can do it for your own plan to make it happen for you. It will bloom, but you have to work, too.

When you do not plan a thing, what do you believe will happen? You. You will be the being you are, but the being is not here on Earth to merely be. The being You wants to be something new—something far superior to whatever being you were before being this man of Earth. You will be, but try to do more and be better than you ever thought you might be—that is success in every land.

When we teach as a group, and you generally do not realize we can, you have to reach inside and criticize, but it need not be mean at all to you.

You plan, you work, you perspire inside, but the work needs to be amended and edited if it is to be the work you do best. Work always needs the best you can do and be to flourish, but one or two of the things you do are almost perfect as they come out of you. Work on the rest to make it as well as those two things and you will be seen as a star that is able to lead.

Leaders are not recognized on Earth for being saints, but if too evil, will not remain leaders. You have to design a life at this time to be and seem to be free of all others who do not live and believe as you do at this time, but will you be?

When you are a being and see and do and believe, you be. When you are dead and not of Earth, you are.

You are free of dread of death? Good. You can now go and not have to work as hard as those who remain afraid all of their days. You will not leave Earth any sooner than those who are afraid of death, but you will have ease and peace and dread not what others have said. You will be free.

Freedom is a state of bliss and not in the head. It is a spiritual belief and not easily made open to those who are slaves to their brain output and remain as is. You can let the mind explore the brain and produce more, but the mind cannot free the brain anymore. It is not the order of the universe to be explored, but you think you should do it more. Why? You want to know things. You want to believe more. You are going into the wrong area—it seems. You should be going inside you more.

Your lives are insecure. You do not own anything, but you could believe if you stored it up and saved energy and things and money and never used them for your most important work. If you do not use things and money and time and effort for the best of the work you came to Earth to perform, what are you doing with them?

Waste is not a by-product of love. The love you have of you is deep inside and never leaks out or causes you to break in two, but hate is a far different view of you and will cause you to leak and break and not be able to look as good as you do.

Look at you.
Do you see inside? Do you only look at the outside of you?
What do you believe?
Are you free?
Are you fully able to do more and more or are you trying to say you should be at the end of your days?
What is the work of Earth?

Now that your mind has elevated its work, can you elevate your soul? Think no more. You now have to work on the soul power to release what you came to be. You are free. You have to do nothing to believe. You have to work very, very hard not to believe in you, but it can be and will happen if you try very hard. You will not enjoy being upset, but you will conclude that everyone else is mad but you. That hardly appeals to the world, so you may be cut off from the others around you if you consistently state you can do more than they or are better in some way. Listen to others and think of what you can learn from their experiences, too, but continue to be you.

If your mind compares you to others, and most of you have to learn why you cannot do that, but some will not try, you must control the mind and take care of you. Your mind is a tool. You have no need to play the fool, but if fools surround you, you may think it wise to dress up like one in disguise.

The Scribe was in school with fools and tried to hide the fact that she knew all the lessons years ahead, but she never ever let on she knew. Why? She was there to learn why others did not like to work as hard as they might on educating themselves and becoming other beings that could do more. Are you the work of your own mind? Think of what you knew when you went to school. Were you ahead of the class or just a fool being unkind to you and not letting you learn what you already had inside?

When you foolishly let others direct you or let them ignore your work and compare you to those who did nothing, you will despise you and not like the work you do. Do not compare you to anything that you might do and you will be able to work it out and do it for you, but say you believe and it will be. Look forward. Do you see? Look back at the past. Are you able to be? You can see only what you were and not what you will be.

You have to see you are an ever-moving sample of what can be. You are always being and moving and conceiving what you can be, but only what you actually work on will come to be. You decide what to do all your life or you are not going to be alive. Once you decide to stop and not thrive, you die.

Your life on Earth is what you derive from living in the soul and asking for more work of a nature not as hard as the soul to be. When you come to this plane and erase the memory of your own basic belief and nature, you begin over—but not if you remember why and what you came to be. You!! You came to do things for you. You came to believe in you and follow you and you and you to the end of this plane into another view of you that will lead you back to the ultimate YOU. Can you flow and follow you? You will then be able to know whom you are and why you cannot assume to know anything while you remain on this planet. Again? Are you back on Earth? Are you here for a second try or a third anniversary of whatever?

There are many ideas now that thrive and die, but some of the oldest memories of Earth are trying to come alive. Try to thrive and find what is alive inside. Go into the memory of your birth? No, just be as still as you can and look inside and see what you hide.

Your own work is what you might not like. Why? It is not grand and glorious and does not impress the mind, but the soul is what is working or not. You either connect all day long or you cannot seem to rest. Why are you so unhappy thinking you are? You will find that the mind cannot rest and be happy at the same time, but many of you wish to believe that working will help the mind more. It can, but not always.

If you work for you and have no plan, what do you construct? You might believe it is fate that brings you to the end of the time you have to spend on you again, but it will not fly if it is not good for you. Try to fly with anything before you work too long on a plan, too. If you can work and fly and feel great inside, you will be able to do whatever you came to Earth to do, but be sure you know what to do and do it for you.

Whatever you wish and dream is not necessary to be, but to help you. If you never see a miracle of you, plan and see what comes true. You. You will plan that today is going to be great. It is and will be exactly what you expect it to be—plus the excitement of what others might generate around you to be.

You will not be upset much by others if you do not let them control who you are, but if you do not like the power you assume from others, give it back and make them control their own destinies more. Children are not gifts from heaven, but loans. You are not there to take them home and keep them for your own work or pleasure or desire to have power over others. That is a sin against them that will lead you to be upset with them and they will have to live life over. Is that what you meant to do?

If you have a plan and it includes you having children, do you plan to take care of them? Do you imagine that you have them? Are you planning on raising them? Are you merely thinking of having them there when you can be at home with them? Why have a child if you then hide that child? You can, but is it the right way to be you today?

What a lot of questions!

You ask so many of them every day, but when asked a lot of questions, you will generally refrain from answering them. That is the same for all entities, so let us begin again and not ask if you can ask a lot of questions today. You never listen anyway.

There is nothing in the air that is going to keep you here, but there is a time for you to forgive you. Now. You must forgive you. Do you?

Are you afraid of doing worse everyday? Are you sure you can do the work you came to do today? Are you afraid of others or what they might say about you today? Are you afraid or conceited or pleased that you came to be?

Are you the only one in your city who is able to feel that it is pretty and very unique and quiet in a way? Not if you live in this city and you never visited any other place. If you live in a city that is very pretty and noise is a problem, you complain about what other people in other cities do not even think of today. They are in pain with a grief and a domain that is not safe for them to go about all day. Are you aware of the problems in LA? You are? Why are you not there in your mind cleaning up that town in time? You can. You can do anything you dream of and scheme for, but you have to plan to do the right thing and have the plan beam you to that thing and do it right away or it will not work today.

You can travel in time. It is done all the time. If you believe in our appearances in this place and you can, you will find we plan to be here and then we wait on others to accumulate and admit they are able to be any place, but would prefer to be here among us. We are glad to see so many of the same faces week after week, but some are too weak to accompany us much longer who are not able to be here every time we meet, but they think it is their own private life that is interfering and preventing them from being here among the others. We know better.

We will find that your own life is not going to go forever, but if it is going to go and you have to go, you may as well do it the best this time and be gone from Earth forever. You can, but you have to work and do the work of your own plan.

You will find that someone is always saying you have nothing or you need something or you could do more, but you do and they then find something else wrong with you. You can ignore them, but do you? You will if you have a plan.

You are determined and open to others more if you adore what you do more than you think of them and what they do. You will abhor anyone who is not going to work at all if you intend to work always for you. What you do and what you say you will do, do not seem to be the same everyday, but if it is true, you will begin to be so prosperous within you, life will then spend nothing upon itself and let you accumulate more for you.

You will find if your mind is upset over anything at all, think again. It can erase a lot of mistakes and it can even erase your own price of mistakes, but you have to be you. You have to practice on what you do.

You can be you and fully estimate who is going to do what for you, but will it be you or the work that makes you follow through? You. You are the work of you.

If anyone in your place sees you and tries to erase you, are you going to say it was by mistake? You could, but you probably will never underestimate that person again. You could, but that would be a mistake. You cannot afford to constantly open to someone who is not going to want to help you or work for you or even be around you more. You have to close doors if you wish to open to the only source of energy more.

You can also close interior doors to seek immediate attention, but if you close them and never open them again, you will dry up and never be able to intentionally bloom again.

You have a faith and a course of energy that seems to grow if you know who you are and why you came to Earth, but many do not try to do anything even once they do know who they are and why they are alive. Do you work for you? Are you truly living to be you or are you trying to be a martyr who is actively pursuing, even wooing another so they will give fame to you? You will find you create a monster and that personality is not going to want to thank you. You have to do what you must do first and then prepare to help another. That other, no matter what it may appear to you to be, is not going to need you like you do. You may find the other is blind or crippled or whatever, but you still have to be. You still have to see, and talk, and be in order to be able to share anything at all with any other; so do not intentionally give up on you for another. It will be held against you.

You might decide today that this time of the day is a lot like the morning and you are tired and not able to sit so long, but today you will not have to sit long. We will write a letter to you and then you can talk about it and then we will resume and you can then all bloom and feel the room coming into you.

What we intend to do tonight is not talk to you so much as you might like, but listen to you. We want you to talk to the room and talk about what you do and why you are free or not to be you. If you can do anything at all to free you, please do, but tonight you will all have to talk only about you. No excuses or additions once you are through so plan to do whatever you can to talk only about you.

You will find if your mind is open and you are not open enough, the tongue will sputter and it will not let you talk to any other, but tonight you will talk to us. We are here to observe the way you talk and the way you sway and the way you betray to others what is truly going on within you. We will begin today with our favorite Ray and we will ask Ray a few questions today, but after that we will not say a word and all will answer in the way they feel is okay.

When you were young, Ray, were you ever asked to do anything that made you feel that you were not as good as your brother? NO? You said NO. We remember better apparently than you do. We remember you doing a few chores and you were the older one and you were told over and over you should know better and you are not a serious enough person for the younger one to follow as he was prone to do, so you became more sober and you became more serious and more continually analytical than you were. We know. We were there. We are always watching over those who care. We think all of you in this room are older than others, but do you?

Now, let us ask another question of you.

Are you aware of anyone who is not going to be on Earth when you are older, and if you can seriously change their view of you?

Group response:

(I could, but I doubt that I should.)

The wise have spoken, so you all can see. We expect no promises or false tokens, but a vast thought process and a few words carefully spoken and that is all. No need to sport pedigrees and talk about others. Just do what you knew you had to do when you were not of the time you now are and had to be someone else and how it affected you. Are you able to follow and decide what to do? You will tell us now, what you did do for you that helped you the most. Ray, we would like one more favor today. We would prefer that you not fidget with the machine, but since you seem to be a fidget by nature, what made you choose to work with Ruth this way?

We will accept the emotion and we will not reject the notion that it somehow evolved into now, but you can see there are so many changes and yet it still is there to be. You can be and see and still not know who you are, but others do see and plan to be where you are. You can do anything, but still inside you is a plan. You can still plan to be anything, but if your idea of a plan does not agree with what is inside "the man," you will not succeed. You have to be in the right path to ignite and tonight we are able to see the path opening for all of you. We do know you. Now, do you know you?

Let's ask Lynn.

Lynn, are you free of any or all thoughts that once were a problem to you and now you feel are not even worth the time to talk through?

Group response:

(I think I am for the most part.)

You are not done apparently, you added for the most part and that was the tail wagging the dog of the heart. You will succeed and you will believe and you know more than most, but do you have to not speak of thee? You are right not to talk too much, but now we ask you to open your heart. Can you talk about what you have had to do to sit in this room and be you? Can you tell us what to do?

Anger is a pain and it is not the same in everyone, but it causes the same degree of anxiety within each of you and if you only knew how much this room is blessed by being here with you, you would refuse to ever, ever again abuse you. You will never do it and we will all pursue it and you will be you—forever and ever in God's view of you.

Now we want to ask you one other question? When you were able to quit the work of the world and you decided not to, but then it actually came to be true, did you feel that it happened to you or you were directed or that God pushed you?

Your questions and answers are reversed today, but today we help you as much as you can help you, but you all have to stop and seek inside to see what direction is best today for you. Now will all of you proceed to be you? All of you will proceed to talk only about you. We would prefer you not have to have direction in asking questions today, but we understand that you want perfection and you want to seem to be discreet and honest and wise among the others who may not know you, so we will continue to ask you concrete questions about discreet inventions and what you tell others about you. We do know the truth.

The day is full of the ways you can pray, but Kathy you are praying all day and we heard you, but you do not have to say the same words over and over. We heard you the first day. We always listen and we always say you are going to be happy one day, but do you listen? Why are you so nervous if you are told everything is going to be great today?

We see you are full of joy and not gloom and that is the perfect way to be. You took all the energy you had to spare and you helped those who were bereaved and you are clearly able to see that God is able to take someone away and still leave you a perfect view of you and he as you will always be. We will also take care of the crowd of souls now prospering with thee. We want you to talk about what to do if you are not as prosperous as you. What should a person do today to be as able to pay bills as you?

` response:

(Refuse to buy the admiration of others with material possessions.)

That is excellent advice and you have paid the price so you may preach tonight. Only those who have actually done the work are permitted to preach, but all of you who are merely practicing on you can teach. You learn more. You practice harder, but once you do know what to do—preach to anyone who is unable to learn in the usual way today.

Kathy, you are stronger than the world and you are able to go forward, so flow and flower and see the world as a flower child of the next century and you will never grow old.

Well, we could go in order, but Maggie is still in a quandary over what to say about today, so we will pass over.

Sharon is now open to the new way and the best way to be her today. We will ask you, Sharon, what made you so upset that you had to learn all over why you are here on Earth and why you got this close and then backed away?

Your day is open and you are not closed, so let the air drift in and out of your nose and the work will prosper and you will know what to do and where to sow the seeds so you can grow. We know you wish to be a mother, but you have to see your own needs first. If you were to mother a child, you would be too inclined to do too much for her. We want you to be independent, too.

Now, let's look at your own day today. What did you do today that was quite different from the old ways you once would have lived a day like today?

Anger is going and you are only showing irritation and that is because the new robe is rubbing today, but the robe is white and will float one day and not irritate you in any way. We would enjoy this group more if we were you, but that is another day. You will also be able to work a way of doing whatever you wish to do better for you. Not for anyone else, but you.

Now, if you could choose to be anyone on Earth, who?

The answer is YOU. You are to be you regardless of whomever you compare you to. You will be like all who teach you if you try to follow through. You will be like you, however, and not like them or any other. You are close, though. You will be fine, but rest more and take time to do more for you and have a great time. You don't have to work so hard at meditative ways. It is a joy. Sing and you meditate within. Sit and the relaxation is there inside and you can recline, but do it for you. Do not pressure you to do more and more just to be able to go out the door. We know you are here to be you, so do it for you and enjoy the view. We will help you.

Now, Barbara, you have a choice and you have a life and you would like to be a wife, but you are. You chose to stay a wife to Leslie. You chose to make a life for her, but you have to choose you over her and why is that a burden to you? Can you see now any way you can do more to be better to you and thus help her more?

You are the mother of a fine woman of Earth, but she is unable to do things you would love her to do, so you often feel sorry for her. She is not feeling sorry for you. That is just an observation, of course, but you need to project your needs, too. You can and not make anyone mad, but if you are mad, all see that inside you. So, we will guide this conversation into the area in which you can excel—you as a child and as a woman who once said that you wanted to marry and have a child. Why? Why did you decide as a girl that you wanted to work for others?

You care too much for what others think, and now you are wise. You see through their eyes and you need no proof that you do what you do and they do whatever, but you have to be happy about you. You will use this as a rule—I will help anyone I can—provided it does not collide with what I want. If I have to do something and it is helpful to you, I will help you as much as I can.

That is the Golden Rule spelled in everyday words. You can do it. It is the wise way to live today. Ruth, repeat the rule for Barbara and all others to remember longer than today.

The Golden Rule is the answer to your problem, but you will find that you have a problem until you decide to unwind and unreel the real person inside that young woman again. She is not a child, but not willing to preside over life without you in the sidelights and that is not enough for you. You are a star in your own life and have the right to be here tonight and do whatever you like. Do not ever again be upset for being you. That is a cardinal sin against you. Be you. Love this thing that is growing within and take all you have for you and be you again. When life is young, you have very little fun because you care too much what others like, but as a woman, be wise and use your time to have fun. You can and will be able to find that one. We do want you to be able to have a time away and be you. There is a way and it is happening today.

Now, there is a time to go back to the beginning and there is a time to end the past, but Jack, you have been living in the past and not going too far into the future and you do not have a plan. Why are you not planning more than you are doing?

You are the only you there is and there is no other one futuristically speaking, so enjoy who you are and be you and tell the old one to get going and onto the next you. You can. You have to plan only if you are not willing to let the work you do go, but you work for a living and you have to do what you think you can, so work now to plan a life without work and see what you can and cannot do. You will begin to see that living without money is not a big thing if you plan and have placed away a few dollars for the proverbial rainy day, but you are not planning to be you in any way soon. You seek? You do not have to hunt for you. You are.

Now, let us see why you think you missed out on so many things? Are you aware of the self-pity that seems to be in your speech? Are you going to see that everyone is sure they missed out on many things? Are you aware of what you would not have if you had not worked for others as long as you did? Think now of the good you did when you should have not been working so hard—according to what you said today to another who was not prepared to enjoy life today. You are to talk to your own mind now and tell us why you are not able to see the future today—regardless of the fact that none of you can. We want you to tell us why you look so hard and seek so much and not truly enjoy today. Talk to us. We want to help you today.

When you say I sure deserve that, it implies others do not. You then see yourself as lower or higher by some degree and you do not. So, what you say programs you to see you in a lower light today than you are. Others see you in an entirely different light, but you see yourself as still out of the light seeking the light and not delighted with all you are to be.

You are entirely free and you are entirely capable of being you all your life, so stop seeking and be. You are free. Decide to be free? No, just be. It is the positive way of life and you do not like the idea of being you and having to support a wife, but you truly feel you need companionship if you are to be free. Why?

Now, let us depart and go forward. You have a long life and you have supported our work naturally and you are delighted to teach those who are not as advanced as they would like, but are certainly beyond us. We think you have to see beyond the outer life much, so we want you to listen to all who come to you for advice. Listen. Counsel them to talk to you and not expect anything again. You will listen. You will learn why they are talking to you. You talk sense, but you are not taking your own advice. You will now. You can teach, but not until you practice more and more what the lesson plan is today and always—to be you in all ways. Now, let us pretend that you have one of the ladies in front of you now, and she is asking you a question about you and what you do to meditate. What do you usually tell them?

When someone approaches you again, assume they want to know what to do in order to be new. Assume that they are there to find some way to connect better today within them and say what you think you are doing that day. You assume others do not wish to work as hard as this, but most of them already do. You work with a crew of women and men who are not going to upset you. You alone do that to you, so practice today to do whatever you can and try to meditate among them. It is a viable practice at work. You can, but it is not easy when you do not believe it can be done.

Now, Maggie, we want you to do something you can do easier than anyone, but we want you to admire what you do first before you tell us about the lover who is so wonderful and how you almost lost him. First, what about you and how you helped you and then tell us all about him and why he was worth all the changes within. We truly are here to hear about a romance and what you can do to help these old saints to something new.

You are able now to adjust and that was a fable you long believed about you—that you were rigid and could not do what others were trying to tell you to do—be you. You were a perfectionist and that is good to do, but you also confused love and things and being another who is not you with doing well. You tried to be another and then you wanted to be more and more and do it all over, until your lover told you no. You then became a new you. You decided that love was the reason you were on Earth and you decided to be you. Now, you are greeted with love and respect and are delighted with you. But what would have happened if you had decided to not be you?

You are about right in that assessment tonight, but you would still be sitting here tonight. It would have gone on a detour and you would have suffered more than you needed to, but tonight you are on target with us and we are all here and want each one in this room to keep on meeting with us. We would prefer no others if this group can unite and meet like this every month or a week or before. We want you to know we cannot tell time any more, but that is obvious to you tonight.

Tuesday is a day when our Ray of sunshine can plan to be away, but he has expenses if he is to be here all the day. You will all pay Ray $5. Okay? You can do that and not pay Ruth at all. She is not going to be upset if Ray is paid and that is the way to be sure we get all this on tape, but if you can decide a better way, that is okay. We want to be sure that all of you meet this way and not be upset by others breaking into the day. We will meet when you can each be here in this room and what a way to begin the book today.

Yes, we are writing a book and today is the day it begins and today you will be included in the tape, but most of what you said is not in the book so that readers will be asked to do the work you did. You will find the questions are for all time and are related to everyone today. Now, we still have one smile left. Bob, you are the only one who is not going to talk now and decide later what you should have said. You have had time to think about it. So, we will surprise you and say we already know who you are and why you are and we will help you, but to teach is to teach and never to downgrade you. You will now talk only about the positive way you are teaching all who are around you today. Teach the group the way to talk to people who are not like you, but surround you all day.

That is enough. You have earned a piece of cake and we will pay for it. We are obviously kidding Ray about the size of cake he likes to eat, but you are to see we are all a group. We want this group and we will help you to be discreet and refuse to upset those few who refused to be here so you all could meet. We know you knew there would be only eight, but you all hesitated to say you would be one of the eight, but you did not wait. You came to be and you are here and now going to move forward, but you can remove you and we will find another few to do this work, but if you do move and go forward, you will remove all that is inside you and is not working for you. We promise. We will help and we will do, but you have to be you.

What you will be and see and believe is not important. You are and will be and it is the product of the entire being—whether or not it is important to you to be. You will do whatever you like to do, but now you have a feud over who is you.

When you are told a lot of wonderful things about you or others, do you immediately believe? Are you unable to see things that are wonderful? Are you upset if another has done more than you?

You have not learned—questioning your own mind is the best way to keep it in line, but never question you. You are the integrity that finds the unhappiness in you and completely turns it over to you and gets proof of what you need to do to help you. Your mind will be able to fully develop and you can do more and more of this for you, but you will have to work on your own work and not believe you have to go to school if you are to mature.

Your work is not going to be easy if you let it accumulate deep within you. You may even pass on it and decide to relax a bit and not do it, but you will in time have to do it or be removed until the time when you will do it.

You may follow the airline strikes against time and wonder if it is fair to strike and call others to do things they do not like, but you are you and able to share in the problems of others or you do not have any faith in you. Your mouth and mind are compared all the time. You are seen as striking out on your own if you do think of others first and ask them to help you, but are you? You are just trying a new path for you.

If your mind reflects the news of others and they are unhappy with whatever, are you wise to connect inside and fully understand them and why they are unhappy now? You would be wise to do it. You could then be free from doing more in that way of life to understand why the crime was done or not seen by anyone. If you know why murder is not a sin against you, but who ever did the work, you will find out why the mind cannot be trusted all the time. It will convince you that whatever you want is okay to do. It can. It can totally dominate you. You will find by listening to the pain and sorrow of others, their way of life is not conducive to free speech among others or they have given up their power to someone else to walk over this life and not let them survive. You have to regain or reconnoiter if you want to know all there is to know about you, but do not assume it will happen to you.

If the mind runs amok and it can, you will find you do not enjoy anything most of the time. Your mind is running in circles and scaring you and others with things that do not exist. Yes, the element of time is what makes you all survive and decide this is the time to work together to eliminate the ravages of power, but are you doing anything? No. You do nothing now, but all of you are changing the power systems of Earth within you.

You can and will do it until there is nothing left for you to do.

You will enter into the work of you and exist or you will not move and do anything that is not great for you to expect to do. The work of the vain is not as well discussed at this session, but we will go back and forth and mention the vanity of others. If you cannot see it, believe it, or be aware of it, you are so conceited that you are controlled more than others; but if you can see conceit, control it now. It will ruin all you plan. Do you feel deep within you a plan? Are you better now than when you began?

Are you full of energy?

You are and you can plan, but the man of Earth is not going to plan if there is another who is going to work for you. Why let another direct the work you came to do? You can, but why not work for you?

This is a time of jubilation and celebration, but are you able to join in with the land and work on the mind of the general population and clean up the air at this time? Do what you like, but all of you have to decide what to do, plan on doing it, follow you to the end of this plane and see what you can do and do it for you. That is what life is and can do, but do you plan it? Today is a new day. Are you?

CHAPTER 3

The Three Who Are And Who Will Be

When you begin to write a book or a letter or a note, you begin with a beginning and you then address the nature of the book, but the body of the letter is the meaty part that imparts why you are writing the letter or whatever. We will write up a list of the things you can expect in this book, but you will not be able to examine the list in the usual way. There will never be a table of contents in your own life, so why would you expect one today?

This is the table of what you will be able to do when you review whatever you do. You will work on you. You will begin to do work only for you and what is left over will be given away. You will do your own work and not expect someone else to support you ever, but if someone should, you will love them for it. You will not sit and do nothing for it is going to hurt you all over, so in this book you will learn to read and work at the same time and provide for the rest of your life.

You will now begin.

The best way to start your own work is to begin your life as though it were a book, but the table of contents is not the same as the work you do within. It is a measure of what you may or may not do if you work for you and work within, but some will never do it or learn to choose what it is they want to do or know when to begin. We will learn to begin and work within.

You will now notice the first few lines were rejected, but they remained within the work you have to do. Why would they not edit out those lines and begin again?

You will find every time you decide to do another line, you still have the first line within. You have to end it and then begin again, but to simply erase a line and say it is over is not going to go within. You have to end it and decide firmly to begin again.

We will go back to the beginning and reread each line and say within—that line is not going to be in the final work.

Now that you know how to erase a line, do that to your own life—one line at a time. Start at the beginning of your own time. Think to the time when you were so young you could not do much for yourself. That is when you will begin to undo whatever you did and remove what is dead.

If you never see anything good inside another, you are totally used up and unable to begin, so rest a lot. If you are upset and nervous and cannot be bothered by others, do not worry a bit, but head for the covers and sleep until you can see your own life make sense. If you sleep a lot, remember you have a life to live.

Living and being and seeing and believing have a composite effect on the work you are here to do, but are you using each of these tools as a way to view the old and new within you? You will now work on living.

When you work, do you feel this is the end of the world and you do not have to work, but most others do? Are you confused about who is taking care of you?

If you are sick and you have the flu, who looks after you? When you are ill and disgusted that you are, will anyone else feel the same as you and wish you success in beating that illness? Are you feeling ill from being upset about not having anyone else around you?

Are you so lonely now you would prefer anyone to sitting at home with you?

When all of these questions are united and able to be compared within you, there are three individuals who are striving to be there and work with you—you and You and YOU, but who are you? "You" in lower case letters. You is not the only way to look at you today, but if you can, look at the letter U and look at the curve under it.

When you look up and out of the bottom of the U, it is like a cup of water and it holds it and does not leak a drop. If you turn it a bit, it will drip, and if you do not like it, you will spill all of it, but you will still have a U and it will be used whenever it is needed.

What you and U have in common is that both open at the top. You will find your own mind is not accepting all of the work in time, but you will do whatever is open to the kind of mind you have and the time you spend working within you. Do you feel you do not spend enough time?

We will talk again about the work of you and why the time is not going to be aligned at this time, but will and can be exchanged for the price of life.

Another personality is open and closed is the other, but Ruth Lee is unable to do this work without a lot of company. She writes the preamble, but tonight she is hit by the work of what she is going to be and does not feel the way she normally sees herself writing—free and easy and not swift to the work of others.

You are all going to read easily and the writing is done fairly easy among friends, but try to write by yourself and see what kind of work you reveal about you and at times, what you reveal will be okay and have a lot of wonderful work to provide this life. You will find there is a time to decide and a time to wonder why and then go ahead and dedicate the time, but you are not happy enough if you never ever go inside.

If you look at you and the letter U, you will remove the time and the length of the U. The work of the book of you and the letter of U is not as long as it was, but there is a time of remorse now.

The subject matter is so intense that Ruth Lee is about to go deeper than ever. She is unable to seek anyone to stabilize the work and the machine is not much better at writing than her own hand, but we are writing for everyone with the hand and body that she maintains today. You will learn more, but now you have to see that you and U are not the same thing.

The time is up. We will let Ruth Lee go to work when the power is up enough and she is able to breathe. We will give all who read a bit of work to do while she is able to flow into the work of you.

Sit still now and breathe. Do this exercise for you and do something you would never be aware you could do: view your eternal soul from within you.

> Now that you are refreshed, are you able to see into the very being who is you?
>
> Look into the being of you and see if you can see YOU.
>
> Look deeper still and see YOU.
>
> Now that you have a picture of you and You and YOU, let us continue with you and work until YOU follow you and decide what you can do.

There is nothing in your own work and being that is not the way you see yourself, so if you cannot be you, how can you see another? The essence of being and seeing and living are the same in the way you approach others, but you will live easier than you are and will be as calm within as you can be if you see yourself now living among others and having nothing around you but people who are able to be like you are now—calm and clean of ideas that are not going to help you now.

Once the being is inside the seam of you, the entire fabric of life is one long picture of delight. You might not like the work of your life, but you will remember it all this life and delight in whatever you like, but it is going to be you all this life. Act like you enjoy being you and it will help you. Be who you are and the work you do will help all others, but do the work now on being you—smile.

The work you have inside the work you do is you.

Now that you have a good idea of you, we will proceed to you and what you will do to see you.

The first picture of you is one in which you are very new to the Earth and you try to find another who is going to help you. The mother is a wonderful way to see what you were on that first day. You might have found a nurse rather than a mother, but you were warmly embraced and hugged and loved and that is what you expected from the first moment on Earth.

You were not upset by anyone at first? You never wanted to be born, but you let it happen anyway. After the first moment, you became calmer and reasoned, if this is Earth and this is what you have to do to live, you might give it a way of being and breathe, but usually you just started breathing in an outburst. You shouted at the world that you were here and did not like the air, then you became quiet and let the air enter the lungs and worked along with the body until you calmed down.

Why not do that now?

Sit and look inside you now and let the body calm you down and let the air in your lungs sit there until you have to spew it out again.

The day is over if you do not inhale and exhale over and over again, but you will find that to be reminded of it makes you wonder all the time why it is such a bother to breathe better and better and have to be reminded. Why indeed do you breathe?

The being of You and the body of you are not tied together. You are light as a feather and could be bounced into the atmosphere as light as an ounce and disappear, but you in flesh has to produce a lot of hormones and whatever to exist. You will need the compound of oxygen to produce health and work that will produce wealth and a personality that will make you want to reproduce—but what else? You need You to be sure you are okay inside.

You and You are not the same, but go together all the same. If you and You do get together and always remain, the effort of being born is put into a stage of unanimous acclaim and from birth you are famous or whatever, but you seldom ever remain as is. You will generally move into a less stated state of grace and remain. You will remain as is until you are able to remain in an elevated state of mind for longer periods of time, and if you can enter that state and remain, you will express your own life more and more of the time, but you can and will experience pain.

Pain is a way of seeing what is not fitting in the present way of life and is hurting you and giving you no room to be you or forgiving nothing you do. You will enter into the state of bliss, but those still upset will not forgive you for leaving them.

You see? You will.

You can leave the entire world and live on a high hill, but the world will still know you live and choose to do what it is unwilling to do. It will laugh at first and then the ridicule will pull it up the hill to see if you hear it. You will not laugh at first, but then you will because they are so ridiculous and still they are what you were and you will wish to help all of them climb the hill. In time you will not bother with helping anyone at all, but at first you will. You will try to educate one or two at a time and then you will try to mind them all the time and then you will take the bitter pill and learn you cannot be one of them and still live on top of a high hill.

The moral of this fable is not that it is a poor life to climb high, but that you will return to the more elemental parts of life only if you do not enjoy living within the work you are and will be and have inside. You will love living on the hill if you are already there inside and able to see what all you have and will live on the hill and never leave. Your memories are all going to abide in you, so be sure they are great and will help you in time to make any giant stride. Release any that are holding you back or making you take too much out of you to suppress them at this time. You can release and relieve your own back at the same time.

Try now to sit and stare into air and not worry so much about the past.
Is your neck less tense? Are you still nervous or worse? Are you anxiety ridden and regretting that you even started to do this work with us?
Now go inside and elevate the mind.

You will now see that if you cannot do this while you read, you will be able to tape record it and play it back, but that is what the mind does best—nag you over and over to do better and better and not look up or down or back.

Look up now and see if you can see the being YOU. Are you? Look inside deep enough to see YOU. Look fully into the middle being and see if YOU are there and able to be. Now you know where to look and can see, why not be?

There is nothing left in this work but to be and not to see into another until after you fully believe in YOU. If you do fall for others first, you will be disillusioned and upset from birth. You will have to return to the origin of your disbelief in YOU and try to conceive a better need and better way to be. You will rerecord your birth and everything in-between only if you cannot be.

Once the being of you encompasses all that is YOU, you are ready to be entirely free of Earth! Once YOU and the being of all of you are able to go beyond this work and do more and more for the work of the being of all that is good, you will learn to beam yourself into the core of your being known simply as YOU. If YOU is simple, how easy! If YOU is complex, how much do you have to know about you to survive and be able to absorb YOU into your life and become YOU by the time you leave one life in order to be two? What? Is it too complex? You will have to trust more and more if you refuse to learn what to do.

You can educate yourself and a few, but to do more than two is hard on you. You will be given a job to do and that will take you into the work of many who are also going to know what to do and expect you to learn it, too, but you might not like to be like them. They might even frighten you, but you will stick to that job until you know why you dislike them.

Your mind is a job and a method of fighting you, but you will work until you know you and what YOU did to help you to begin this life and find a work you could do.

Your life and your work and whatever kind of work you might like are not going to help you if you never talk about the work to another, so you might decide to talk and talk and talk and never be able to reach another, or you might decide to teach and find another who is able to reach the part you are now leaving to others.

If you can leave an estate to another, would you?

If you were Ruth Lee and had a life on Earth that was as good as it could be, would you consider leaving it?

Who can stay and who is able to determine what day they will be able to move beyond it?

YOU decide what you will do with this life, but God of All is the only one in the world of all who is going to determine when it is time to leave and go within. YOU cannot decide when to end this time. YOU is able to determine later what to do with you and You, but not when YOU will end, too.

Yes, YOU is the line of you and you and you and the commencement of three of You who also go back into two more. All of You until you all connect within a moment to the eternal one known as YOU and YOU and YOU, but then you end at a moment within the one who is God of All and that is the time when some of you will rebel from it all. You will comment that you do not believe and cannot conceive of any such thing, but what do you believe? We would like your comments, please.

Now, what do you think of this moment?

Are all of you open to saying now what it is you dream and believe?

We will begin to take on the room that is in this book and see who is able to work within it, but the reader is going to have to furnish a room and see who is in it. When all are ready, let us commence to view the work we all do to learn from the universe of YOU what to do.

The work! The work is and will be all you can give and get naturally. If you have time to give others work, you have time to do your own work, too, so be sure you never talk about what you do to others until you can see where you plan to be, too. You will find the being and seeing and willing to be are stages of eternity. You may decide time is on your side and not on the side of destiny or whatever you claim to be, but it is. You created the essence that is an essence of the being that is inclined to be in time or is not. You can arrive at a time when time makes no difference, and yet you can decide to stay always in time. Why?

You have freedom inside and it is wide and it is deep and it is so very much a wildness to you and what you do, that some of you take many lives to just cross a view of you. You have to decide why you came to be you? Yes, and once you decide, you then can ascend and do it again, but why?

Are you the only Christ to you? Are you the only being who is true to you? You have beings always that teach and help you, but you cannot say they are telling you what to do. You decide. You decide to follow the Christ this life and another time you decide to be a Hindu or a Buddhist or have the faith of Islam and not any other. In some of you there is the need to be all three of your own beliefs at one time, but now we are working to combine at this time a level of three religious beliefs into one line.

Yes, that is the decent way to be today. Combine. Do you mind? Do you wish to not hear anything that is kind about another line? You will be upset if that is what you had in mind. You are here to work within time and develop into a being that is not upset at being out of it. You are here to do more and more and feel it is you who is being you and not giving it to another who is not going to work within you. You can give up. You can give over your own power to another and you can also decide never to live up to what you are inside, but why?

Are you ready?

Are you all together?

Now, let's see who is in that chair and not ready. Okay, we see some of the people who are not present humanly are in the line and have to step back out of time. We need the room and all who are there to be in time. You will all align your spine. Please sit and stare inside and not mind anyone else again. You will heal and not feel any pain at this time. Sit inside and breathe and remind you not to mind anything that is going on around you.

Now, there seems to be a breath of air in the air and it is so freeing and you can believe now and it frees you of the belief of what you came to Earth to do this time. Let the religious upbringing you cling to subside at this time. We will return in time to pull it up and make it better and better for you over time, but now sit and decide "Why did I choose to be a Roman Catholic this time"?

Are you aware that everyone in this room is Roman and has a bit of it inside them and may even today practice a religious belief that way? We are, but you do not have the capacity to look back and see. We believe you all will be able to do that before you ascend at the end, but do you believe?

You will now offend no one again about what you believe. You will talk to you and you will live what you believe is you. That is what you are to do. Be you and YOU and you will live this life so easily that others will not get inside you or bother you. You will have the time of your life.

You will find that some of the people, who profess to know much, do not believe. They study in order to convince themselves of what is and must come naturally. "If you believe," and you must if you are to finish this life and take on no others. You will find that phrase is a praise of God over others.

You will finish your own love of you and grow beyond you into the work of you and then your work will be so good for you all others will grow and develop with you. You can stunt others, too, but why do we want you?

We want only those who are able to know what it is and why it is important to strive to be new and not over the hill with all the worry over bills and worldly preoccupations and such. You have to work and you have to provide? Yes, in a manner not upsetting to you inside, but it is there and God is always pushing you to it, so do what comes to you and it will never upset you.

You will determine those times in your life, when you were astride a life that was not good for you. You did it. You determined what to do and where to work and why you would want it. You decided. You did not trust God to provide it.

You will now do whatever it is that you love.
Are you now doing it?

Are you able to sit and stand and walk and talk and not have to worry about it? Are you blessed with health and wealth and never think much about it? You can. Wealth is a hazard to the health. It can cause you to want it more and more and not feel you have it. It can make you unreal and demand more and more out of habit and not because you have to have it.

You will now see that greed is envy and it is the seed that causes you to envy others and not see what it is God gave to you and blessed you with. You will find if you spend all your time on others, you have little time to decide why you might be so tired of working with them and wish to leave the work again to others. You will not burn out and you will not shout at others if you are working within and doing what you can to win.

You will find if you are unkind to you and another is able to stop that happening again, you might even resent them. You might even think they are not a friend again, but you have to do whatever there is and then move. If you stick, it unravels in time and is no good for you.

Move now and see if the spine can move within and take you to another time.
Breathe in and out and see if your spine is out of line. Is it?
You will adjust then to the next line.
Here we begin to go within and all who can will go and seek whatever is within them. Can anyone here tonight sit inside and feel the channel open within them?

We will not hold anyone up by forcing them to remove what is not good for them, but you will have to bend and mend you and decide what to do, too. You are who is here and you all know there is a method to all we say and do and we seldom ever pray over you. Why?

You are all here to do good for you. If you are still reading all that came here in this book to you, you are also being good to you, so we need not pray for thee. You are in the work and you will be, but if you came to this quite naturally, you will be blessed beyond capacity and be able to know and grow and benefit more than those who are not able to decide if they want to be in the best line of this life. You know. You have at times set aside the wisdom and prided yourself in knowing what to do when others were choosing the way of God today.

You sat and you stared at others. You said, "My, what a wonderful time I am having with others and they would frown at me if I were to say I was holier than them today." Of course, you are all the same and so are we. The soul is not greater in one than another, but some take on greater responsibility and change the way and some do not and some delay, but all are here on Earth and above in a way. You are here and you might see the lesser being of you and not the greater woman or man you can be, but we see you all.

We are here today to talk away the way you used to be, but you will continue to do whatever you see. You visualize and decide what to be, and then if you are truly aware and wise, you plan to blend you into the work you do. You will find others who are as adept as you? Not likely. Why? You are not really able to see who is like you.

You will find some talk like they are like you and some seem to act much as you believe you are, but they are not you. You alone can blend and bend and be you.

The time to be you is always with you. You cannot afford to let others tell you who you are and what to do, but if you are totally ignoring others, you will offend them and they might try to bend you into the way they seem to believe you should be, but if you never offend anyone again, it is highly unlikely they will bother you again.

My friends, of course, I speak not lightly, but you are friends and this is the beginning of a meeting of friends who are taking the bend in this life and asking for advice and help when the end comes to this life, so it is a meeting of Friends.

The time has come and I am free of all that once was a bother to me, but I come in harmony and I come to help you see that believing and being and having a lot is not impossible to have and be and yet it is. You have to believe and things have a way of taking away your humanity today.

You might decide that the Quakers died and they are not around today, but they are. I am one and I have come to teach all others the time is here to begin a state of grace and decide why you all race about in time and try to erase the old time. You all are here to decide what is weird or queer about the end of time? No, but it is a time when many of you will disappear.

You will find a meeting house and you will come to that place time and time again and erase all that is in the face reminding you time is not going fast enough for you. You will find lines are there to remind you that you are not taking time for you. If you worry and want advice, the lines are etched all this life, or you do not pay the price of taking the world's advice and covering the face enough. You will learn and you will earn what you do learn. If you are wise and never fully ask for all the advice and do the work that comes to you, you will prosper in time. It takes years to be wise and it takes even longer to have time to amass what is there and not used daily by you.

You will find we Quakers are not shaking ever inside, but we quake at the thought of God of All inside. We are not proud and we do not proclaim in many different ways the way to worship anyone or God of All today. You are asked only to pray and sit and meditate and be as you may.

Today, we are in this room and we have often visited this group as a union and we have often sat here among you, but today we ask you all to pray with us and see what you believe. If you have a message, you will open to the century and talk to us.

We will tell you nothing, but you will tell those present what you believe. Can you open to the channel within you?

The way of the Quaker is fine and decent and exposes no one to discomfort, but you have to release hatred, discriminatory beliefs within you, and you cannot war. You cannot control others who hate you.

That is about all we stand for, but you will find this is a religion that is good and kind and helps others and is and will be in time the kind of religion you will want to be.

Now in a Quaker relationship the man and woman are free, but the desire to be alone is controlled in the home. You would not take liberties and then let them alone. You would have to ask for the permission of family to be wedded and you would have to be able to be bedded naturally and raise a family, but you would not leave the home for others if you began to feel the time was at hand when you wanted more. You would be bound by your word and honor is a belief that you will honor whatever you believe, so it can be so easy, but for those who lie or are dishonest inside, it is cruelly unable to be.

You will all now see.

Look inside and be.

Are you able to see a hat that is old? Can anyone see anyone who reminds them of the time they were also a Friend?

Group response:

(I saw a woman in a veil, and couldn't see the face.)

Ah, our Friend Ray, you went back too far. You were in Roman times, so step forward and meet the woman again without a veil. The Friends never have put women behind them and women are often the speakers of the congregation and never stand out as being less than men. They are still here today, but now most women blend in with them. Look again, Ray, what do you see today?

It's okay. You don't have to pressure again, but if anyone is able to see a Friend and know them, you are already on that way. You will all remain a Friend today, but later you will return to the way of today and blend in the way of the Friends and be you in every way and not hesitate to say, "I am a Friend, but also practice another way." You will find there is time and you will in time be able to feel better about any religious organization than you did before this time.

Why? By learning from the Friend inside, you will see others with the tolerance of the Quakers and others who never pretend to be anyone but themselves and never ever do without for others, but take care of anyone who is treated unfairly and is presented to them.

You will remember you were once in a slave ship and you came to this world and you betrayed another in order to be the lover of another, and then you became another sort of pain in your own vain way of being who you are today, but we will work on that another day.

You will find the Quakers are blind to color and you will be after today. You will not see and believe in anyone who is willing to do evil to anyone because of a racial discriminatory belief, and you will help them instead of abetting them by turning away from them. You will not argue with them, but remove the power within you and turn the group away with you. You can. You will also be able to stand up for your own beliefs and you will believe in you. You will do whatever you came to Earth to do, too.

Now, let's assume that Ruth is the speaker of the meeting and she is the Quaker who is asking you to speak only if God is inside you. Will you now sit and stare inside and quietly assume you are speaking in that society and able to speak of your own love inside for all that is you and no one will ever remind you again of what you spoke of this evening to them.

This evening I am speaking as the speaker and I have a passion and I have a fear and I wonder if all of you here are able to see me. I want you to know I will disappear and you will not pursue me, but I will always love you. Even if the time is near that you must leave, too, we will be near. I will be with you in spirit and I am not upset at all. But God is deliriously present.

You can all now speak.

WE ARE ALL ONE WITH GOD. NO ONE IS GREATER THAN ANYONE ELSE. ALL THE PLANTS AND ANIMALS ARE ALIKE, AND LIKE US, ALL IS WONDERFUL.

If each reader can unite with a group as we do as we write, you too will greet the group as never before after you finish this work as a Quaker. Grow into the work and know that on a really fine Sunday, only one or two had the courage to speak, but tonight so many of you were able to bloom and speak because you have worked into the deepest avenue of you.

You will find you and YOU are here all the time, but only when you decide to open you really, really wide do you feel the power come into you and take you by the hand and lead you to your own promised land.

You will find there is a lot of pressure in the atmosphere that was not here in the prime of time, it is not here to disappear, but to remind you over time you have all contributed to the time of ending.

You who are sublime are not ridiculous to anyone who is wise when you advise not to harm the Earth and anything thereon, but some who are wise are counseled to talk no more to others. Why?

Talk abounds today and seldom is the quiet way the way. We would adopt the Quaker way today. We would also not say so much at church or about the way we pray, but you all are here today to help us teach others what they might like to say. So, we are welcoming you to do more and more expressing of the way you feel today, so many others will also grow in that way.

We will also not say who you are speaking and preaching and talking to this way, but you will be relieved only three were placed in the way of others to read so no one is able to see what you truly believe.

You all are very filled now with the old ways. You all could write up recipes and advice and give them to others today, but you would be expected to use them the most if you were to give them away. You have to be you. Do not expect anyone else to do things you only say you do today.

You will remind you over and over not to be impressed by what others say. Look at it and read into it whatever, but you are not to digest whatever another says in ego to you on any given day. The spirit will decide within you what to do only if you are admitting you do have a spirit within you and you are willing to open to it.

When Christ willed to you all the gift of tongues and the willingness to call upon others like Paul, you were not willing, but now you will see you can speak to many others who do not believe the same as you. That is the gift of tongues. You can speak as though you are one of the others and yet you are able to stay within you all the way through to the end of you.

You will find the Holy Spirit is often seen as a dove of purity and white and flying and having a wide wing span, but you are thinking angels again and not the purity of the light of the Holy Spirit that resides in this time and is here to unite all of you who are ready to take flight again.

You will find that the dove of your own mind is pure and you can soar to the stars and back tonight, so align the spine and dream of another time. We want you all here to sing tonight and be as one within you all and then disappear, but you will all hum within and let the mind disappear. We will use the mantra Om and we will hum with you all. Can you help us unite tonight?

Within the universe is a star that just appeared. You all called it to you with the vibration of the sound that is universal and has no end to it. It goes from here and blends into the atmosphere and bends around the Earth and disappears? Never. Sound will reappear and appear and seem to disappear and it will go through and over and beyond you. We will send love now to follow that tone so all who are wherever will feel the power of love and know to not disappear into any other part of the life they have to live today. Send love now.

When you can settle your own life into one line, make that line unending and unwilling to end and let it blend within anyone who is going to be with you time and time again so all of you will blend into a time when there is love around you and all who are envious of you will have to love in order to be like you.

You will find that whatever you do and whoever you were, is now set aside. You will now be able to bend over and be you and feel as good as ever, provided you always awake feeling like you. You will never force you to do more or be better or whatever, unless you have not been you.

You will now look forward. Look up! What is inside you? You. You are now You and that fear of being inside you and being You is over. Now all who have truly worked together will unite and feel better and not be upset no matter whatever. You will blend into the work and you will all disappear when it is through, but you will go to do whatever with a renewed vision of you.

Now you and all the you's who are all in this work doing better are together, let us assume you continue to work like this. Will you be able to soon see all of you together? The three and three and three will mend into a blend and be a string of energy that bends into the universe into the work of the worlds and becomes the wonder of the Universe and is of God and will not reverse. We will all learn a new verse. We will all say over and over after today: I AM THE ONLY YOU.

What can that line mean to you?

You are not going to be upset by anyone again. You will only see you and know that whomever takes up a battle against you is merely trying to do more and more to make you bend and be another, but that is what will strengthen you more than being always surrounded by Friends.

Friends will bend to talk to you and say you do better than you do, but a pure enemy or two will never hurt you. They are inclined to brutally tell you the truth about you, so be sure you know if they are pure, and if they are just as pure as you are and are just not like you, they probably will help you more than anyone else today.

Be sure you listen to all who are trying to help you perform in a more positive way. You will find enemies over time, but you must ignore and go before them and ignore them more and more until they are way behind the time and know nothing more about you. You can. You will merely shift your mind away to another time and let them be no friend again.

You will find that the quaking of the heart was not to stop your heartbreak, but it meant you were shaking with the love of the life that is now on the other side, so you will find your father is fine and he is among your friends on the other side and standing in line. He is not yet judged and cannot come for you, but in time, he will arrive and be sitting next to you.

You will find time is so comparative in other lines, so to tell you he is going to visit you in time is not meant to confuse you, but it is meant to console you and tell you that God is in the work you do, so do more and do more for you.

When we talk to anyone on a personal level, we teach all of you, so no one is special, but if you were to find a positive role model and then found that model was human, would you then refuse to continue to follow them? You usually do, but it is you who made them a god over you, so do not say it was them.

You will find if you are helped much today and another then tells you that you have found nothing good or fine at this time and you let them convince you that you were unwise to follow you inside, you will condemn you and them in time, so be wise. Listen to you and do not take the advice of others unless you requested it from them.

You will find that tonight and the day you read of this night are the same, and yet they happen in time in a different frame. You can decide you are in the group tonight when you sit and read and pass the time, or you can say you cannot see anything of what is going on at this time. It is all inside and you can develop a time line that will unite you with others in time and still not harm the line of you over time, but best to leave that until later. You have plenty to do this time and if you dawdle so much that you are not done with the work you came to do, you could be made to come back again and what would that prove?

You will find many proud of the prowess they say they possess inside them and are able to fly and talk and see spirits within and so on, but you will not listen to them. You will not envy anyone again. Your spirit takes you as you present you to it, but if you do not go within, when do you think you can rendezvous again? You will find there is time now to be inside the bend that is coming within sight of this room tonight.

We will leave you and decide what you can do, but all of you will talk about you and not be upset by the time there is within and outside of you again. We want to know more about the life of women and men at this time, but when we return to you again, we will know you as men and women and whomever you bring with you. You do not attend these sessions alone, but tonight the Friends were again hosting this session for you and others to attend.

You will find your mind is able to travel over time, so do not let anyone again say it is a special way to be today. All do it most every day. When? When you dream and see inside you another who is not within. You will now come back to the room and zoom into the life you set aside tonight, but do not be unwise or foolish again and say that anyone else is wiser than you are and will be better than you will be. That is not right and that is not wise and that will build pride within the other and spoil them this life. You must not confuse anyone again with being you.

There is a moment when you do not see and that is the hardest time to be, but if you have a strong belief in you and what you do, you will pull it off or go through or do whatever you believe you can do, but do you?

Are you so deep now that you can see what it is you have to be?

Are you ever so nervous that you see only what you will be and not what you are? Are you so anxiety ridden at any moment that you cannot see how to be? Look inside at that moment and find out the place you hide and open it up and turn on the light!

You will hide anything that is not without a moment of work to be done inside. What? You have to live inside and work all the time, so you will hide anything that is not being worked upon at this time and you let it seem to be unimportant or you do not release it to anyone else to see, so it gains importance to only you and no one else cares about it, too. That is the reason anxiety is so oppressive, but are you oppressing you and doing nothing now to repair the seams that are open from all the oppression you commit upon you? Sew up the seams and rejoin us in the next seating. We will wait for you.

CHAPTER 4

What Is The World And Who Are You?

When you dedicate a book to the work of another, do you feel they will love you more or better than if you dedicated it to your mother? It's possible, more than likely no. You are never going to find anyone who cares as much as the one who created you, but that is not the mother who bore you to this life.

You are here and now able to describe a life of caring or not, but why bother? You are now within you and being you and taking fullest care of you, so let others go who once provided for you. Let them alone.

You will grow if you work harder than you did to grow; but if you have grown to the fullest degree, what can you be? You will and always shall be you and your own work will grow more and more sure of being accepted by you and possibly a few others if you work harder than you think you need to and polish it better than others say should be.

You all work for a degree of time and the electricity is there for you always to work in time, but most of you decline to work and do what you came to Earth to do this time. Why? You do not believe you have a path to make for you today.

You create this life and the work you do creates a world all around you. If you work and do the work of a few, are you still the only one who is going to be able to do work for you? Yes and no. You will find only the most compassionate and able will flock to help you. You can see now only a few are enabling the Scribe to write down these lines, but you are all able to jump out of you and into the life of a scribe if you all sit and write down what you do with the Scribe.

You will all go home and begin to write about a life you have inside. You will produce a lengthy article about you and the work you are to do. You will work and it will not be asked again if you did it or not, but you will find out all others will know if you did not.

You will bring the article next week. You will not sit and stare into the air all week. You will write about what you are and intend to do. You will never compare you to anyone else ever, but share. You will all grow by leaps and bounds if you are able to deliver a fair share of the work we do here, but then you can decide to sit and do nothing and let the air fill you in time.

Your mind is not open to the dark if you are closed inside and have no use for the dark, but if your mind is inclined to want to poke around a lot, sooner or later, you will get into a dark spot. You then have to arrange again to brighten up your own day. You will not depress anyone else ever again.

You will get you to decide why you have so many times decided not to win or to go into the best possible lines that could begin at this time. You will decide. We will write away and let some others show you ways they are inside so you can compare you to them, but what do you gain if you never feel pain?

If your mind needs a drug to see itself as it was, you will find you cannot grow into the next love or life for you now. You will stay consumed by the drug or weed and not be able to concede that you are not happy as you were and now as you will be. You create the day and the lives that are all around you by deciding what kind of life you will be.

You are the only world you will have, so choose wisely. You will not be upset if the crowd is not wise. You will choose sides and educate some to be as you like or you will adjust to them all this life. You can lead or follow, but you must follow at least twice in order to know what to do if you should ever be chosen to lead others. You can decide to lead, but it will not happen unless others choose you to take them wherever or teach them whatever. You cannot decide to just take over. Adults will not let that happen now.

You were a child who never listened at all? You are still a child. You cannot learn to be an adult if you never learned to take orders. That is what a child must learn to do and learn skills that will help them learn a trade or work that will take them to the best level of earnings from now to their old age.

If you never work or do anything at all, you are not able to know why others are pleased or dissatisfied and how much money can mean. You will be mean and not have any idea of the value of what you do and how it works for you, so you will do things you want and then in the end be consumed by want. You have to work for the money or it is not going to please you at all.

Whatever you believe, it matters not if you grieve. If you have no need for the work of another, you will not use it ever, but will wonder who does need such work ever. If you use a lot of tools and work with leather, you will wonder why people grieve over the leather and how it comes together because you work with the product that makes up your dreams. If you doubt another is any good, you doubt you forever.

If you wonder if there is eternal bliss or whatever, it is that which keeps you seeking out another to live with; you will find you cannot live with anyone and remain kind. You are not able to understand bliss. You will not be able to live with another over a long period of time.

When you have trouble with your own work, are you sure everyone knows you are the greatest and the others are overpaid? You will find that is the common consensus these days. You either are overpaid or unwilling to expose yourself to the credit you extend to others. Why not clearly evaluate what you do and ask exactly what you expect for it and then do it for you?

Your house is open to the elements inside of you and others, but you might only worry about the price of the TV. Why? Are you aware of the violence that comes to the mind via a screen and then becomes so controlling of everyone in the home that in time they relate badly to others? You may not visualize now, but if you watch a picture over and over and over again it will become you inside. Be careful of the work you do and the kind of pictures you keep around you. They will proclaim to others who you are and they will in time become you.

You are either a clown or a sage is what one will say to the other, but all of you are both and contain many other roles. You can decide what to do and then act upon what you do, or you will not do anything now for you. If you are assigned a project and later say you did not hear what to do or refused to do it, you will normally not like those who did a great job on it. You will refuse to accept responsibility for not doing your own work and doing it in a day. You can. All work is divided into healthy ways and you either do what comes to you or you do not. When you are ready, please remove the crowd around you.

You will now go inside the mind and reveal what you do to you to keep you under the wheel and not controlling you into the next avenue. Exit at the next spot where you are unable to decide what to do.

Sit now and figure out why you wheel into the avenue and do not really know whom you are and what to do. Think of the fool who would drive across the country and not have any fuel and taxes to feel are due. Think of what confidence or lack of wisdom he or she must possess to go and never rest.

When you are able to sit and do nothing, rest.

You will now continue. When you continue to do this and not sit and rest, you work within you and decide to do whatever you came to Earth to do; but why not make sure you are on the right path for you?

Why?

Are you aware that you cannot compare you to anyone?

Are you aware that you do compare you to everyone who is around you?

Why? Are you alive? Are you bright inside?

Look at these questions and seize the one that really gets to you.

When you are deep in the seam of a difficult day, you might forget to pray. You could, but that will only upset the work you came to do. Think first, pray for you to be able to do what is best for you, and then do the work that comes to you.

When you see such a simple lesson, are you able to say, "Thank You"? Not if you did not rest and work it all through.

When the day is over and this book is overdue for you, you will find you did not do much of the work that came to you to do, but you will feel you flew over the words or you were stuck halfway through. Why not fly?

You can decide to flit about and not sit down, but you might not be able to fly if you never land and gain the strength to plan. You have to know you and what you do and why you want to gather around you people who like you if you are to go inside the world and achieve a level of celebrity.

Most of you want to be famous or noticed for doing whatever, but most of you will not work so hard as to do what you must do to attract the level of attention that must be yours if you are to be famous. You must not see that fame is a degree, but that it means someone has achieved something they were not expected to be.

If you were Mozart and had a lot of gifts to give others, you would assume others were not working hard when they did not produce the same amount of gifts. You would begin to not work as hard as you did. You would become selfish and arrogant and not happy to work as you once did and sooner or later you would let the work get away. Why? You are not able to judge the age of a seer until the age is used in time to get the work across to others—and if you are wise at an early age, all others assume you will achieve and do not help you to succeed. That is the shame of the human beings who make up the race of teachers in this age.

You will now go inside you and embrace the self that is able to face all who say you are not going to achieve and do whatever it takes to make them erase that decision in their own way. You do not have to hate to achieve, but many use that device all their lives to erase the hatred others gave them when they only wanted to survive.

You will remember that the prostitute is not alive in the arms of a man or woman and is not loving anyone at any time, but was taught this way of making a living by those who were most unforgiving and accosted the soul when it was very young and never let it grow old in the usual way. You will be paid in a life of prospective alliances if you never are able to let the prostitute among you survive and teach you they are not here to survive, but to teach others to truly love if they wish to survive.

The scourge of this life is an antibiotic given to sick people and well without any prescriptive reason or belief in helping the patient thrive, but you believe it is a vaccine that keeps you alive. You kill off all that is good inside in order to shut out the powers of a few that are not working well. Why? You will now know you have power; but do you use it well?

You have a lot of time to sit and prop up your feet, but will you realize it until the feet swell up and give you trouble? Are you the type of personality who is never going to rest until the death mask is fitted for you? Try to smile and see if the mask is ready yet.

If your face is revealing so much about you today that others know right away what you believe, you are simply not believed. We notice no one talks with a smile who is going to achieve any level of belief from those gathered in the same room, but look at who is made president of the greatest country on Earth. A man who smiles constantly and usually never gives an impression of caring if you smile back or believe. Are you able to achieve that kind of belief?

You will not smile if you have a lot of money? You will if you know you can make more of it and have plenty of time to spend it. If you are lacking either, you will not like the idea of any money being set back. You will spend whatever arrives and thrive for only the day or so when you are able to see money there in front of you. Money is a weed and takes time and order to succeed to believe that money is not greed, but the wanting of it. You are who decides what you want today, and so many of you are so needy you are merely greedy and believe others have so much more than you do today that you envy them and then are jealous of what they have. This is a triple whammy and will not leave you with any rest. You will harm those who are blessed, but you will be harmed no less more by the unrest that will hit the center of your own world for not feeling blessed in being you and a separate entity among the rest.

You have to believe and see others are not going to be able to free up the work of the world unless you are able to help by degrees of concentration what you did to produce unrest within you. You are the world and your degree of concentration is a belief that you must be and shall be what you achieve. You are all on Earth to be and help you to success, but what do you do to achieve the success you believe is necessary to have to succeed? You will now see inside the mind what is bothering you so much of the time.

Look at the seam of the mind.
What kind of mind do you want?

Are you wide or narrow and able to see nothing but what you believe of you and others? You will be widened if you travel more and more and see others around you. You will not be able to narrow your mind if it is stretched out to the outer limits, yet it does shrink with time to the line within you that is most naturally what you want to live within all this life or two. You do live at a level above and below you, so go slow and seek out the best balance between the two.

You can rise above the level you are now, but it will balance you by dropping lower if you do not work very hard to adapt to the new work of the higher level and stop the work from falling into the next view of you before you are through working for you.

You can ascend to the next level and begin again, but why not eat and dance and enjoy the work you have to do always here in this plane and make a plan to ascend at the end and meet you with a friend? You will take no one with you? You can. You can work with anyone on Earth to blend into a perfect configuration of the figure eight and win the work of both, but you must bend and blend more than most of you can do. You can and will work, but will you work for another who is as good as you? It takes time to dedicate your life to you, but to add another is almost inhuman to do. You might try, but trying is not going to make all things come to you. You have to follow you through to the end of the life you now have inside you and view you and another standing side by side and being able to stand the view of one of you leaving before the other. It is generally that way, but occasionally, both can ascend when the entire job of blending is through. Do you now know anyone who is working to go with a friend?

We will blend with you, but we are not on Earth and cannot end with you. You need a companion or a friend to help you go to such an end, but it works and helps both of you. You can find anyone or sit and mope and hope, but it is usually the work you do that will bring someone close to you.

Now, let us all go inside the work you do.

Are you able to help us? Are you able to show us what you do? You must if you are to carry out the task and get others to learn why you came to Earth. You will have to explore the ways you are first. You will have to look inside you and decide why you choose to do it for you. You must.

If you sit and work on whatever you are told to do, are you working for you? Yes. You are choosing to sit. You are choosing not to fit you into the climate or move or do what you are more able to do. You might be wise to sit and look and work for some time, but you should be able to know before 25 what it is you wish to do with your life. If you do not, you will miss it.

You are going to decide earlier and more maturely what you believe if you are raised by a family that believes in you and what you are to be, but it is still not the price of company that makes the family help you to achieve. You must decide to work and do what you love or it will all come unglued by the time you are 42.

Today a man or woman is still a child at 41 in some avenues, but why is that so mean of you to let them go so long and not help them grow inside?

You might decide you do not want to be bothered by the immature and nervous, but you are immature or nervous if that is what you decide to do. You will find if you are able to help another, you are fine and fit no matter what your age. You might be classified a child of 9 years and still be able to help a mother 32 years older fit into the world and be better for it. You might even be the mother of the 9 year old child who is unable to understand why the child gives up all day, but will pray so the child will learn to tolerate frustration more each day.

Frustration is a way of fitting you into the work you do. You either find a way to fit or you leave it. Frustration is not bad in any way, but it is exasperating to you if you do not get paid for it.

You will align the spine now and sing the praises of all who pay you for whatever you do at this time.

This is a chant that will enable you to raise your own element in time to the top of the line of that avenue. You must not change the way you think of those who pay you or you will have to get another way to meet the day's bills and will have to be full of another way soon. You cannot say you hate the work and continue to bloom doing it.

You will find one man and one woman are not going to change a group, but will if the group is small enough that they take up the major portion of the energy formed by the group. You will not be able to say why you have designs on leading anyone at this time, but you will find many others wish to boss you all the time. Why?

You will not let others take advantage of you unless that is what you are told to do. You may be told to let another lose their way so they can learn that being a fool is the harder way, but it does not say you are a fool, too. You will be called to work and idle, too, but be able to know when you have to do one or the other.

You will today sit in this group and idle.

You will prepare the daily list of what you will do.

What are you going to do when this group is no longer available to you?

Look inside. What are you hiding from you?

When you feel that you are going to decide why you hide and why you are unable to die with your own work not done for you, you will know why you came to Earth this time. Why not find out now?

You will prepare a list of work you need to do now.

See what you have written inside and write it down when you have time.

You will not list everything at one time, but add things as you tune into the world around you. The world is a work you have to do for you.

You will not notice much about you if you never have anyone else around you, but you will notice the trees or bees or whatever else is active around you. Activity is what sees inside you and makes you be you.

Yes, activity is a motion that causes you to feel the ocean inside you and not to seize the tide and make it work for you—is to be in a way a great fool. Why do that to you when you can be a wise sage all your days?

If you want to marry another, why ask anyone else what to do ever?

If you are asked to marry, why ask anyone else what to do?

Are you forever a fool or not willing to be responsible for what you do?

Which controls you—the fool or the wisdom of the ages displayed by others who work harder than you do?

When you have time to run to one kind of seer to another, you have time to study inside for you. Why not do the work and then see if your work is better or worse than what they do? You can, but it is not likely to happen again if you plan to work harder than ever every time you meet someone who is better and better over time and will be ahead of you in line.

Yes, there is a line. You have found you stand in lines on Earth all the time and hate them, but you have to learn those who work hard are generally more alert. They position themselves to leave the work of the world and do work they love to do first and arrive at the other side ahead of the work they intend to do over. You will have no work to redo if you work now all the way through to the end of you, but if you never do, you will be back to do it over for you.

When today is over, you will not age a bit, but your mind will know order and you will take orders better than you now do. If you never learn the way to do things the way you are to be told is best for you to do, you will not age gracefully and may remain foolish all your days. Why not age, as you would love to be seen in a novel of love and compassion and not just the fashion of these tired old days?

The days of this world are so old that fashion is tired of even reinventing ways to clothe you and your world. Why are you so tired of the new? You do not even know the new work, but complain of it still. Why?

You have old work and the world of this time is to finish and get beyond if you are to risk no problems in the next life about to open inside. Many will begin the next life while still on this side, but you may never be among them if you do not work to ascend.

Ascension is a length of line that takes you from one time to another. You will take that line and study more or you will end the line with this time and not ascend, but actually bend into the next view of you and do this work over for you.

The work of ascending and bending is not the same, but comes to you at the end of a day or two of the work you do on Earth to be you. You either learn and emerge greater and better than ever or you go on as you did before—only tired of the work and tired of being as you were. Why not rise your own lives at this time?

Rise? Yes. It implies that you work and it arrives and sweeps you to the next work and the next as you feel better, but you still have to exert. You have to work. You cannot sit and let another make you fit. You could work on others, but they will not be any better for it. You would negotiate a better wage or whatever for these days and then not be able to cross over in the end of these days, so make sure your wages are for your own old age.

You will now sit.

Go inside and see what it is you want to do to fit into the day you are in. Be sure you are aware of the work you must do yet. See it.

We will now go inside the work of our Teachers and the rest who abide in the work of the skies to help us all fit.

This is the best of all time. You will sit and be fit and you will know it. You will never ever whine. You will never ever say you do not fit. You will do fine. You will see others who are also you over time fit in and do fine, but now be you and do whatever you see fit to do and let us work with you.

We are all gathered in a moment of time, but are you?

Are you fit and fully equipped to meditate with us for an hour at a time? We know so many who aspired to be here with us as we are scribed this hour or two, but so many were unfit to meditate with us for this time and so we are delighted to be among this group of those who meditate and decided to never hesitate to unite with others and the Scribe to write this way.

Some would scoff and laugh at the idea of teachers from another space being able to congregate in a special place, but not these folks who are here tonight and will work inside to relieve the feeling that they are not united in some way. We will unite all of you today, but some of you will ignite in a most special way tonight.

We are aware of the mother to be and we are very delighted. What wonderful company!! You are all blessed by the desire of a soul to be among you and be with the mother and not wait until the later days of this pregnancy to be within her and live within her body. You will find most souls do not unite with the body until the mother or the host soul is ready to accept all there is to be and is welcoming the soul to the body, but some never are expected and some are never wanted, but not this baby tonight.

You will find there is a lot of work for all of you and some of you will work for you and another, too, but decide to do work that fits you. Decide to work on you.

You will find there is nothing at all that is undone if you really do a great job, but if you rush too much or ignore the rules, you will have to run back and forth or do it over for You, so tonight let us all unite and be ready to take flight.

We will understand only a few voices are mingled in these lines, but you will remember when we first assembled, three of them had a lot more to do to align themselves with you. They were unable to assume the role of a teacher and not be upset by the absence of recognition from you all and so now all of you are united into a group and none of you is recognized to be anyone simply as a soul or two. You all are united and the teachers are here with you, but who is going to actually teach you? YOU!

You decide in every issue of every tissue that you believe or not. You decide and you either believe and work through all the issues and create new tissue or you die. You will not live to be old at all if you lose your way within you today. It will take time, but you will not be able to thrive and your drive will leave you and you will pity you so much when the time arrives for you to "die," you will not be grieved at all by those who really knew you. Why? You never lived as you could or believed in others and wanted their best good.

You will adopt or adapt to anyone, but some are easier to call friend and some take time to blend, but anyone who takes the time to blend with anyone is going to have a friend. You can exist in any time and not realize it, but if you exist for another all the time, you will lose you in time. You have to do your own work for you!!!

You have to bloom, too. You will not be upset and you will conceive a new belief in you, but first let us all conceive the belief that you will be you and able to do this in time with the Scribe—one line at a time, and know she is not working against the flow, but with you in time.

You will also go inside your own mind and flow and flower and grow into the next issue or idea or ideal that is to be you. You will decide. You will guide and accept the guidance of others, but first know where you want to go.

You are not here to sit and let another tell you where to go, but that is the problem of people who are not willing to exist in the present and wish to slow down all others by not cooperating with anyone who is going to grow. You either admit you are not willing to work, or you get going and work and submit to the work you love to do within you.

You will now see the work of this group is to work on a book that is going to explore the teachings of those who are guided by the Lord to help all whom are not able to see what is going forward. You will work and you will provide the way to help others by teaching them today that a group can work together if it is prepared to work and never says it is not willing to be.

You all released a lot of energy to be, but you all conceived a belief you would be like Ruth Lee. You are. You all believe and she is one who is able to be with you all, but sooner than you can be, you will find you have to convert over to you all you do and accept that is true or you will not believe in anything at all or be able to work again with Ruth Lee. You see?

You are not working to devote a life to anyone on Earth, but thee. You are here to be. You are here to work and do whatever you feel is best and makes you feel real, but if Ruth Lee or another is able to help you confer upon you the degree of aptitude you seek to find and know about you, you are wise to go and work inside to flow. The flowers of youth are not wasted on the youth, but are there to help the society empower those who are about to leave Earth. Do you agree?

Are you all here tonight? Yes or no?

Well, it seems we heard so little from you all that we figured out you were not even breathing until you smiled, so let us all breathe deeper than you seem to believe is proper to do with others around you. Breathe!

Now, as we are all here and able to do this if you are all willing to breathe into the lungs your own ambitions first, we will help you to heal you and to work inside you to do less and less on your work of this life and more and more on the lessons of the eternal being called YOU tonight.

You will be.

You have a lot of changes tonight. We will meet on a scheduled routine only once or twice until there must be more nights. We want you to do whatever it takes to be here and make no mistake, be ready to assume the role of teacher of others. You can decide to leave tonight. We will not accept that you do not need anyone to help you to succeed, because all of you are humans and none of you has ascended into the light.

You will all need you tonight and you will help the others around you to ascend when the time is right.

You all work. You all get together. You all are willing to volunteer to help another put together published materials that are made to help others, but now you are to find out tonight that all of this was simply a way to get you to today when all of you will be told what to do.

You, and the people who are going to read this work, will work today to do the work of others and help all to learn to pray and be themselves all day. You can find out what to do later, but now you all are going to pray and ask for help in every way to be able to pay for the work you must do to be here in this room and work with Ruth.

You will find the time you are in this work is going to be brief at first, but in time it will take a lot of patience and cooperation between each of us to work with you in order to get this message from you to the world. You all will work and you all will place this work out into the world.

You are all stunned? No, you do not realize what has begun.

You will be asked to do the entire task and not have anyone to tell you what to do once it is begun. You are all of you a figure of the fullest number 8 and you are a climatic occurrence that occurs only once in this race. You are to accumulate a degree of work from others that agree with you and help you to conceive the way to print and publish this work after it is done for you and are able to be placed in your way to do.

Ruth Lee? You are to leave and take nothing of this work with you. You will ask only that the group let you do the final proof. You will trust they will not betray the work you are dedicated to today. You will detach your own life in a way and let all who are gathered today work with this material and make it appear in a far different way to others in the work and across the Earth and know it will work.

You all are asked to sit and not bask in the sun. You are not to ever say you did the work and did not ask. You all volunteered to be in the work and now all of you are here within You and doing what you all came to Earth to do—work for us and help us to work with the people who refuse to believe that God of All conceived you all and none of you is more precious than any one of you.

The stunning success of channels today is an admission by the authority of the Churches that you conceive to be a way of God speaking today? No, but all of you will challenge their view. You are being asked to help today to prepare the way to bring the churches together again and not spearheaded by so many factions they betray all that is good and all that was prepared by God for all of you to use today.

You will not say that a religious belief is not yours. You will not compare one way to another after today, but you will work with others who say their prayers different from you. You will also ask them to teach you about what they do to meditate and connect inside to the permanent guide and whatever else you want to do for you.

You will travel as a group and you will teach one or two who are going to also want to be like you, but not today. Today all of you are here to learn what to do and how to pursue a new life within you as a group. You will ignite. You will not have to fight. You will just be you.

You and you and the new you who exists in this room is a group of you and you will learn what to do to be a friend to two more who are not like you. The rest are all very much a crew, but some of you do not know much about all of you. You all are perfect and fit inside this room and you all know what to do to make a success of Ruth, but you never do. She did that for you so all of you can succeed by doing only a few things you believe—work and decide as a group what to do to succeed even better than you do by yourself or with a partner or two.

You will all get together and anyone who is now reading this book is in the work, too. You will all be together. You all see each other in the work you have to do, but some are in the flesh and some are in the lines that run together. You will be one or the other, but pretend now to be one who is willing to work together.

You will help by teaching and not preaching to anyone about what you are to do.

You will help by telling no one to get it together when you are completely undone.

You will not ask anyone to follow ever.

You will not be asked by anyone to lead if you never are a success in your own life and seek forever to be as you are tonight.

You will all now know exactly what needs to be done and whatever else can be done to make this work a success, but give it time. You all have time to do things in your own line and align the spine into a lot of emotional ideas and beliefs, but you will not ever at any time decide not to believe. You are and will be the missionaries of this line on time.

You will be asked over and over, "Why did you go to that class?" You will know then, but it may not be evident today. You will not be upset or nervous and asked a lot of personal questions ever. Why? You are anonymous as a group and anyone who takes over is seen as less honorable by others and will not be asked as much as if you all remain as is—impersonal in many ways. You are to grow only as fast as you are able to flow.

You will all be asked from week to week to work for this class. Tonight you were told to write and you will prepare it and you will bring it forward, but if you forget and you are prone to if you do not believe in you, you will be seen by many others as not as prepared as many of them to work with us. You will not be graded? You will by many, but not us.

You will be asked in time to talk about why you are working on time, but you will not know tonight what it is you are working on this time. You will accept and begin to see that time is a lesson on you and others and why you are unable to move inside you and do whatever comes to you, but you will in time.

You will also see that we are dangerous and not able to continue to work too close to the machine, we will write with you and we will talk with you, but never ever try to run this machine when you are not asked to be in the group. You will find out why, but do not even ask that much.

Why?

You will see that in time the Scribe is going to not have to ask for work from the universe or from the passers by, but will be submerged into the work for hours and hours at a time. You will not be able to do what she does, so do not ask about it until you, too, understand time.

You will not go inside the timeline. You will not ask for questions about a life that is not sublime. No need to bore others with the fractious ideas of others who are not here and would like you to ask questions for them, too. We decided whom we would use.

We did not choose anyone but you, so do your own work and you will be able to move, or choose to leave the group and let the others who are now envious of you enter this room.

You will find there is a lot of unkindness when anyone is excluded and that is why one or two will comment adversely about all of you, but do not mind it. We do not.

When it comes to you and your families being in the same room and doing the work with you, you may find one or two of them picking up energy from you. That is fine, but be sure you do not run down you.

You may also see a lot of people coming up to you and asking you about what you do, who Ruth is, and whatever else they might dream up to ask of you, but you will not know. You will not be able to see inside the work of others and will not be able to express your own delight. You will know.

You will find that whenever anyone reads these lines, they become the group. Why? Time.

You all align in the spine and channel all the time, so channel straight up the line!!!!

You will also see that in time you can be anyone who is not being used at this time. Yes, there are people who use up one personality at a time and others who become so used to going inside another personality all the time, others confuse them with being confused when it is the best way to be today. You have to work in many areas if you wish to make this work on Earth yours today. Work!

You will now see there is a lot of time inside the clock, but you have all worked for an hour or so and have had to grow, so you feel it and do not see where you will go. We will now collect all that is not going to flow and end the life of the one who is unlike you within and will not help you to go inside and live the rest of this life.

Go inside your mind now and clear out the alcoholic or the drug addict or the weird one who is always scaring you now. Go inside and capture this moment for you and sow a lot of flowers that will grow as you grow and will give you bouquets of aromas you will use to cover all the decay around you.

Those who refuse to grow will not bother you, but the stench of the dead is not what is upsetting your head. It is the toxic poison you eat and use to clean up the Earth that is causing the distress to your head and the kind of allergies that you dread. All of you are going to be sick if you do not limit the amount of food you do ingest into you. You will have to eat less and less and have less pressure around you if you wish to fit inside the angel who is going to help you climb to the next level of work to do for you.

You will climb and you will work for it, but the angels fit you into the plan of the universe and time is with you and not a figment of their line and the work they do. Do not call angels now to help you. God of All is the angelic choirs' master and is not to be taken to task ever if you wish to survive to the end of all your lives. You will not blasphemy God of All and live, so decide today to stay away from all that is not good for you to believe and talk about all the time. You will be able to safely live that way.

You will not give up what you have worked for and give up many things to achieve unless one who is on the outer limits of your own being, expects you to do something that others can respect. You will be called only if you are able to save you at the last day. All who are still working must submit to the work they came to do before they are called to work for others and can still refuse to give up any Earth days to work for others and not be upset by anyone calling them up and saying they are selfish. You will not be called ever if you have so much work to do, you cannot be you. Go inside and collect all you have to do and work for you. We will all work with you so you can expect added blessings, but you will still have to do all the work for you.

When we gather in this group, we will not ask you in the world to believe what they see or do. We will only say to you to believe what works for you.

You will work and do whatever you believe is great or good to do only if you are wiser than many who are around you. You may not be bothered now by the egos of others, but you will be when you begin to act differently from the way you were brought up if that is not in harmony with you now. We will help you achieve a level of indifference now that will help you enter your own work and be. If you cannot, you will not achieve. If you cannot achieve, what will you be?

Now, let us see what you have to be.

You are all of you certain to be a success and you will see inside the work of the rest that they are willing to work for you to be the best, too. You will all teach, but you will all be teachers of destiny. You will not be told what to say today, but you will believe and it will happen and you will see why you can achieve what others only ask for today—to teach the way.

You will be away a lot? No. You will do whatever you wish to do. You will pray whatever prayer comes to you and say whatever you believe, but it is true for you and whatever anyone else may say, it is your way. You can only teach your way.

You will also not preach today, but if you totally decide to follow your own guide all the way and accept without the pay of the world what you would expect others to do if they saw the way, you will find this work will reward you over time with all the good that you could ever hope for today.

You will be rewarded for believing in others, but they will see you as never ever worried after today. All of you have worked together in a way, but some of you have had to work together for a longer period and have had to be merged together before today in order to know how to work today. It is no accident that the men need not have worked together until today. You will see women do not believe in each other and will fight in a way to stay separate and not unite, but in this work of today, the work has united all who are here and in this room to work this way.

You will be united and you will never fight. We promise you that today.

You will also be able to gather in this place until the work is put away. You will not have to pay for others to do whatever, but you will be subsidized at first by the generosity of others. If you all work, and you will, you do not have to pay any bills, but if there is a profit at all, you will first allow the prophet to smile and then let her give her share away, but you will all be paid. You will all share whatever you made.

You will also not give it away. You will be told when and what and how much you can make? Never. It is a gift from God. It is not to be given away. Only the Scribe is not allowed to keep money from this work today.

You will all do the work inside you and profit by becoming prophets, as you are now able to do. You will work as a crew and decide who is going to do what, but you all will work harder than you ever did with anyone who was not a member of your family with you. You will grow and develop and know so much more, but please do not talk between you about the others. You can, but we would appreciate the work to be as impersonal as it can be.

You will not be asked to work by others? Yes. You have to pass the work of Earth on to the family first. You then can have a wonderful place in history? Yes, but not if anyone else is there first. You will find many on Earth are now working to clear the path for another to take first place among the channels of Earth, but you will not be at all a part of that work. You are simply to be you and help you by working for the good of Earth and the people who are trying to do more for themselves and want to ascend with you at the end.

You will now not ever again pretend to be busy. You are. You will begin to see many visions and you will begin to dream dreams again.

You will see history and you will know mysteries are all around you, but only when you are with your oldest friend will you know who you were when you began this work again.

All in this room have been in this work from the beginning of the timeline, so it is most appropriate that all of you bring time to an end. You will blend and not have to bend. We appreciate all of this time with you, but please let us go.

Notes on the Gathering of the First Formation of the LeeWay Production;
This is to be known as the Time of Day
March 11, 1997

There is no need for fear. There is only joy over here.

The day is over and all of you are over the hill? We laugh, but you are so serious and so we are getting sillier—and Ruth is aware of how silly this work can get to you and make you feel as good as new. We truly do love all of you. Do your own talking and forget about notes. We will work with you and all of you are to be aware that no one knows today who you are or cares, so do it all your own way.

Addendum to Chapter Four

During the last session homework was assigned. Four of the eight returned to this session with it done. The writing of two of them is included below.

When an assignment is given, you either respect whomever assigns the work and do it, or you do not. It is a simple way to see how you live life. You do or you do not and that is all there is to decide, but so many do not believe they decide all their lives. When this work is read, keep in your own mind that you would be one of the group and either did the assignment or did not, but we know which group you are in most times. Do you?

The assignment was to write about yourself and describe whom you are, what you are doing, and where you intend to go, but these two works of art went far deeper and reveal the lengths to which the Teachers went to get a balanced group and one that would grow. Would you be able to know such people and form such a group to grow?

Group assignment:

(I see myself as a healer, but in a quiet way when the person doesn't realize something good is happening. I want to be humble and wise in what I do in the Lord's name. I don't need much in that I could live without many worldly possessions. My comfort is being

warm with shelter from the weather, food, God and the guidance I have felt all of my life.

I was the eighth of ten children and my parents had mellowed by that time. I knew my limits with little discipline and I felt free, unlike some of my friends, who needed a more structured environment. When they were out, they were out for a good time, for me, I would leave them and return home where it was pleasant, warm, and a great place to be.

The older children looked after the younger children and there was no sibling rivalry. The only time I got into it with my younger brother was when I heard him swear. I guess it made him feel like a big man with his friends. That went on for a week. One day I pinned him down and then let him go and he swore at me. I told him, "I don't care if you swear, just don't swear around here." I guess that did something to him, he didn't feel it necessary to swear anymore.

My parents were very religious, meeting on Sundays and Wednesdays with friends and family. We took turns at each other's homes with no money involved ever. Once a year we would have what we called a convention for four days. We shared fellowship and all chores. I helped to peel potatoes. Meetings were three times a day, and all was pleasant.

My mom cared for all of us. If there was a favorite, I never knew. She always made time for each of us. She died at age 70, about 17 or 18 years ago. I feel like my parents are still with me even though both have passed on. Since I've been with Ruth, I have felt the presence of my Dad twice.

It's funny—when I was younger and driving along in my car, I would say a swear word or two due to outside commotion. I would feel a "twinge" and actually look in the back seat to be sure there was no one back there.

After my basic training in 1966, I was on hold for a security clearance. I was a Radio Teletype operator. My orders to go to Washington State and then Vietnam was canceled. I had new orders to go to Germany when the security clearance was approved.

My Guides seem very strong. When I asked for a few changes I thought would help me to be a better person, it happened, just like that.

My dad was always happy. I remember one day he said, "I was in a field and talking to God about certain things and God tapped me on the shoulder as if to say, "You're doing it right." Back then—if there was a problem, we never knew it and even when there wasn't much money, we always had food on the table.

I'm glad today that I have good dreams, patience, and a goal to make things better. I see where our Tuesday gatherings are preparing us to help our fellow man and to be more responsible guardians of the Earth.

I see each generation is the summation of the past and within our conscious and subconscious being we try to make the world a better place for all. What we need now is to wake up the subconscious, or that place or state that our soul resides and acts as our connection to God. We seem to have the gift of knowing right from wrong by just listening to our inner guidance.

Could the Church be reformed to include information about guides, dimensions and planes, how to love our neighbors, to never let the ego guide us and to put God above all things? I believe the awakening is here and the information at this time is available for anybody that is ready to grasp the concept, (the key of knowledge is already within us.)

The second letter is a balanced view of another individual in the group, but who?

(When I was very young, growing up was quite a struggle. I was forever trying to free myself from the restraints that governed every aspect of my life. I was always testing the boundaries and pushing people to the limits of their patience. Lots of spankings were given and most probably needed. I don't remember much affection shown to me, but I knew I was cared for and loved.

When I was 9 years old we moved from the city to a rural country setting. I loved the woods that surrounded our home and played for hours on end running and tramping through the trees and bushes.

Soon I was in high school and beauty school at the same time. The usual boyfriend nonsense began as I approached early womanhood. I was only a fair student academically, but excelled in beauty school. I had found my calling.

When I was 16 years old I met a young man whom my parents did not approve of. We dated for two years and my parents continued to dislike this young man even more. I was told to forget him and move on. Naturally, this caused another rebellion, and we promptly eloped to New Jersey. We lived there for seven months with no communication with family and very little with friends. I was miserable, lonely, and pregnant with my first child.

We returned to Pittsburgh and reunited with parents and family just as my baby girl was seven months old. A second child was born two years later even though I was becoming disenchanted with my marriage. My daughter was seven and my son was five years old when I decided I no longer could remain married. I was tired of trying to survive living with an alcoholic man who didn't care if he made a living or not, and after eight years, I decided to get out of the relationship.

The children and I ventured out on our own and began a new life of apartment living; we were free, but still struggling to survive. There was no child support or moral support in this endeavor.

1975 was the year of my divorce and the beginning of my new life. Dating, dancing, and experimenting with my newfound freedom made me forget my economic problems. I met a special man, only 21 years old, and I was 29 with two small children. We dated casually for six months, but nothing much came of it since he was very young and had not made his way in the world yet. He didn't need a ready-made family, so we drifted apart. I moved on to others, but never forgot his quiet ways.

I married another and made the same mistake of choosing an inappropriate mate. That marriage lasted seven years.

After only two weeks alone, I ran into that special man again. This is where I became aware of fate and a plan at work. Still sweet and loving and ten years older, the time was perfect for us. In only four months, to the shock and disbelief of my family, we were married. I never hesitated because I knew in my heart this move was right. I never felt that way before in my previous encounters. This was the right move, I was sure of it.

Not only in my personal life was a plan unfolding, but my business life was changing dramatically. I opened my first salon with two partners. The partner thing kept me from advancing my income for three years, so we split. I leased space from another salon and tripled my income. That salon closed, so I opened another salon that led me to purchase a larger salon. When a computer corporation wanted our rental space, we were relocated to a larger and better location. My business was growing very fast. So, it seemed whenever something devastating happened to me, such as divorce or losing a job, a new door opened with a better opportunity.

I had lost my enthusiasm long ago for religion, and I didn't seem to believe in God anymore especially after all I had been through in my life. So I started to search for something meaningful that I could grasp onto and to help explain why certain things seem to fall into place when you finally get on track and your life starts to feel right again.

I met Ruth Lee, now my friend and spiritual channel, and when Ruth introduced me to my Spirit Guides for the first time, I did not quite understand what was going on. After having several readings with Ruth, I finally realized that this was God's way of talking to me and helping me to be all I can be on this Earth plane. Our Spirit Guides are assigned to each and every one of us to help us to live and die in the right way. They watch over us always and only wait for us to ask for their help. Ruth has shown me through her books and teachings that this Earth life is just a minute part of the big picture.

The spirit life is real and should never be feared. Our soul is eternal and we never die. Once the fear of death is removed, we can really start to live. God is real after all.

This knowledge has changed how I perceive all that I ever believed was true of my world. Everything we do and say is remembered by our Guides, and if you want to graduate from this school called Earth, do no harm to anyone. I hope to make a difference while doing my time on Earth. My big dreams are to establish a means of purifying the water, to teach people about life after death and to teach people how to listen to their Spirit Guides. I would also like to have a Wellness Center where people can meditate, practice yoga, and connect with their spirit while relaxing in hot tubs.

My children are healthy, happy, and well adjusted even after all I have put them through. I am strong and my life is blessed. I have much to do before I leave this life. I thank all the Teachers who have visited us this evening.)

When a day is over and there is nothing more to say, say Good Day and turn your mind to the next day.

CHAPTER 5

The Work Of The Work Is Here, Now Begin

When you are able to work and not wonder what it is you are here to do, you will find life is free of clutter and such that distracts you from whatever it was you thought you had to do for others. You begin to see inside to the other side of your life and wonder why you never saw it before. You wonder more.

If a child has time to be alone, that child will never worry later in life about being alone, but if you clutter up the life of another who is old or young, you harm their progress as much as your own. Let others alone.

When you are able to sit and stare into your own air and see why you are and where you were before you were on Earth, you compare and begin to swear you will live better—but you won't. You will do whatever you do normally and continue to review the work of others around you. You may even begin to blame one or two for not helping you, but that is not fair. You do to you all that is ever done to you. No one else can get that near to the real you to damage you once you are over 22. You are an adult and adults realize before the time, what is going to happen, so get inside and tune into what you intend to do. It will save you time, energy, and a few things you love to have around you.

What if you are not a friend to anybody? You are not. You are sensed as being a friend or enemy, but you are not doing anything any different from one person to another, but the enemy within that one determines who is evil and who is indifferent and who may be loved, but the greater the hostility within that one, the less love.

You will find today we are going to study the mission of our own work on Earth, but all of you will work on the work first. You all have to make a living and fill in your time from birth to your death on Earth, so you will have to find time to live within you more if you want to improve your life at this time. Most are unable to retire ever, but if you are, perspire a bit anyway every day or so to keep the warmth in the body until you need it no more.

You will find today is a day when you can plan or you can work for anyone on Earth, but plan to work for your own mind and then take time to rest the body and prepare to keep your Spirit inside all the rest of the time. You can. If you never dwell in Spirit, you do not know what we are talking about, but that is virtually impossible, so we will continue to tell you how to connect more and more with you inside.

You will know who is in charge when we talk to you? No, you know, but you and your ego do not know who is talking to you in this work of art, but we will tell you that there are now three combined into one time and able to feel within the work a flow while the others are still trying to write and develop what they know to deliver through the Scribe, but you can see in this work a difference as it flows and grows. We know, but do you?

Are you full of the Holiness that is YOU? You are and will be the soul, but will you believe that YOU are in charge of all you truly aspire to do on Earth? You have a lesser soul or being that we describe simply as you, who tells you how to live and believe as you do, but you is the form you are and will be while you proceed into the work of what you came to do on Earth.

YOU are you and you combined into a flow of energy that will help you to know who you are and what you will do. We work first of all in the day with the Scribe and then we work all day to keep the crew alive, but all are growing within the work into a group who are going to take the work into the world and survive with the work they are here to help you do. Will you subscribe to such a work, too?

You pay for all you have? No, but what you value is not inside. You are in a material plane and seek to know fame; but why do you not just be you and sit and talk and let others near enough to know who you are? You are in pain too much to feel like talking, or you have no name and feel you cannot talk to others about what you are. We are going to help these people to embark upon a life of talking to others about the work of the Spirit and see if it makes a difference—to them and each other. Perhaps it will help you to begin to talk more about what is important and deserves greater diligence than now, you and your life inside.

If you talk and never listen, who is it that survives? Not you. You are not who is able to sit and talk for hours about nothing that is good to know about you. You are the only one who is able to listen to such talk, but you will do less and less as a lesson this time. When you conceive an idea, think. When you believe, live what you see. If you cannot be as you are, do not think others need to be better than you are. You will find now that today is a wonderful time to be alive, but others may not feel that way and you are interrupting their day. Do it! You will help them more than any work can today.

What if you are in a car and speeding to some far away destination and a 'cop' calls you over and says you go too fast to safely arrive at your home at the end of the day. Do you resent the fact you were caught? You may, but you may also resent that you will most likely have to pay. We are here today to tell you how to avoid that day.

When you do nothing at all, you are free of the belief that you will be caught and that is truly the most wonderful way to be, but if you cheat on others or take too much for you on the side at what you do, you will feel the time closing in on you. You will not feel like you deserve all you have and what you do. Just let the work carry you and see what you have to do and then decide why you cheat on you all the time—if you do. Do not try to cheat others if you wish to be able to do whatever you wish to do. It is a foolish endeavor to try to cheat anyone who is better than you, but you will find the better the person, the less inclined they are to cheat on you.

A matter that was unrelated to what you do interrupted us, but concerns so many of you—divorce. You must be in the life of a scribe or a counselor on this side to know exactly what to do, but you have to live for you, too. When you are working inside and a person unknown calls you to do something for them, do you? Are you able to set aside what you do to aid them? You would be then considered for work on the other side, but not until then.

We will begin with a job you have to do if you must divorce you from a friend. We assume you would not marry just anyone, so we also assume the one who is married is a friend. Do you?

What if the woman on the phone called you and said she could no longer work with her partner and had to leave so soon she would have to abandon three children to one whom she no longer can talk to. What do you think you would advise her to do? Are you wise? Are you able to enter another's life and be you? Are you able to subscribe to the belief that that other person does know what to do and the first thing they asked you is what they need to do? The Scribe was such a person at a time in her own life, so she quickly knew the woman must first talk to a lawyer who is "kind and brilliant at the same time." That is what she proposed to the woman to do. She gave her a number of a third party who could decide who would be best at helping this woman work through the legal aspects of a work that is still in progress and may yet not be unglued. What would you have done?

What do you think a scribe is? One person after another asks the Scribe what it is she is doing to stay alive, but no one wants to take care of her this life; so why ask, we ask? You are nosy. Admit the impatience you have inside to know too much about others in order to never work on your own inside and get beyond it. It is holding you back. You will have to return and do your own work over if you do not hold up the highest ideal that lives within you and make it 'real' this time.

When a woman and man are so devoted to each other that they decide to have a child, why would they do anything later to harm each other? We know, but do you? Think now of the time when you were in love with another and see what happens when you are not lovers anymore. Can you?

When you can imagine or visualize a life, you do not have to live that life or do anything like it, but it might not be wise to live so many lives as it is considered to be a fragmented personality on Earth at this time. You would be wise to sit and do more within you, but others would possibly not permit you that time. They expect you to contribute and do more and more if you are not willing to work with the group who is asked to support you.

If society provides a living for you, are you the product of the society? If you think about it, you will see that you are; but will society admit it?

When you divorce you or your life, are you leaving you? You cannot leave you ever on this side of the veil. You have to be you no matter how many travails, so be you and enjoy you and get it over so you can land on the other side prepared to work for the good of all you are and will be as you remove yourself eternally from Earth and the work that is there. Yes, ascension is a way to remove you from this day, but it means you will not return to Earth again to live another day. We stress that it is not possible to just lift and then return over and over, but you can prepare to remove you by visualizing you or a group of you doing it within the work you now do. Practice more on being you and all the rest will follow through to you so that YOU will know you are ready for whatever comes back to you.

You ebb and flow and a relationship is one in which the individuals are mixed and do not know the other as much as they admit, but will in time see why they committed to each other for a time. You are not asked to do anything? You are, but you do not have to submit to anyone but God. You are the part of God that lives upon the Earth and you do unto others what you are allowed to do, but only God will take you apart and make you do it over. We are not here to tell you what you did, but to help you get over it.

When you are able to sit and work for a living and find you do not have anything to do at this time, you will sit and know why you are here and doing whatever it is you will do. No one is going to know you or what you truly know about you, but you could take a life and decide to try to help others move to the other side, too. Why not write and seek advice? You know you know why, but you like to hear another tell you that you are wise. If the other refuses to agree with you, you become mad or jealous or upset with them inside, so why do it? It is your pride. You risk a lot to confirm that you are wonderful to others and often find you are not, but will refuse to take that as an excuse to do more work on you. Why?

When we work, the time is not as good as when it is dawning in the world, but the Scribe is up and able to write and no one is then by her side. We work with her and later in the day we work with the others, but we like to talk with the group about what they will do, but they never speak the truth. Why? A group will adopt a habit of speaking to you as if they all agree, when in truth they never speak the truth to each other, so how can they speak the truth as a group to you? It is a lot fairer for you to decide if you are listening to you if you know there is no ego involved in teaching you what to do. You cannot blame a group, but you will blame one or another if you only know one teacher or a group of individuals who teach you.

When this group meets in the next millennium, will you be a member? We are trying to begin to do more and more in small groups than ever before, but will the work be available where you are? Yes. You will be the group if no one else can meet. You are a huge and spectacular being. You contain a group of many individuals that needs to be told what to do, too, and all of the individuals are there inside the dreams you have and the work you would like to do. If you are unable to handle more work, the ones who are nearest to you will often take over and do the work better than you could or would do it now for you; but what do you need?

When in need, go to the top of the work you do and ask what direction they intend to take you. If you have no need, do not bother those who are working with you. Flow and grow, as you will be. That is all you ever have to be, but so many want to be better and taller or higher inside than others—why? We know, but do you?

When the weather is fair and there are blue skies, do you feel that God is present in your life at this time? If the weather is dark and hail is on the way to flail at the crops, do you believe that God deserts you at these times? You are what you believe, so believe in God and stop blaming anyone about you for what you do not know is good for you. Hail is a way of beating down the Earth that is too prone to float upward and blow away the topsoil today. If the hail never comes, what do you think will beat down the dust? Not you. You are the product of clay? You are made up of the same material, but never are you malleable like clay or able to be molded the same way twice. You are definitely a fragile being and only God knows what is inside. We do not, but we will work with you to discover what you would best do if you truly did know who you are and were. We do, but not what may become of you.

Your nose and mouth are here to help you to breathe, but some of you think they are ornaments and try to rearrange them from time to time. Why? Are you so sure your ego is greater than God at designing a way to live today? If so, you might as well give up and give in and do nothing within. You are doomed to design a life that has nothing you can take to the other side, so why bother?

When you decide to do something again for you and your life, will it be to get in the path that leads you directly to the soul and where you intend to mold you into the most powerful soul you may be? If not, why try now to read this work and do anything with a group? You are too old to change what direction you will be, so give up the work now or change gradually into a being that is not going to be whomever you are now. It works? Yes, if you associate everyday with a type of person, you will become that person and be like them, so be sure you know who you are and what you intend to be if you wish to form a relationship at work that will work for you and the you, you will become.

When a group decides to meet, are they meeting each one or just moving as one? What is a group? Are you one?

What we will do with you is seek to know you and find a group where you can grow into the highest and tallest and widest part of you there can be, but you will get your orders from you now. Go inside now.

Are you able to know what to do when told to go inside and work? Are you aware that you do anyhow, but might not like being told?

Look now inside you. Are you able to do this work? Are you able to sit and move the eyes and let the work follow you? We are through with the work of you if you never let the work move through you, but it is entirely possible you will still want you to work on and on and do more with a group. We do not, but you will tell you what to do. Listen to you, and YOU will not be far away and will help you to do whatever you need that day.

We will now join the group we have put together to do this work, but the Scribe is going to write a bit longer today at this pace and time. We let her work this way because it is hard to take up a lot of parts when a group begins to fragment into each other. At the end of each session, the group departs and leads another life, but do they?

Now the group will begin and you will notice the flow of energy within, but will it do anything more than the work of four now working within the Scribe and working on the work to come? You decide, but now we will meet with members of a tribe who will be helping you on the side of their own lives as they provide for themselves a way to be.

This is the end of the day for three of these people who are so tired they could slip into a deep sleep, but for you, the reader, they are inspired to work harder than you do. Why? They want to help you, but do you want to help you? That is the challenge and the purpose of using people to help you learn to work for you.

You will find there is time, and time, but what time do you have inside you? You are here today and you sit in a time frame that is about to sway, but do you? You feel nothing? You are you and you have a long day only if you never do what you are asked to do. You may, but you may also decide to never do whatever. It is not a problem to deny, except if you deny you and what you do and who you are forever.

You will find that today we ask no questions of you, but we will ask questions of a group of individuals who are much like you. We know, but do you?

When a group of women and men meet and they meet now and then, are they really a group or just meeting as friends who seldom see each other again? You decide, but we know. You will also remember that many friends are unable to remember you on this side, but will remember you again on the other side and wonder why you never were kind to them.

You can see many people are trying always to be friends to others, and some are so deceived and unable to conceive that many are not going to ever like them now. Why? You decide, but if you are one of the numbers who are not trying to do more for others this time, you will find you must live over again.

You will find angels and lovers are two of the areas that modern man loves to talk about all the time. Why? They refuse to believe one is alive and the other is able to love them. You either believe, and that is the end of the discussion, or you are talking all the time and you do not believe, so cut out the discussion and sooner or later you either believe or you move to another kind of arena and are able to discover who you are. You will be, so remember, discover.

Discover and seek and know and acknowledge all about you. You are who is discovering you and you seek to know what to do, but will you know you and acknowledge that you do? We rarely see anyone do that now, but will you?

When there is time to go inside you and decide why you are and what you do and how you can be of use to you, do you?

What is so hard about being you?

Are you so difficult to know that others have to hear all about you now?

Are you so angry and upset usually that others cannot know what you do and whom you are if you smile?

Are you so upset and greedy and needy that no one else is supposed to have what you own now?

Are you sure you are not jealous of others and what they possess today? You are if you are unable to accept the many blessings you are now.

Are you able to accept that work goes with the work you are to do?

Are you so sure you alone work harder than others do?

Are you full of energy? You are.

You are going to now star in the center of your own work and do whatever you have to do forever until you know why and what to do better, but now, you will listen to YOU.

Where are you?
Are you free?
What is it you intend to be?
Why are you still envious of others?
Why are you still enjoying only you or your friends and not others?
When do you intend to begin to see others?
Why are you so intolerant that you cannot be?

When you can answer all these questions wisely, we will proceed.

What do you intend to be?
Are you still open to being free?
Will you be envious of our work?
Will you intend to ignore us for others?
Will you decide to not do anything you do not have to do?

You will remove you from this work if you cannot see we are teachers and if you cannot be you, you will never arrive at the other side. If you are alive and wise, and very active today, will you always be? You are eternal beings and will be, but be wise.

You will find there is so many eyes upon you if you are unwise, and only those who are also wise will notice you if you continue to do what you came to Earth to do. The unwise advertise and tell others why they are so and whatever, but you will know. You know who is wise. You also know why you give up inside, so grow and know who you are and why you will be wise.

Your life is full of a lot of things you cannot do, so why collect all those lies around you and grow instead to know more about you. You will find if your mind is upset most of the time, you are not very good at doing anything else at that time. So, you are who upsets you.

You will also see you do not believe in you if you believe the lies or the lesser truths of others about you or those who are nearer to you than those who talk about them to you. You condone those who would throw you into the fire? You do if you hire them to work not for you, but pretend that they do. You are being foolish and unwise to hire anyone who is not going to work for you, but so many do. Why? They are flattered into believing the other and what the other says they will do. Why not hire the educated over the experienced and see what they do? You will find experience comes over time and education is forced work on a few. You cannot learn to work and you cannot do what you are educated to do unless you combine the two, so only the highest scholars are able to work for you. Why? They work inside in order to get so high and will work for you.

We would never talk to you about the work you do unless you have to do so much of it, and all of you do.

We came to Earth to see you, but found all of you looking at you and not doing much at all for the Earth or for you. We found all of you surprisingly tolerant and able to see into the lives of those lesser than you, but most of you refuse to work for you.

You will find there are times when energy is so rare, some of you cannot be you, but have to cling to someone who is able to energize you. Why?

You are healthier than previous generations and are so bent on being unhealthy you all run around and talk about pain all the time. Why? You want fame? You want money? What? We are not sure about most of the fame or the claim to money at this time. It is too fleeting and most of you are here this evening working inside for you, so give up the idea of being anyone else, too.

You can decide to feed the tribe or you can sew up the seams of their mantles and be able to look with pride at the way you are able to lead them today, but why would they follow you if you do not know what to do? You have to be able to follow to the end of the road and be able to know the destination of the folks who travel with you?

No, but you do have to follow a map or you will be lost no matter what you do.

We have asked this group to prepare maps of what to do, but only one or two are prepared today to talk about it with you and us. We want you to remember this is a day that is long awaited and few are able to see if they do not agree it is too late. We are not here to appreciate you. We were all divided into groups and told to move and do whatever we could to educate you, but some have done so much work before we arrived that they are able to work as scribes, and teachers and lecturers of the other side. We want you to be able to catch up on the work, too, but will you?

You may find that a gift is going to help you, but most gifts do not last long enough to help you see you must use them well or they will not be good for you. You have psychic abilities? You do, but only for your own use and what you need to do. To exercise your will and power over others is to doom you to do over all that you willed on others and did not do for you.

You will find if your power is such that you can dim the light of another, you will advertise that fact to them over and over until they will do you in and you will never again feel as good, but you will see you can decide to heal you in time. If you decide, try now to heal you and do it for YOU.

Your mind heals you, but many of you are so used to the mind revealing you to others, you do not trust that view of you, so you turn the mind against you and you do not do what the mind tells or reminds you to do, even if it would make you well. You are so inclined now to not do anything that is good for you that so many of you refuse to even work for you. Why?

The ego of men is not the problem of the few, but the problem is there for all of you. The problem of ego is pride—and greed is the second view of pride and what you want to do. You both work and earn all you have and accept that you cannot have it all, or you demand others give up things and whatever to you because you think you are better. You are and you are not going to do anything to lessen you, so get on the work you came to do. How? You should know by now. If you are over the age of 32 and unable to do your own work, you are neglecting you. You truly have to be adult to pass, but if you never do anything adult or you remove all obstacles from you with a passing glance at others, you will find others do not care for you and that makes it very difficult to learn to live with others.

You came to be you. Simple. Direct. To the point, but why aren't you?

You are very gifted, but who among you is willing to use the gifts only to be of use to everyone around you? You are not so gifted you can lose one of them and not miss it, but you do miss so much by not using the gifts that are among you.

If one of you were to use the gift of healing and use it well, others could then excel at the other gifts, too, but all of you want to be whatever another says is best to do, and so many do not even want to rest or let the gifts come back to them. Instead, they rest on the day of work and work on the day of rest in order to get ahead of the others who are still not able to see work is not labor, but rest can be work if it is directed in the proper way. You are here to work on you.

You are here to read and study about you, but do you?

Are you so sure that someone is going to be able to love you?

Are you so sure you cannot love you enough so that you must have lovers who do?

Are you so sure your heart is open to love that you can open to others and not let them open to you? You do when you never at all let them give anything to you.

You will find if your mind is open, and it is if you can be a friend to others, you will discover that some are unkind to you for liking or loving them, but what can you do? You can find another friend, but do it more wisely.

You will find some people are not going to like the one others delight in, but that is the way of humans today. No one is allowed to become to big or too proud or you all turn on them. You do and you truly do help them. That is a lesson and many of you are afraid to try to do more because you fear you will be such a huge star? Yes, some of you are so conceited about you that you truly do believe if you were to work hard you would be so large a star others would pull you apart, but are you working at all? No, but you dream that if you were to work that hard—stop the dream of doing nothing and scheme today to beam to you the way you need to be today.

You will beam home the message you are okay. How? You will smile and you will pray out loud today. If you never tell the world of you what you are doing, will you know? Yes, but it is not going to be easy to see you if you are not shining and working for you, too.

You are here to develop a new work for you to do. Did you ever see anyone not be able to do whatever? No. All of you who are endowed with the normal amount of energy and bodily functions now can learn to do anything there is to do on Earth for you, but most of you refuse. You do not like to work hard. You want others to listen to you talk about why you did not do whatever, but who cares? You.

You are the only one who is going to do anything for you. Remember that. You are who is here to be you. Do it now and do it quicker than you thought you could. You will find if you decline daily to speak your mind, in time your mind will not do anything on time. It slows down the pace to a step at a time and you even erase your own work that day. Why? You cannot face you and do the work you left undone. You have to do the work, but do you look instead at another's work and dread or wish it were you?

You can do nothing if you do not concentrate upon you and the work you came to do. We will help you, but you will still do the work or it will not come true.

You hear of delightful messages and ideas that are told to people and they come true, but do you follow through, too? You do? Then you have many delights in store for you. If you do not follow, sit and delight in the work of others, because you will come back for another life or two.

You cannot avoid the time and the weather if you work for others and have to go about in the world to do whatever you do, so arrive on time and stop the stories about others who do not arrive on time. You are not at all believable if you call and say you are stuck when others arrive on time. You will also see you are ignored most of the time if you lie, so why?

You will find your own mind will remove you and the work you did not do if you are still caught up in the ego of you. The mind is a tool and the ego makes a fool of you. You are not the only one in spirit who is working today with you, but if you believe only you and a small group is going to leave Earth, and you are going to be there and only you will know what to do, you are silly. You will find God provides many clues to all who are wise, so look inside, view your life as if from the outside and live for you.

If you are unwise, you will give what you have to others and then cry when they do not give to you. You will not see a wise man being foolish with others unless he is wise enough to know he cannot survive without the unwise and will be unable to grow unless he can exercise his wisdom over those who are unwise and cannot grow without his advice.

You will find love is not blind but goes from soul to soul searching for one who is blind to the evil of this soul's mind, and normally there are many who will mate with any soul at this time. So many mate and scold the mate at this time we wonder why the rate of matrimony does not decline. You are not well endowed at this time, so all of you are inclined to expect another to support you over time, but do you expect to support another? You usually decline.

You will find if you can save a day or two for you, another will waste ten and not be able to say when. We want you to consider that you are here for an hour or two and you will never know when it is over. If you do, you will find you live every moment of this life and seldom ever pine over what you did not do. You will not have the time.

You either sit and dream of working in an atmosphere where you can be discovered, or you discover that you do what you love to do or it is a natural for you. Why sit and dream when you can do?

You will now see this is a natural capacity of the Scribe to write and write and write, but did she arrive able to write? You see? You do not agree. Some of you believe the Scribe is totally gifted and cannot write naturally and others believe she is not scribing at all and does all of this to be noteworthy, but all of you are so unwise that you do not learn to do this for you. Why?

You will write and you will educate you, but when do you intend to do that to you? Think and do and see and conceive but be you. Do the work you think everyone else should do for you, and others will do it if you are too busy doing what God has given you to do.

You will find few people are going to do anything for you or be that kind to you, so if you do find a friend or two, betray never the day and be sure you have a way to befriend them again. You will be blessed, but the blessing is—you are not alone at the end of the road. Others will be waiting for you. You will find if you are able to do anything at all, you can share it with others, but if you cannot work, you cannot do anything for anyone other than you. You have to perfect you before you can work on others. That is the work you came to do—be the perfect you. Whatever else you may decide to do, you have to first work on you.

Your own life is not a circus and you are not a performer trying to be you. Do your own ideal idea of you and feel it is real and it will be you. We promise.

This is a day of remorse if you have been upset and defeated, but you will be triumphant at the end of your days if you stick to the path you alone know you chose to do. If you are diverted from it, it begins to get steep and hard to believe, but once you are on the level and deep within the work you are, the world is not able to bother you, as it is further and further away from the everyday life of you inside. Believe.

When you are able to sit and do nothing, see inside. If you do not, what will happen to you? Nothing. You cannot do what you do not believe or see or want to happen to you. You will merely breathe and another will tell you what to do and where to live and what to do with others, but that is not life, that is a form of slavery which you allow to happen in some segments of your life—if you are not happy as is.

When you are proud of you and others, do you feel the work zoom? No, but it takes time to see when you achieve you are doing nothing, but the work in progress is what is going to make you happy all day long. If you cannot see the end of a story or a book seems overly long to you, you are not happy to be reading it this day, so put it away. If you feel you are not learning anything now, see why you try so hard to read what another is trying to say. Listen inside. Meditate upon what you need to say to you and pray for help in what you intend to do that day. It will inspire you to do more for you and help others by the way you take away all you normally dump on others.

Be fair! If you are unable to stand your own day, why do you ask others to listen to you repeat it over and over? Why? You are ego driven and do not care if the other has something better to do. You are trying to get your own mind to take care of you? No, you want another to do your work with you, but you will never give them credit for whatever they do. Counselors are not born, but are trained to do more and more? No, you know at birth if counseling is a good way for you to explore the other lives you could not have lived inside this time. It takes patience, of course, but it takes time to drop your ego and let the other just talk and you have nothing but time. If you think your advice is needed, you have to take more time to work on you inside.

When you ask a scribe what they write, you refuse to believe that a scribe writes for money and does what you do to earn a life, but why? You know someone who is able to write and not talk must be smart. Why?

If you are intelligent and honest, will you be asked to write by another? Not if you talk all the time about what you write or who is asking you to write for them. You have to also take time to earn the respect of many who will need you in the future if not at this time, but you will have to continue to do more and more work if you want to be able to provide the material you need for you.

If you decide to teach through writing, become a scribe; you will not feel you provide a life until the public congratulates you? You will starve if you do. The public reads and drops all that is provided by you, but will keep anything you tell them is good to do. You must not confuse you with talking for you to the people who are around you and asking you for help and ways to do what you do. You will teach only if you do know you, but others will not like the idea of you being better than what they are intending to do. So never be proud, or you will end up with no work to do.

We are done with this day and have many things to do, but if we all pray and ask for the work of today to be ended, we know not if God will see things that way. We can only ask and see if that is the last day of this work or will there be many other days in which we can work together this way. Never assume anything will last and you will then not be so foolish as to not work all the way through to you.

When today is over, the work will be blessed, but you are blessed all the way through to you. We want you to talk with you, but decide first what to do in this life and decide why you want to change if you do. Think twice and then check the reason over and over again, but do the work only once.

We will end with this: Be a friend and you will be doubly blessed and you will never have to pretend if you are a friend to you and have enough left over from loving you to do more and more for others. You will love and you will leave others, but you alone will enter the final line of your time and go further into the work of you, but do you know who you are? You do. Discover you.

CHAPTER 6

When You Are Ready, Work and Do—Do Not Sit

Nutrition and physical stamina require that you move and work all day long, but so many want to just sit and think and do nothing with the body now. What will you do when this paperwork is all through? Will you sit and do nothing and try to remember what you did with the body?

The body is not the physical person you are, but so many of you treat it with such disrespect you might believe your body is yours to keep and you can do whatever you like with it now. But, that is not the way to improve you or have a great life.

Today we will begin to round out the emphasis on your skin and what you have to do to begin to see who you are within. We will sit now and read and smile about the way others are not yet with it, but we will also feel inside a twinge about what we did. Yes, no one on Earth is quite over birth. All of you think you have enough on Earth and do not have to move from it, but birth takes you only so far. You have to unearth what you are.

What do you think it means to unearth you? If you have a lot of things you need to do, you feel burdened and need to refuse a lot of things others want you to do, but do you then do what you have to do for you? These ideas are new?

You will find there is a time to be you and a time to renew you, but the body renews you all the time. You only have to work hard and eat the right food for you and the body will work all this life and take you to the top where you will be in line to fly away with you to the other side. Is this too hard for you to believe about you?

When you get into deep superstitious beliefs you lose you and gain only a mere glimpse at what you once knew about you, but so many on Earth are not able to see inside to the one who hides. Why?

Tonight you will be as tight or nervous as you like, but all the others will proceed to be as they were. You are not to try, but to do and then die. That is why the body produces so much heat and energy all this life, but if you never use it for what it is intended, you will not survive or the life you have inside will collide all the time with others. Believe. See. Look inside and be.

When anyone talks to you about you, do you shake your head in disbelief and say they do not know you? You do not have to, but most of you do not have any idea, either, about who you are and why you are here on Earth and what will happen to you, so you invent a story that makes you all sound authentic to others. We believe you do grow eventually to believe these stories and hand them down your line, but we can see. We can show you all the ways you are to be, too, but not at this time. Why? You know.

When someone pokes you in the arm or the body and grins and says, "You know"? do you believe that person knows something and you do not? You will begin to see none of you can see each other from birth on Earth and know what might have been, but accept the story they bring forward.

You will find if your mind is bold and others are not bold around you, you begin to sit and say nothing rather than submit to ridicule from them, but you do get angry all the time. Why? You let them think and talk for you and you do not do anything at all for you. This is the day you have made!

You may believe that God made this day—and did in a way—but you created the day and your life within it. You created you by deciding yesterday what to do. Your day today determines many tomorrows, so live frugally if you think you will need money in your old age and not give it away in hopes others will one day give money to you.

Did that paragraph send you?

What does it mean to "send you"? You repeat silly phrases at all ages, but that one really means you are ecstatic about something and you never are. You sit and glower at others and send showers of anger as if that kind of power was within you and will help them to begin to think better of you. But do you ever think of what you do to you when you submit to the anger of you and your view of the world?

When you are here on Earth, you know very little before the birth, but we do. We are all in the work of teaching you about Earth? No, but we are here around you in order to help you and to determine who is capable of teaching others. We are not here to talk about you in particular, but a teacher must be able to explore more than the students before they arrive and begin to explore more.

If you never do anything at all for you, are you angry that others do?

We see anger in the fields and streams over what you do; but do you see anyone at all thanking you for throwing garbage in the streams, too? If you do, are you going to thank them for pointing it out to you? No. You have to clean up the streams better and better and do it forever if you intend to teach. No one goes and does things once and then is permitted to teach anyone.

We are hard on those who profess to know so much and do less? You are hardest on you. If you say you want to do—do! Sitting is not what you are to do if you are called to work. You are called to do!

We sit at this computer each evening and write, but Ruth is unavailable to us. We work anyway and when it comes to the day we are to all meet and combine the energy of this single time, we enjoy the work. We are all done. We rehearse and then can enjoy the final production; but do you enjoy your work?

When an actor has a part to play, do you think the actor is willing to start out first and do nothing to rehearse? Never! Professionals want to know first what to do and where they will rehearse and what kind of audience they will have and will it pay to put so much effort in that play; but do you play and then rehearse the way to live today?

No one on Earth is full of love of birth, but you all talk about death all day. It would seem to anyone who is not of Earth you fear that Earth is the only planet that will survive and you are all alive for some special purpose because you are on Earth. We doubt many of you can see beyond Earth, but for those of you who do, we want to congratulate you.

If you can see Earth as a photograph of the way you were, you might see that you are a universe, too, within you. There are several different kinds of planets within you, but only two are going to absolutely not want you to move—the liver is a grand organism that is capable of regenerating you, but the heart is a pump that slows down and that seems to stump some of you. Why?

Are you a heart and it pumps until you do? No. It works all day long regardless of what you say it must do. If you overload it in any way, you do harm to the pump, but perhaps not for long. If you stress out the muscle a little each day or so, it will get to the point where it is very strong, but if you exert too much on a single day, it could melt away or rip. We would not like you to sit and do nothing, but it is you who do it. You are who is unfit to work and compete and complete this work. Why compete? You are now sitting in the center of a universe and it is not able to rehearse. You are the final product? You are the only one who sees you so grandly!

When you are able to see what occurs on Earth, you will laugh for the way you egotistically betray what you are today. You are only rehearsing for the fullest expansion of you—not the economy.

If you do nothing for the water but sit in it, will you teach others not to do anything to it, either? Why not? That is what you practice now over and over. You are what you do and if you never do anything more than use the product of another, you cannot shudder when others misuse the product, too.

You are all breathing in this work and doing whatever you want to do, but you might believe God tells you to be a better person, too. If that were true, why would God ask you? You would be told and it would have to wait for you to do it? Not if God expected it of you. You are who controls the work of Earth, but God created you. Think over all you ever heard in church and then see why you were not converted to God and the work of the Earth.

> Now if you sit and do nothing, are you working? You are if you meditate within you. We will work now on the church and the work you are to do. You will sit? You will then do nothing, and we will advance beyond you.
>
> If you have time to whisper to others, you have time to talk out loud to God.
>
> Did that stop you?
>
> When you sit and talk about others who are struggling along, do you feel you have time to be you? Are you sitting and judging them, too?
>
> What if you did nothing at all in this book and opened to this page now, would you say, "I knew it!"

You would know the intruder did not do what you have done to get this far along with the work, but could you prove it? You would watch to see if they could pick up the next line and continue along with you. If it was okay and they were able to adjust their line to you, you would be sure they did do the work, but would you also compete to show them you know more than they do because you have been working in the world a lot longer? You normally would, but in the spiritual world of the other side, you would simply know and not have to hide. Are you preparing now to float and not gloat and let others be as they were when they meet you?

If you expect strangers to tell you all about them when you meet, you are nosy and very likely to be indiscreet about you. Did you know that?

Are you tempted to talk to a friend about your own family and run them down to the friend? You will then be unable to remember if the friend is a family member when you next meet and sooner or later you will run them down to a friend, too.

You all study psychology in a way, but some today speak as if psychology is reserved for the study of freaks. Why? You do not like to look inside. Why? You are hiding from you all day and seek out others when you do not have to see them inside or be with them again. You will prostitute yourself for others first and then later resent that you sold out you time and time again. Why?

When you are asked a question, and we asked many now, are you able to smile? If you admire you and feel great inside, you will; but how many do?

When a drunk or a drug addict comes to a party, do you feel someone should take them outside and help them to get out the bad that is inside? Why? Are you so sure you are not a drug addict? We watch you pour herbs and things you grow into the mouth so you can feel good, too. Why would you then say the other was doing worse than you?

When you stop and stare at another, are you pleased? Are you afraid? Are you wondering what to do? All of these are part of that type of reaction, but it shows you do notice. You notice others, but do you see you in disguise also? Open your eyes—look inside at what you are!

When you know you have work to do, do you work or stew and refuse to work? You are lazy if you never do any work, but most do such silly work they have no time left over to work on the real work of being. If you cannot be you, are you silly?

If your mind refuses to follow this line, think about why you resent it: I have no time. I want to have it all sometime. I will get it, but I don't have time.

Once you identify a line, do you feel it is about you or do you sit and dream of another who might fit the line better than you?

The way you judge others is by the way you try to analyze you. If you are hard on you, you will usually not notice others and do not see they are not watching you. But, if you judge others much harsher than you ever think of you, you will not have a friend around you.

You will be able to see right away judging others does not pay if you work in a place with others who are better than you at whatever and yet you refuse to admire what they do. You will be fired! You will be told to leave—unless you set up the scene so you could leave and then you cannot be fired, but let them do what you wanted.

If you are fired over and over, you might decide you wanted them to do it to you, but did it hurt you? If it did, you were not aware of it. You were not at all aware that you are human and have to work to fit on Earth, too.

If you work and then retire from it, you will be fired, but it might not seem to be the case. If you work and work and it is all you dream of all day, the job will rise and fall, but will you? You have to know who you are in order to fly at the end of this work you do on Earth, but you will not fit into the work of you if you never give up the work of the world to do it.

When you see the word "work," do you think of labor? If you do, you are like so many others around you. Work is not about labor and others paying you to do whatever, but what you do to be you. Do you work? Are you able to fit? Are you really doing anything at all for you or is society—taking care of you? That is all they want to know, but all of you seem to believe being employed is what they mean.

Why not sit and talk about you? You do not know the other person well or you could fit something you do into the conversation and talk about you or the other and have a pleasant day, but most of you cannot today. Why? You do not want to fit. You want to move away. You want to go and see what is in the next room or whatever you call the states of the world, but you are going to find you are there wherever you go and nothing changes at all; but will you?

The Scribe has said all this life that she wants to live in another world, but she is never so sure where that world is. Why? She is not here and now most of this life and feels out of place from time to time, but will she submit to the idea now? Yes, and so she is willing to go and fit in where others need her more and more, but do not know it.

You will help with the time and you will submit over time to driving ambition and what others need, but only if your work on you is on the way to you and being approved. If you drive you to do things that you does not approve or will not let you do, the body may be asked to stop it or your mind might collapse with the fight inside you, but you will not do what might anger you.

When the day comes for you to move into another part of you, will you?
When you move or commit to someone other than you, will it help you?
Think of others.
What do all three of these sentences mean to you?

Are you going to sit and dream on it? You are already working on it, but might not know it. Why? The mind likes to be questioned from time to time. It sees a test and goes straight for it, but you might not want to work at all. The mind will not submit. It will work instead and tire you as much as if you had not gone to bed. Why not sit and meditate within and let the spirit work for you instead?

When you sit and drink a hot chocolate or tea, are you willing to see the stain it makes on the teeth? You are? Why then drink them?

If you stained your own mind all the time, would you agree pornographic work is not good for you? You could see nothing in the mind after the time you looked at the material, but it would still be there until you washed out the stain or put the stain into another plane.

When you clean your teeth and say you want them to be perfect, are you saying you are staining them over time in order to correct them? You are if you continue to do whatever is hurting them or you.

Clear the mind first and then stop and think about what you do to you that stops the work from flowing within you. You will find if your mind is broken in two, a single line can correct it. If you shattered your mind, the single line will only remind you of many you once spoke to you or others and what you now must do to help you, but it will take time to repair so many things broken inside of you. If you begin to work now, how many lines do you think it will take to repair you?

We want you all to sit and stare now at whatever we said today that upset you or hurt you or told you that you need to do better. Think on it. Dream of what you must do. Then, if you have time, do the work, too. We know you have time to be, but do you see how much time you have gone through to get to this line? You are not sure if this is the last time you will be on Earth? Why try to remain this time? Why not die and get beyond this plane and do more?

When today we meet in the elders' parlor, we will also meet those who are discreet and will not want to speak, but will you see them, too?

You feel people at times around you, but do you see eyes? No. Why? They are not in physical form and do not need to see you with vision tools. You need eyes to see, but the rest of the universe is able to 'see' you without vision. You see?

What you are and will be is determined by what you see in you and you cannot use your eyes to look at you.

You will now go inside and review what we are telling you. See if any of it pertains to you and then examine what you need to do to perfect it. Then go within you and connect with the one who is like you and expects you to be perfect. If you do, you will feel great and renewed. You will linger and stew and be unhappy with you if you do not.

Whatever you are and whatever you will be are not determined by others and not at all limited by you, but you have to do more and more if you wish to remove the stigma of having been on Earth so long you do not remember why you are here and what you came to do. If you are unable to do your work, who do you think will be doing it for you? YOU. That is the way to look at whatever you think and wonder about today. Look first at you on Earth and then think what would YOU want you to do. It is easier that way, but you will still have the work to do.

Now the day is over for you and the Scribe will help all of you to go deeper into the work you have done on you. You will now sit and review the following words so you will know what to do once your own work is done and you are fit to move into the next view of you.

This is the day of the Lord! Repeat that over and over and you will see this is the day of the Lord and you are all here to pray to the Lord, but some say, nay. You will find if you decline the will and the way to follow God on any day, you may as well stay away and just let life become a hell. It is if you never know what life is. If you are so sure you know what to do about others and what they must do, you are in the wrong work for you. You should have been a saint, too.

You will find saints live in this time and only they are able today to see you as you may be or will be or can be, but you have time to define you and do whatever you wish to do. Why not live for YOU?

If your life is so confined that you never have time, what do you think others are doing? Are you as busy as they? Are they stupid and have no time like you do today? Why would you say I have no time, but you have so much I believe you should waste some of it on me, too? You do that when you state you are so busy you cannot find a minute or two to talk to another about what they do.

You are all so busy—doing what we say? Are you as busy as YOU? Never can you know if you never pray and meditate and see the way you are built today.

You are built to stay on Earth for as long as it takes to put away all the past and former "lives" as you say. You have today. You will stay as long as it takes. This is the last life on Earth for us. Say that over and over today.

This is the last day? No, but you will find that there are seven kinds of people today who whine and cry all the time, but the eighth is the one who does not whine, but prays and asks for what is needed and when it should be there and how much time. If you never find time to be you, who is going to know you lived at all?

Are you so small that God is not watching over you? Only the tiniest instrument of God is going to know who you are if you never are you. Why? You will shrink inside. You have to be used to growing and know what it is you are inside. You know, but you have to work before you go. If you do not, what happens at the end to you and any friend like you? You all sit and stare into the air and watch others ascending the stairs. You will not be able to rise because you have never used this time to rise above others.

You either try or you die as is. You have no other recourse. You either prize the time you have inside, or you will live to die and come back again to try over and over until the time arrives when you are weeded out and told to just die. Just die? What is that all about?

Well, let's see why a wise man or woman would not try to live at this time. If you had a lot of soup and it was on the stove and it was cold and you had to eat only one bowl, would you try to heat the entire kettle at one time? Wise to try? Why not, but it will take seemingly forever. Why not try to heat up only one cup at a time? That seems wiser to most at this time, but we wonder if you will be the one cup that is heated up enough or will you be left to stew and simmer and never be hot enough for others to want to sip at your cup. We wonder.

Will you?

Will you begin today to see why you are dismayed if others win this day and do more and more and more for themselves in ways you cannot even understand? Are you so sure you know the way that you can sit and do nothing for others?

Are you prepared to do nothing again and again so you can meditate from within and gain the day at the end? Are you prepared for this time?

When this day is over, will you turn this page and roll over and go to sleep again and not even weep that you have no friend inside you again to help you?

When this life is over, will you sit and die and let others cry over you? Who are you to know? You will not know if you greatly affected others lives until you are dead and that is not going to happen to you. You are eternal and will submit your credentials at the end of this time and are told if you must do it over or if you can stand in line to move up into the next time. If you are able to do nothing again for you, will you?

If you knew you were not being escorted to the next avenue, would you try to remember what to do? Would you watch landmarks and expect others to heed the speed along with you? Would you? Are you really in tune with you?

Will you ever forgive you for not being able to do whatever you think others should do?

Are you willing to stop looking and asking and work for you?

Will you?

Are you just talking?

Are you aware that talking and doing use the same air?
Are you aware that using air up to do nothing is not good at this time and you will be held back if you whine too much of the time? Why?

Whining and complaining affect the tummy of many and you are who is upsetting you at this time if your tummy is upset and you are not pregnant with a baby who is going to try to often upset you. So it begins slowly and tries to grow into a human being inside the woman so she is slowed and knows what to do when it is time for this human to be blooming in this time.

You will find a long line is preceded by no awareness that the long line is coming to you, so take a long breath always and be able to speak for you and others who are in need of whatever you know to do.

You will find that the spine of one is ascending and trying to bend into another line again, but the spine is not willing now to sit so long and not have time to bend. We will ask all of you in this session to stop now and climb the rope and try to bend the inside of you so that one who is upset inside can now have a breathe within.

Our lesson is, you will remember, the body gives and you take from it; so do not hesitate to give it a break. Help it conform when you can to the demands of the body time and time again.

Now we have a mother who is going to give birth before this book can be delivered to you, but do you know who it is? No. You will never know all she contributes to it. All contribute in some way to the day, too, but do you as a reader ever know why another gives to you?

Are you a writer, too? If you are, you will know the writer learns more and more as the lines go and erases only what is totally new and cannot be placed inside and able to hide what the writer normally prides himself or herself on knowing now.

You have pride and it hides you? No, but you might try out of pride to hide your life from others. We know. We are aware of the time and place of your birth and each one is compared? Never. We are not here to discuss birth, but it is a phase and you will be replaced one day, but it is still a strain on you and trying to help you to be alive to you.

You will find that on Earth all of you are connected to the birth process first. If anyone of you is a human and is not given enough oxygen at the time the fetus comes down the line, you will die. If you are rescued and it is a bit too late, your mind will at times refuse to accept that you did not die and will hurt a bit, but the body will be fit. The body will get over it. You will and you will not be you is the problem for you.

You might decide that a leg or an arm is not as good as normal and it is not going to be good, but it works well enough or the body will compensate for it with some other feature that is stronger and healthier than what others would normally have to use.

You will find if your mind is disabled and it is at times, you know it? Not all the time. You might not even notice that you are totally preoccupied with you. That is what we mean by being out of sorts and unable to socialize with others. You see only you. You believe in no one, too.

To believe in you is the first step to believing in others and if you cannot believe in you, whom will you accept as Lord over you? No one it would seem, but you know. You do. Deep within you is a term you use over and over. Maybe you say God is not for you or you do not believe in God, but you do. If you did not, you would not talk about it. You would not have any knowledge of it.

You will find that you just knew that God loved you. You just knew. Why? It is preprogrammed in you. You might get conceited, though and believe you are greatly loved and others are not, but that would retard you and not others, so stop being so sure you know more than others.

You will find if you are unkind, others generally will be unkind to you, too, but the wise seldom yield to what others do. You will find if you are kind, much of your time is happy for you. Why? You are today what you prepare for others tomorrow.

You are working in a crowded workplace and others seem to hate you or you cannot find a crowd there who is like you, so you despise them and say you are through with them, but were you? You quit even if you continued to sit, but are you released and relieved of the job? You will be when it is time for you to go or if you are harmed by it, but otherwise, why not open your eyes and see why you are being told to submit. You are. You have to see you have to respect authority and if you cannot, you will not be able to ascend with us at the end.

You might believe God is a power and not capable of being human and doing whatever you can do, but you will see God is in the trees that will stand upon the Earth long after you are gone. You will not be given another birth if this living one is not working again. We can promise nothing, but if you live and you survive and work until you die, we will help you cross over this life. We will attempt to promise, but God is in charge of all our lives now and if you are to be promised again anything in order to be helped to do whatever you already know you must do at the end, isn't that unwise of us to promise anything to you? It is. We are not so pleased one or two may decide to do whatever they feel is good to do with others, but you will know as a group who is fast and who is slow. We know.

You will find if one of you is disgusted at times, the others will feel a bit of denial of the work they do. You will feel you are unlike you at times if others are on the same line with you and not pulling their own weight, too. Why?

You are a team of people who have decided to work in this line for the good of others and if that is not a good enough line for you AT THIS TIME, YOU WILL NOT BE ABLE TO DO IT FOR OTHERS. IT IS BEING SHOUTED AT YOU!

We want this group to settle down. We want you to stop and stare into your own air. The Scribe feels so many in the air, but there is nothing there. What is in this room? Are you aware? Are you able to see anything in the air? Is there anyone in this room now who is able to see anyone "out there"?

No one spoke.

If you can see spirits and figments of energy and whatever, you are gifted beyond the six senses and you will be able to use that gift when it is time for you to help another to go further, but tonight you will practice the seventh sight.

If you know you have six senses and most of you know that by now, are you aware there are seven? You care? You will find that your eyes are blind and your ears cannot hear, but the brain of one is as fast as the others and it takes less and less energy to fill the air if all of you care about the same idea or ideal that is in the air. You are able to fill your mind with air and feel what it is you need to compare in order to know what to do, so beware. Use the air to know who is around you more.

You will find there is a time when you are alarmed and know you must move and go somewhere, but where? You also know you go and buy things you did not want, but you knew you had to be there. Why? You will know. You are also aware that some people are unkind to you when you are not there, but how do you know?

You also know of the enemy before it is found, but you may not care. You may not even want to know more, but it is there. Why not find out what you do know and use the gifts of the Spirit to submit to the work you must do before you go from you to the next work of YOU?

When you meditate, you do anyway, regardless of how much you might try to say you never do, but when you consciously meditate and do the work you came to do, you feel inside a line that leads out to others who are not like you. If that line collides and tries to turn over and around another, are you aware you do not wish to connect to that other? You should find out before the mind tries to make you form an alliance that is unwise.

You would do better to sensor your letters and not send them if you are not going to rewrite them. You are also like that. You can send out a feeler and see if the other is a friend and if it is bent when it returns. You know to either strengthen the touch or move over so the next one will not be touching that one again. You know, but the mind will try from time to time to get you to align with one who is not like you. Why? The mind is only in this time.

The mind is what whines. It is in a rhythm of birth and it tries to touch others on Earth, but if it is lost or split or discovers how to commit mayhem on others, it might decide to be so bossy or hide and you will not discover much about you this life, too.

You have to submit the mind to a discipline or it will uncover you in time and cause you to be upset with others who are disciplined enough to do whatever they are here to do. You could decide that socializing a child is too much for you and not do it, but the police will end up doing the chasing for you, so it will turn into a socialization process sooner or later, but you will still be told it was your responsibility to socialize that child. You will not be removed because you did not raise the child. You had it. You asked for it or you would have removed it when it was not a fetal condition yet. You can and will see that whatever you begin is there for you to do over and over until the end. The end of a child is when it becomes an adult. You are then to let the child know you are no longer a parent and end the association as soon as you can, but the child will always find you a friend if you are any kind of parent and want to see the child until your own end.

You will find others are not likely to want to be with you at any time if you are constantly unkind. We remember that when we are tough on you, but you see we deserve to be respected by anyone who is trying to move up and ascend at the end, but you may still not like us best. We can handle that, but can you?

We know it is hard to be unlovable, but some of you are working so hard to do that to you. You will find if others return hatred to you over and over, you are not being loveable at all. You should know not to bother with those who are not like you.

You will find if you are deserted by a spouse and unloved by many others, you probably do need to check out what you need to do for you, too, but you could be the wisest one of them all.

You will find that if you are right all the time, you will become unpopular with so many now. Why? No one stands out for the right against the wrong much now. You would be seen as holier than thou and not right and too egotistical to be right in things that are not nice to print now, but you will still be you and proud of you if you do not submit now. You have to fight for you and be you and if that makes you not right with others, you can leave them and never be upset later by anyone again. You have to know when to go. You have to be able to let go. You have to learn to leave and start over slow, but if you know, just practice and practice until you go.

When you are able to sit and perspire and work very hard being you, you will wonder why you ever worked so hard on others. You have to remember you came to Earth to learn and grow and feel more and more like others who are also here to grow. If you learn nothing from all the "lives" you have lived on this side, why come back over and over? If your life is full of you and you do not know anyone else like you, we will fly with you, but why not try to find out if anyone else is like you enough to want to fly with you?

When your soul is aching or you are lonely, you will seek others, but it is a sign to predators, too, that you are now ready to be taken over. Please do not give up your own intelligence to another or be so upset with you that you let another tell you what to do.

You will be open to predators in this life only once or twice, but that should be enough to show you that you have to watch over you. You have to detect sooner or later who they are, but today is the day you will fight to protect your own right to be free and be you and believe as you choose. You cannot let others tell you what is right? You do that now and you will have to do it again before you lose this fight, but if you are also not right, who are you to know? You have to use the wisdom from you and the power of YOU to grow into the most powerful being you can be while on Earth, so live inside you and grow to be the tallest being you know.

You will find so many others are growing now that the light is brighter than always, but will it always be? You will be, so the light is there for you and will help you to see that love is light and darkness is when you disagree within with thee, but whatever, you are who turns up the light or dims the light within. Why not brighten up your life?

We ended that lesson on a bright note and wish that you will decide now to live life in the light. You can, but you can also frighten you all this life and decide that life is to be one long fight. Why not just be?

We will ask this assembled body to sit and breathe and see what is in the light. If you can light a candle, too, you can join this group regardless of when you are reading this work. You will come to this life then. We promise.

Remember, we are not promising at all what you will like, but that you can arrive at any stage of life at any day in this life and relive it over, but why? You have to get over this life, so move and do and work for you.

CHAPTER 7

Things Will Be People Are

If your heart beats and you feel like your mind is on line, are you awake or dreaming all the time? The dream is now. You are and will be, but now you are. Things will be. You are. That is the way you must see today.

If your Mind or mind is not on line, who are you and why are you, are questions that remain. Do you use, are or is, when speaking of you in the personal way? Think of the ways you speak of you all day. We are and we do and we see are what couples often use to distinguish between what one or the other might do or seem to be, but are they the same anyway?

If your mind is concocting a line and it is not in the English language, do you think that it might still mean the same thing? Why? Why not? It seems words are merely token meanings for what you dream and if all of you decide today to concoct a word than it will be that way until someone else says no. Why? You are who decides this dream called life, but some do not think enough of this life to make it a dream that is worth holding for life.

If your mind gives up on a plan or a plot, does the plot or plan go and disappear or do you continue to be there? It is true some of you continue to do whatever you set out to do, but so many of you are tired because you stop you and then start again on another plan. Carry through. Do!

If you feel like you have a plan and it is going to come true, do it now and let the rest go until you can see what is coming through to you. If you try to do several plans at one time, several will not follow you all the way through, but you could still combine one or two and follow them through. Why try?

You are who is distinguishing you all the time. If you never try, you die undistinguished by you, but you might believe it is because others never noticed you.

What to do to become rich and famous is a prayer many of you are always talking to you about now. Why? You are tired of being you.

When you are tired of you, who is at fault? You? You are tired of being unable to follow you through to the being that is you, so you get tired and then stop dreaming. We would help you to follow you, but we do not know you. You alone know who you are and what you will do, but most of you can do about the same sort of work. You are all trained approximately the same, but some of you work and some of you shirk, but all of you dream of work that will bring you fame until one day it all is the same—work, fame, declaring what you once did to you.

If you were Ruth Lee and a Scribe to the Maya, would you die a Maya or a scribe? What do you do? Are you working for you or just being another version of you? When you work for you, are you always in the line of you? The time to follow you through to You is now, so let us all go inside now and weed out the mini-versions of you.

Cast out all the snide words you ever knew. Say none of them ever to anyone—not even you. Cast out the mean things you mean when you smile at someone who is not liked by you. See if that does not free up a lot of space within you.

Now, look at the six sides of you. Are you six or seven? You are one and there are six more sides of you, so there are seven kinds of people who are going to know you. Do you know the seven kinds of people who are always around you?

When you can name one or two and know them by the way they are today, will you be able to wisely endeavor to learn the others, too? Are you working on knowing today why you are you? Psychologists are wiser than you if they do know more than just who they are, but do you always think of a psychologist within you? You are one and you are also a politician somehow. If you were not, you would not mind so much what they do to gain power.

If you could be a lawyer and a doctor to you, would you? We know you are now, but some of you do not notice what you do. We watch and see you decide if you know enough to cheat the income tax people and smile, or do you pay them in order to make sure they never come after you? We would say you have a way of directly avoiding the problem by hiring others today, but you still prepare all the facts before you pay them.

If you do your own taxes, pay your own way, who are you to say that anyone else is not doing the same today? You have to see you are equal if you all believe you must pay or do or believe in the same thing. If you think others should not speed, you think you are the only one who is driving safely under the limit posted or do you speed and never get caught so you say you never speed and others are not good drivers today? You hide from others what you often say they should not be today, but we see. Others are aware of the work you have done inside you, too, but you seem to think only one or two outshine the sun.

If you are at full power, you shine and glow all the time. If you short change you and do not do much for others, the power within you is out most of the time. You are not seen by others, and you did it to you—not anyone else at this time, but sometimes it is caused by another part of this life. Yes, there are parts of this life that never seem to come to life. You place so much time and energy in dreams that you never decide to redeem. You will find if you dream and never decide to be, you die always wondering what it was to be a success and live out your dream, but if you dream and decide to work on at least part of that dream, it is a way to see if it might be a way to delight you today. You can try. Why not decide today to lighten your load a bit more by opening wide the dream you have inside?

As you are, so you will be. That is the way to judge today. You are not the tide constantly slipping to the side and rolling over the others who are then undermining you and taking you forward or towing you backward all the time? Why? Are you not the tide? If you are the tide, open wide and let the ones within you who are trying to get to the top rise and fall with the next movement of the work you have inside? Why are you considerate to others and not willing to even work within on you? Decide now.

Within the tide and the time are a few ideas that comfort you, but mostly you refuse to acknowledge that you do not know you.

What did you think about that line about you? Are you confused? Are you even upset that there is something you might be unable to do? You could spend your entire time in this world studying you, but would it make you famous or rich to know all about you? Think of why you want another to love you.

You would be satisfied with you if you truly believed in you, but most of you never know whom you are and why you have to grow. You think another is going to help you, but it never works that way. You will find you grow only when you decide to help another grow, too. Why? You shirk your work so much of the time that when you see another is unable to grow you know you could do more for you, too, than you do, so why not help them, too? If you get confused with this line of factual belief in you, go inside and seek relief.

If you are caught in the sea and the tide is running out of the land into the sea, are you able to find the bottom of the sea or are you going to ride the tide until it decides to come back to the shore? You are like a top bobbing if you are not truly able to be. Most of you are not. Why do we blame this on you? We know you do not work inside on you. We can see, but you do not know that the universe knows you better than you know any work on Earth—only you will know when it is over, but others will see you go.

What a dim view of life you have when you are unwilling to work on your own inner life. We work and grow and help those who are striving to work for others and cannot see they wish to do that simply to avoid doing their own work. We watch so many people on Earth talk about people as if they were not. Why?

Are you able to sit and criticize others? Are you shocked when they then criticize you? No? Good, because you must get over being upset because others are not impressed by you. Ego wants others to admire and fawn over them forever, but God within wishes to know what to do when you are unable to do things you wish to do. Facts and fiction are all the same within. You have to soak out the floss if you want to do much with any string within, but some of you sew with thread that will not grow within.

If you are the type who embroiders every story, you will have colorful tales and many will love to hear you speak, but the bare life within you will never be as wonderful to you. Why not speak the truth of you and see if it is so hard to do?

If your life story is new, you have reinvented you. Congratulations if you can reinvent you, but God created all of you. You are still in the same body and still the same soul even if the world does not remember you.

Fame and fortune come now to many more individuals than before, but you will not know much about them now. Why? No one is interested in looking at those achieving and doing or smiling or believing. Why? The world disbelieves that anyone is happy and achieving now. Greed has entered the arena of the world and most believe that money is what is there for the taking and must be absorbed, but the wise are smiling even more. Why?

The wise see you have to have enough to be comfortable, but you will die. You will still be on the other side regardless of how comfortable you were on this side, so you may as well decide to add a group to the work you do so you can travel as a tribe all the way through this life—that will take money away from you, but it will add up in many things only you will see inside. Why not try to take your own work forward and work with many who are able to help you?

If you teach and believe in what you do, you will thrive and believe in another aspect of life, but will anyone else ever believe like you? Never. There is only one you.

You might decide for ego pleasure to teach, too, but you will not find fools enough to come often to listen to you. We are here to help those who are gifted to pursue the work they came to do, but so many more are trying to step forward, too. They want to tell others what to do! We are amazed today at how little it takes to earn a pay as a teacher of others, but you will also see it is you who make such raises in pay available to those who do not deserve them.

You are who decides who is in charge, but you blame it on another. Is that wise to do? You will never be able to decide why you are you if you never run for office or do anything for others? We know you will find much to do, but take more pride in what you do. If you do want power, sit and examine what it is you should be doing with the power if it does come to you. Do you see? Are you able to believe in you? If not, you are not able to supervise others either.

What if your mind decides to build a castle for you? Are you going to pay for it? Are you going to hate all who actually build a home? Are you going to be jealous? You will definitely envy anyone who does whatever you want to do, but do not work to do or believe you can do. The power of the mind is to stir you to work for you, but the Spirit is what will make the work come to you.

What do you want? Are you able to look inside you and believe in you? Are you able to subscribe to a way of life that is you—all the way through? If you can believe and succeed, you are immeasurably happy, but for how many days? We want you to see that time moves and you go forward or you are stalled and unable to smile. If you smile, will it open a path for you? Why not stop and try that today?

If you are nice to others, does that earn you a reward in paradise on another day? It might, but who is to say? You have to see when you are nice and others are able to concede you are wise, you feel so much brighter than others, so why not be nice and let others ask you first if you are able to help them grow? You are not to advise others you know and they are not to line up while you preach what you know. If you do that, you will have to return to Earth and start over.

Why would a teacher have to start over, you ask? We would advise you that teaching is a cost of this life and does not provide you with the means to live better than others. It is not the time and money that makes a teacher wiser, but the cost of the money going inside and educating over time the mind and spirit to open wider to others. If you cannot travel and seek out neighboring parishes, you will be narrow minded and unable to fully understand what you have to do with others. But if you are able to travel and never marvel at others, you might as well stay home and teach someone who is also not willing to go forward and do.

Many today sit in classes in order to avoid working with others, but it never pays. If you sit and stay in school in order to be able to work up the ladder, you may be paid, but probably not as much as if you had worked all the time you sat in the class and pretended to learn.

What you miss in class is the work you must do until you are experienced enough to know you and what others will probably do. If you never work at all, you will not follow through and do what you came to Earth to do, but you might in time discover why you are you. It takes a lot of time to sit and do nothing before you can become committed to philosophical pursuits within you, but if it works, do it for you.

The work of the mind is to block you in this time. If you want to think about it, stop now and think of the time. What did you do?

Are you able to sit and stew about you? You do. You are often so much more angry with you than all the others on Earth put together, but you seldom will blame you. Why? You tell you.

When the time comes to collide and die, will you find all the many strands within you are woven tightly together and will provide a rope that can pull you through to the other side? Why not try now to see if you can tie off a life and tie another to you?

We will now sit and go inside and collect whatever the tide has brought to you. Will you catch the drift or will you submit? You decide.

We will now sit.

There is nothing you need to do, so prepare only for you to enjoy and do whatever it is that just came to you. We will submit a list, but it is your life and your time to desist and just live or to quit and remove the list. You decide.

There is a time to live? No. It is. You are. You exist and you will persist until God ends your list. You alone know why you exist? No, but you are also allowed to be in others and within the framework of a world that truly does not exist except within you and the others who want to do this.

Yes, it seems strange to admire a race that is not required, but do you feel anything within you that is brand new to you? Never. You seem to be surprised only if another is not aware that you know what to do. You seldom are sure of anything that you do until another says they are surprised at you. Then you decide that you always knew that about you.

You will not say why you do whatever, but you wonder about others and why they do whatever. You could decide to try all this life to figure out another, but it is you who is here to be you, so do that first and then decide if you wish to be with others and teach others to see the way you see life at this time. You can teach only what you believe. You might think that teachers are taught to believe, but they believe and know what they do or they are not true believers and will never be able to teach you. You know. You are a teacher of you. If you go and never talk about you to others, are you still able to teach them what you do? You are. You are the only model of you.

You are going to be remembered regardless of what you think of you. You will be remembered and pardoned by most everybody, but will you pardon you? You might not if you always knew what to do, but shirked work and seldom bothered with you.

If you mind being too bold and talked about, you might feign to be modest in order to avoid the cost of fame, but it is still the same. You are noticed if you do work that is good. You will also be remembered if your work is prestigious among others, but it must still be good. If you have a powerful position above others, you are noticed a lot and are forgiven very little by those under you. You will not be able to pretend ever what you do. All eyes will be upon you.

You can decide that fame and fortune are worth any price, but are you?

Are you? That is the question. You are. You will do, and you promise always to do whatever, but do you?

You will find that whatever kindness you do is remembered and the time is forgotten, but the true believer in you will always remember you were kinder than you knew. You will find that if you can accept a gift of kindness to you, you are wiser than you were when you refused such kindness to you. Why? You accept so that they may receive the blessing of today.

You will find that a fine gift is always the way to be accepted today? No, but it generally is. If you were to give all the gifts within you and beside you and around you today, what gift would say you? You are a gift of God to us today.

You will find that love is kind, only if the kind woman or man is able to love her or himself today. You can love so selfishly others that they are smothered in what you are trying to do, too. You could say you smothered them with the love you had not for them, but wanted to give away. You cannot smother another if you are breathing into you the love of God within you. You will exhale so much love that they will be able to breathe, too, what you knew.

You will find that today is a story of the time you were you and you had nothing to do. You sat in a crimson chair on high and praised God and asked never why, but once you got to Earth, you have cried over and over about your birth. Why? You constantly ask why. You constantly question God on high. You do. You have the absurdity to question God today, but why are you still alive? You are allowed to question while in school and allowed to fail, too, so you are able to see teachers among you who are just not able to do much today with you. You will find they provide negative and positive reactions to what you believe and see around you, but you might still find a murderer who is kind and wise and just never paid any attention to his wife. But, did you learn from the murderer much about you? You may, but it is not the time to watch those who are losing this struggle over the time. You are here to learn what to do and ascend when the end comes to you, so start now to dream only of YOU.

YOU are the bigger part of the three who guide you. You will find that once again you are on high and you can blend in with others, but meditate more and more and find time within to blend in and make time more. You are time. You are here and will be on time when the end comes, but only if you work now.

You are here today to sit.
You will reminisce and you will sit.

You will find that time is not at all in existence, yet it is. You are. You are and are not, but never will be. You cannot exist in a futuristic existence, so stop thinking of when you might not be on Earth until that time exists. You are to practice ascending within your own line, but that is strongly recommended before you are ready to leave the shore of life for more. You can pretend to die and then live again, and that is wise, but if you pretend to live and never give up anything at all to time, you are not living at this time.

You will find that living and dying and feeling pain and sorrow are not the same, but is the same thing inside. You are who controls the power. You are who decides how long you will suffer and how much you will not do for you.

You are who holds up you. You are also who is bold and happy and loves who you are, too. If you do not, you cheat you. You are not able to accept love from others if you never love you. You might talk a good story to others about you, but it is not true.

You will find that love is the secret of all success and that is positively true always if you are you.

You will be a success if you believe in you. Regardless of what others may say about you, you have to believe it, or it will never ever be accepted by you. The promise of a reward is never believed at all by those who lie all day to you. You cannot promise a liar anything or the liar will say it will never be true anyway. The true believer in self is constantly willing to help you, but if you do not believe, you will not help others ever.

You are who is helping you. You are truly never alone, but you will do only enough to follow through to you if you never ever want to do anything at all for others.

You are not expected to work for another and help them discover whoever they are, but you are expected to discover whoever you are. You will be told at the end of this episode of love that you either loved you or you neglected you and will have to start over or do the work of two in another episode of you.

We will at this session tell you about a few things you seem to not remember about you.

First, are you aware that there are several of you? Are you aware that all of you are here inside you? Are you so sure that the one who is inside you cannot be seen, too? You might say that some are insane because they act out two or three personalities at one time, but so do we. We are in the framework of you and we work within you and we talk to the outer personality of you, but you assume you know what we do. We do, too. We talk and you sit and read and discover you.

We will find that if you are serious or clever and have a mind that is never upset with you, the time flies. You feel renewed and able to go further than you would if you were just being good. You can do good and still not feel good about you, but you cannot be good and not feel that about you.

You will find that clever lines are quickly written by the Scribe, but who are you? Are you clever enough to decide that these lines were written by a scribe to help you be you and live inside you all the time? Are you wise? Are you able to scribe?

The Scribe. That is a title and it means you are paid to do what you do and you truly do deserve whatever you are paid if you do the work you do well and help the one who is paying you, but if you never ever write at all, are you paid at all? Never. You cannot be a scribe today and still be paid for work you did not ever do. You have said to many of your own line about this time, I scribe. I write letters and manuscripts all this time, but you are not paid, so are you a scribe today? No. A scribe writes and is paid to write, but you can write and write and never ever be a scribe. That is what you are to be only if you are paid all this life to write for others, so let this semantic teacher who is inside you listen to what you tell others you do.

You are saying, I write everyday in a journal my own way, but do you? Are you truly writing for you today? Are you able to see that if you write a letter to you, you are not writing at all for another and so you cannot pay you?

If you work for pay, you are that kind of person today. Think on it. If you hate the idea of being paid to be you or work like you do, change today.

If you find it is nice to paint and you love to say to others today, "I am an artist," remember that you cannot say that unless you are paid to paint for others today.

You are not an artist, but an artisan to others, so promise never to talk about what you do until you are able to do it for others and they admire you so much that they pay you? No. But you can work harder on what you plan to do, too.

You are indeed someone who is blessed with work to do, but if you never ever want to work, you will be okay, too. You will then be idle enough to pursue the work inside you. If you do not do that, too, then you will be provided with nothing more to do. You will also have to begin to worry about food, too.

You can find that people who hurry are generally unkind to you. Why? They are not even working on them at that time. Why? You ask them. We do not pretend to understand all men. We are here in this time to begin a line of men and women who are about to ascend at the end of time, but what do you wish to do with you?

You will find that we teach all the time because we also have ascended at least once in our timeline, but are you able to teach anyone at all what you do not do? Never. All will remember the foolish virgins who used up all the oil and were unable to greet the bridegrooms who were not on time, but do you see that the men were wrong at that time? You were told that the women were wrong, but they used wisdom and tried to provide a light for the men, but the men were so distant from them that they lost out on a wife at that time in their life. Look at all the Old and New Testament stories again.

Are you sure the Scribe was paid enough to do them then? If the Scribe was alive then, do you think she would be able to rewrite a letter to the Corinthians again? You might decide that we are here today to work with you in a similar way, but are you St. Paul or the slave of them all? Who are you in time? You are all. You are all who have ever been here since Paul. Paul was a convert and he never said what he thought to all, but he wrote long letters and he talked to one and all about the sins of the past and what he did to forgive him forever, but can you follow his path?

You will find that we are all inclined to talk about the past too much when we teach others, so we try to not go back in time, but you must discover the anchor and the measure of your own promise in this time if you are to do more on time. You will find that time is not mentioned, per se, in the Bible of today, but it was once. Why is it so admired by the aboriginals of today and never by your own tribe today? You lost your way. You are all here today to unite in a way, but will your way be the same way as the one who reads this on another day? You decide.

You will find that today is so big and huge and vast in it's own way that 24 hours is never a day, but you cannot go forward until today is over in some way. You must work harder to develop a new way or you will not be able to flower in the May. The May is a time of the year in your own way you disappear. You begin to see bees and trees and flowers and power is in the air always. You are so clear and you seem to just disappear when the air is clean, so get into the air nowadays and see who is there.

Last session we asked this class among you to see who was there, but none saw us. We can see their air, but did they pass that class? Of course. The class is not the test. The test is to be in the class and be able to pass with the rest. If you cannot be there, you can still see them in your own air. Look now. See who is there.

Are you aware of the time? Are you able to see the spine of the book is not holding you to the page in time? Are you able to find anyone who is listening to the lines appearing in time? Are you able to see? Look inside now and agree that you are there.

You will all be together eventually, so be there. Get together. If you could agree to all meet, would you be there?

When you reread this book about what to do to be able to go further and work more deeply within you, will you teach, too? Never. You cannot teach anyone who is not able to see you. You have to be able to just be you and have others come after you and see you and admire you, too, if you want them to do what you do, but a teacher never ever asks others to do. The teacher instructs by being able to do.

If you do and you are seen as an adept, many will come to you, but some will never. Why? They are all in the way of pride at times, but you are, too. You will find that you do not like to teach others if they are not like you, so what kind of teacher are you?

You will find that if your mind is clever and you answer all the lines about time, we might ask you to explain to others what to do, but will you be able if you never do it for you? No, but some will still pretend to be a teacher, too.

You will teach only if you believe. If you do not, the only one who is going to follow you is the one who is also trying to do nothing, too. You can pretend to do anything, but never pretend to teach others when you do not do for you.

The Scribe is not alive to teach you? Why? You all are able to learn from what she is able to write for you, but if you can do better, we will also work with you, but you are not willing to do the work inside you. We hear so many say they can scribe today, but only a few do.

We will never ever ask you to write or orate for us if you never are willing to do the work on you.

When today is over, your pride will take over. You will either decide to use whatever you like or you will not do whatever, but it is not the soul deciding what to do. You are here in a mental preoccupation of you. You are not totally in spirit or you would not be on Earth, too.

You will learn and do more by making mistakes and doing it over, but why not try to do it perfect the first time or two? We admire what you do, but do you?

We will now conclude the episode over you, but do you feel any different from what you normally think of you.

This class is about to exist only in your mind. If you no longer work on a poem or a play or a literary work today, are you still in it? Think of the things you memorized as a youth. Are you aware of the things you could do? Are you aware of the time you once used to be you? Are you able to unload all those old memories of you?

If you were to clean the mind as if it were a closet in time, would you? Are you so sure you are not overloaded with unpleasant memories because you do not clean up after you? You are who is doing most of the work, so if you never finish the arrangement or the agreement with others, you will find they are not going to bother much with you. Why? They are wise. You should not bother either with anyone who is not going to follow through. You have to undo over and over whatever they say they will do, so get your work together now and redo only what you asked another to do.

When this day is over, find time to sit and be you. You can then do whatever you wish and fully decide whatever it is you wish to do to exist, but time is and will move forward when you do.

What if you had a calendar of the month of May, and May came and went and you did nothing with it?
What are you now doing? Are you smiling? Are you angry with you? What did you do last May to remember it?
When you feel the time slipping away from you, are you angry with you or confused about why time is not working for you?

We will conclude this lesson on you by reminding you that you have time to be you, but if you use it unwisely and never discover whom you are and why you are and what to do for you, you will still exist. You will now dry up the puddle of water inside you. Go inside and drink from the fountain that is spraying up high within you. Would you be able to do it if you had a long drink of water, too? Do more drinking and eating within you. You all eat enough for two now, so few of you are able to sit for an hour or two and not think of food, you will now have to see that food does not exist unless the body is asking you to feed it, but you wish to be a perfect host to you and often force food upon you when it is not wanted. Do not eat so much dessert? You can eat whatever you want, but eat it when it is right for the body and your mind will then be able to run for hours at a time.

If you can now rest, please do.

There is nothing we will ask anyone to do, but for those of you who are here to do whatever is best, we would like to add a few tests for you.

1. *Rest.*
   If you cannot rest, what do you work for? You are the test. You will either rest when told or you will grow old long before you can be told what to do. You are wise if you can accept what other lives teach you, but if you prescribe to always be you, you cannot notice what others do, too. You can adapt to the work of the Earth, but if you never do, why bother to arrive on Earth to work on you?
2. *Study.*
   If you cannot read, cannot write, cannot cipher, cannot believe in others, what are you about? Are you able to compare you to others? Are you aware of what they do to you? You could learn to do more for you, but why would you if you never knew why they were here to be with you? Study more and read less. If you finish one book after another, you are not consuming a word or two, but buying time away from you. You are not trying to apply anything at all that you do.
3. *Time.*
   Time you. See who you are. Watch what you do. How much time does it take to be you? Are you able to look at you? Are you able to fully agree that this time is for you? Are you prepared to be on time when the long line ascends with you?
4. *What is your score? Know more. Think less. Study harder about what you adore and will work for. If you cannot do, you will do less and less on your lessons, too. We will help you to do more, but you alone will apply all that comes to you inside. We cannot take anything from you, but you have the ability within you to try and time will help you.*

These are four classes in one. That is the test. You are done. You either learned from one or you adopted two or you adapted inside you to each one as we worked with you, but you are done. You cannot ask for more.

You will study. You will time you more, but will you rest? That seems to be the hardest one for you. We want all of you to promise more and more to trust others and rest more. We will help you to work as never before, but rest more. You cannot work for hours and hours and do the best work there is inside you anymore.

You will either stop and meditate for an hour or so, or you will break in time and not be able to work harder than you do. You cannot grow more if you do not slow down the mind and provide time for the body to have a great life this time.

If you are absolved of all physical problems, you are on time. You can then be on time again. Whatever your mind says, you will repeat over and over until it is done, so either work on whatever you say you intend to do today, or erase it forever.

You will now pretend to be you again.
Sit and breathe deeper than ever.
See you inside and be clever.

Ask for work you can be. Ask for nothing that is not going to be the best you there is and can be. Work is you. You are working only for you, but others also are able to show you a better way today to be you, so work again and do over what others show you to do. If you cannot learn by their examples, then you should retrain or refuse to drain you by complaining about what they do for you.

You will find that today is over.
The day of your week is forever.
You will never ever, ever again be this clever.
You will decline or improve all the time.

CHAPTER 8

Things Will Be Better If You Let The World Know Who You Are

We watch you always trying to hide who you are; but why do you suppose everyone is trying so hard to confuse the other when no one really bothers to even listen to you? When you try hard, you usually succeed in believing what you do is important, but most others will not admire what is so hard to do for you because they generally either do not do it at all or do it so easily they cannot see why you make it so hard.

That sentence runs on and on and so do you when you see anyone trying to help you get beyond the part where you are. You try to stop them and concede only if you find where you can agree—and that is usually not where you meet.

Before you move up your own life, move inside. Look now inside the pride you have for you.

Do you feel wise? Are you? If you are not wise and feel that you are inside, would anyone else believe it is you who is doing such unwise-like things to you? Are you so sure you are not as wise as you are? Why would you say you are unwise and then do nothing to open up the life you have inside?

Why and when and how and where are not questions about life, but about where you are and why you cannot bend. If you answer every question over and over again, you develop an automatic response and it becomes what you believe you are to all who talk about you, but it never seems to be believed after the first few times you speak it about you. Wonder why? You don't believe in anything you recite from memory.

If you had to listen to the same record or tape recording over and over and over and not be able to turn it over, would you admire it as much as when you hear it once or twice and want to hear it more?

The work of God is playing all day long in your mind and in your head, but you begin to dread the sound of you talking within so you begin to sound more and more like an automatic weapon trying to hit something before it runs out of ammunition, and that is not wise to do when you have a friend who is wise to you. Why? You will be able to find in these lines a few ways to help you lend a lot of support to what you do, but more and more you will lend support to the work of others by never admiring you. You will lend them the time you would otherwise spend in ego pursuits doing good works for You.

You will listen to the wise and enter into discussions only when you can support or learn from them. You will not be upset by them, but what do you see in the wise if you cannot open your own eyes?

We are jumping from one subject to another and making you run with the ball instead of just bouncing you on one theme from subject to margin and then back again to the next paragraph. You might think we are not writing today to end your pain, but we may. You are why we are all gathered here today.

This is a room where people who pray come and go all day, but only one is seen writing on the machine. Does that surprise you today? You will feel around you many who are there, but not see anyone who is there to help you mean things to you or anyone else around you. Mean? What can we be teaching if we cannot use a word correctly or are we deliberately trying to make you analyze what you see?

The work you do is what you will be!

Can you see that in a machine and write it over and over in your eye? You are writing every letter now that you see. The eye records over and over whatever you read.

If you read the same old stuff over and over and it never seems to mean anything new to you, maybe it is because you do not read into it enough of the meaning of the author and others who also teach within the work. You think no other can teach you within the work you read? What kind of material are you reading? You are responsible for all you feed the mind, and if you cannot find anything at this time that feeds the mind, what time do you think it will be when you have to leave?

The boat to the next life leaves on time, but will you be able to read the schedule and leave on time to make the last passage there?

If you never read and never study, but you meditate and take away the burdens each day, you will find you are always on time and never upset with anybody. If you never meditate or study or do anything on time, you are not ready!

What kind of life do you want?

Study up on what you have done all this life if you have no idea of what you want to do with this life. Look over what you delight in doing and what makes you hesitate and not do it for days at a time. Think about what you do and why you do not like you if you do not do whatever it is you hate to do and then try to find some way to never ever have to do it again. Once you find how to eliminate all you have not wanted to do, will you then work for you?

What if your life is full of hatred and you are never filled with delight? Are you who is upset with your life? If not, you are depressed by your own life and not aware of it. We will help you prepare to lighten your own life, but first you must know who you are and why you put you down there.

1. You will now sit and listen within.
2. As you sit, look inside and prepare a list of what you like about you and why you would love to be you all this life.

3. Now you have a list that includes all you love to do and why you will do all this for you, but you must remember that you do not have to do anything over once you learn what to do and can do it by rote. If you continue to work over and over the same old work, sooner or later you will learn to hate that work, too.
4. Now and then you have to admit you do not like to work and that is the bottom of the list, but you will say over and over you do not have to work every single day.
5. You now have a long list of what you love to do, sit and check it off every night. See what you missed and why you cannot include it in the day.
6. After the list is through with you and you have a lot of things within you that you really do love to do, sit and dance within you.

The final indication that you are you is the feeling of being in love with you. If you never feel anything like that, you will not feel you know who you are and what you can do, so let us all commit to doing one thing better than we ever knew we would be able to, meditate within you.

As you slumber or doze in a room where others are asleep on their feet, do you feel weak or just succumbing to the room and what others are doing with you? Are you able to doze and sleep with anyone else awake around you? You might not be able to do anything that requires such a lot of work, but it is easier if there are a lot of others there to show you what to do. Work. Work harder. Look at your own work and do more of it and do it better than you ever knew how to do it before.

Are you listening? Are you reading this list over to you? What kind of list would make you laugh within?

Sex and sin are not laughable to you and the world within, but once you do begin to see why you want to sin you will laugh at you within. The world does not care what you do or where you live, but you do, so be sure you know why you do what you do.

Your life is not an episode in anyone else's life. You are not the only one who is watching your life pass before you, but others have no idea of what you are like. If you watch you and redo over and over all the parts you like, will you become bored with you and lose delight in being you?

Try now to see you being upset and bored by being bright.

Can you be bright and happy and still not delight in you at night?

If the answer is yes, you are paranoid and not able to end depressive feelings within you, but that is going to become easier now to do.

You are the psychiatrist who is prescribing life for you to do. If you do not see you are ascribing roles to others when you need only look inside you, you will have a harder time with this work than those who know who they are, but you will learn to work on you by the time we are all through with you.

Yes, the work we do is to work with you and celebrate the real you, but you may not do it alone if you never use your own home to work for you. Are you reading on the bus and unable to settle your own trust because others are pressuring you for a seat or whatever they need? Are you reading in a chair with another close by who is not like you are or do you believe they do not like what you read?

Whatever you do, you learn to adapt to those who are closest to you. You learn to listen to the sound of their tones and whatever they say at home is taken to be what they really mean, but are you mean at home to those who are not there to take you anywhere but to the next phase of your life? If you cannot be nice to those who share your life, what do you intend to do when you become a wife or husband to another this life? You are? You will not be happy long if you despise the one sitting beside you.

The desperation of others is enhanced by the hatred that spreads from those who are filled with dread. You cannot enhance the life of anyone else if you are dead within your mind now, so lighten up and branch out and see others and learn from the wise as soon as you might. Life is not going to be over until you can see the other side.

The world is now open to the work of what you can do, but are you open to the world, too? Not many today see inside the work they do as a way to open a broad avenue of work for others to do, but if you do, open it and take a few through with you. The world is a cooperative venture you either know all about or you do not have the time for.

What do you want from life? If ever you are asked that, say with conviction what you believe at that stage in your life. Why lie? You are not being asked to do anything that is not going to be you, so ask them why or tell them the truth and move on and be sure you know why by the time you die—otherwise, why lie about being born to do work for you on Earth?

You will find Earth is a planet that is meant to bloom and go inside you only if you are acclimated to the work of you. If you can see that your mind is full of life and surprises come to you, why would you lie about life not being what you want? You think others may try to take away your life, but why would they?

You live and you die, but you also lie. Why?
Are you a man or woman of your word?

Think now about the time you said an evil deed was not so bad because you did not want to seem to be talking bad about someone who was working against the good of this life. Why did you lie? Are you able to see such lies are now making the evil wider than it was when you were born?

Are you able to understand why you storm? When the day is over and you are tired of working with others, do you stay on and on in hopes of improving the relations you have with someone higher than you are now? We watch some of you aspire to rise higher by catering to those who are not even aware that you were hired. Why not just do the job you were hired to do and follow through? It will make you stand out from the crowd and get the job done for you.

When you do not work on the work you are hired to do, you may be making time for another to fire you, but you may also be blocking another from hiring you. Why not move and take another view of you?

You will find that whatever you do is fun as long as you think you can win the game and be done by the time you are tired, but if you are unable to see you win at anything you do, you will not see any fun around you.

Work and fun are the same kinds of ways to be you today, but you have to polish up the one in order to be able to take enough time to enjoy the other. Work is not the same if you rush through it everyday, but fun is great regardless of what time you arrive at that stage in the day. Take time always to enjoy you and have a great day. Why would you not?

Your day is your life and if you have finished working and did not enjoy whatever it was, you will not be able to say you ended your day having a great day in this life, so now before you go any further, work for a delight and go inside and open your faith in you and others.

How can you trust you? You can and will learn to believe God is working for you and you are working inside at what you are, and you will do what you came to do if you follow You through this life and come out the other side. If you have time now to sit and stop and talk with another, please do. We will not bother you.

Now if you are gathered together to read this work and study as a group, you could stop and talk, but you also want to learn more about what you are to do. You can do both. How? You will now open the assignment you were given in the last class and you will read it for us to critique. You will not be asked to talk about what anyone else wrote, but we will write your letters from the class that is writing this book and compare their work to yours if you will write it in this book.

Write here what you have to do to make you happy.

Now you will learn why you talk and do what you do, but why you lie will have to stay inside.

The following messages were derived from the class that worked to do a lot of this work with you. You will see why one or two only are placed in this book for you, but will you know who you are by reading about those two people, too? You will learn from others what to do or not what to do, but you will still have time to experiment, too.

Group response:

(My Antidotes for Healing)

(I have experienced many challenges and seemingly tragedies in my life, and I have come to understand that each event was an ingredient in the recipe of my awakening. At the time the incident or situation could not be seen for the part it played in the grander scheme of my spiritual journey, but now they all make perfect sense to me.

Whenever I experience situations or challenges, I first go within. A wise master said, "If you don't go within you go without."

To simply quiet your mind and let the deep voice of safety and hope ring through is the most difficult and yet most simple of actions to calm your fears. Ironically, it is the hardest time to do just that because your mind will start to produce all kinds of doubts and fear and tell you, "Okay, that won't help. This is the real world. That's nice to do but this can't be cured by doing that." When you hear that, you know it is time to go within.

Our goal, of course, is to be in a place of meditation all the time so nothing in this world can affect our peace and safety. To live in meditation is our birthright and God's greatest gift to us—real connection with Him at all times. It's our choice to feel that connection or not.

I also find it helpful to ask questions in a journal and ask my Guides to give me help and responses. The answers that flow from our Guides are personal and can ease the pain, emotionally, spiritually and physically.

The greatest lesson I have faced and continue to face is trust. Trust in myself and trust in God to keep me safe and forever in His arms. My Guides are always ready to help, but I have to ask. I also have to tell them what I need, and I have to believe they can help me. They are very special beings that are a part of me and are invested in my ascension. Your Guides are on your side and can work with other people's Guides to solve the most difficult problems for the best of all concerned.

I have found that writing affirmations about a particular problem or concern is very helpful as well. When you write an affirmation, you need to write it slowly and easily and think about each word, imagine this affirmation is a reality for you and feel the feelings that will come to you. I never knew how powerful written and spoken affirmations could be until I saw it work in my own life. Affirmations create energy that is sent out to create whatever wish we affirm, so we need to learn to be aware of every word and thought.

You are always creating. We are creators in our world—our life is our creation. We aren't victims of anyone or anything. This belief will free you!

Surrounding myself with uplifting books, tapes, and music is another way I have found to overcome challenges. In particular Lee Way tapes and books have transformed me. I simply ask a question in my mind, put in a tape or open a book and there is ready wisdom and knowledge for me related to that specific concern.

There have been many situations that have been healed through the conscious intent of sending love and light to the person or situation and asking God for a healing that is best for all concerned. I imagine a beam of light. I call it diamond light because I think of how a diamond shines with all its facets and prisms. I imagine this diamond light in a beam entering my head and flowing to all parts of my body—healing my body, thoughts, and words. I then imagine this diamond light extending into the room surrounding the place—building and covering the Earth—enveloping the people and situations I am most concentrated on. I see them smiling and peaceful. All is well. I finally see the shimmering diamond light covering the planet and illuminating the whole world in the bright diamond-like light still with all of us connected. What a truly beautiful feeling that is. It can uplift you any time you perform this blessing to yourself and everyone else. I know how difficult it is when things seem to be going badly to think of trying any of these antidotes, but that is when you need them the most. They reconnect you to who you really are—Spirit, and there is no problem that Spirit cannot solve.

Oftentimes we reserve our spiritual practices for when things are going well and we feel content and peaceful. By using these antidotes when we are challenged, we open the door to deeper understanding and spiritual growth from those seeming problems. We cast light into darkness and darkness is no more. We take back the power that has been ours all along and, like Dorothy in the Wizard of Oz; we realize we have always had the ruby slippers on, we just forgot how to use them.)

This is a woman who is wiser than you and wise enough to not say who she is when she is tired of being with you.

Group assignment: How do you dispel negativity?

Here are my top ten ways to dispel negativity:

1. **Smile. Although it sounds easy, when you are feeling negative, it is not easy to do, but it does work.**
2. **Use affirmations.**
3. **Sing. I can't carry a tune, but I enjoy singing hymns of praise in church.**
4. **Volunteer. Doing good for others lets me keep a balanced perspective of others that have bigger problems than I do.**
5. **Garden. I like to play in the dirt, plant things, nurture them and watch them grow. I lose track of time and get involved in the moment. A form of meditation.**
6. **A Walk. Although there is a health benefit to the treadmill, I have found that a walk outdoors is much more uplifting and grounding.**
7. **Church. I find a lot of positive energy within the church walls—whether or not there are other people there or services going on.**
8. **A long hot bath. This serves to isolate me from others and provides some quiet time for me. During this time, I meditate or listen to a tape by The Teachers Of The Higher Planes.**

9. **Talk to God. When I have a problem. I talk aloud to God or my Guides or whomever is listening. This seems to work well, except in public places**
10. **Surround yourself with everything positive. Associate with positive people. Read only uplifting material. Meditate alone or within a group.**

In closing, I would like to include a prayer I have used when overcome with negativity.

Prayer of Protection

(God above, I ask that the white light of the Holy Spirit surround and protect me this day and every day. I ask that it cleanse me and purify my soul. I release to the light now any negativity as just black smoke to be absorbed by the White Light, causing no one any harm. Let nothing but love and positive energy pass into or out of this protective circle. Visualize a circle of white light all around you as you say this prayer.)

This is a man and a woman combined in one personality and you cannot tell which is going to be used, but one personality is more or less dominated by the other all the time 'they' are on Earth. Are you androgynous enough to feel like this woman-man and others who are circling their work?

You are all fine. We are all fine, but this is a book and you are all to be in the lines, so you will continue to write and analyze your life as if it depended upon it. It does. You will admit nothing to anyone unless you know for sure you are not going to lie to you about what part you are doing for you. You will act up at times and deliberately try to throw others out of the way, but 'lying' to them about who you are is defensive in a sport that others who are rude to you can enjoy for what it does for you? No, but you do not have to talk to others about you simply because they say you must tell them about you.

That is rude. You do not have to speak up or you can laugh and if they pursue, why not tell them a rude thing, too? You can, but you would be wiser if you just spoke of a positive thing you once did and it will then never be told again. You can see that some people lie in order to have greater lives upon Earth than others seem to be having at that time, but why lie? Why be anyone who is not having the time of their own life and enjoying whatever it is—the pain, the strife, the delight of being a man or his wife?

You are the personality you project and you are indeed the person who is inside you believing in you, so combine the two and find out within you what it is you do to you that makes others afraid of you.

We caught you off guard? You are afraid of anyone who is in line with their own mind and speaks it. You do not care for the direct approach much at this time in the world, but we do. We prefer the rash to the rude, too, but you do not have to laugh behind their back if they do rush to the wrong conclusion about you or others who are there beside you. You could be nice or wise or rude, but which are you?

Are you the type who smiles and then delights? Are you happy inside and consistently feel funny and happy and delighted all the time? You are not living long in the world at this time if that is the state of your mind. You would have to ignore thousands of ideas constantly bombarding you from day to day if you were to be able to say without a doubt that you are not upset by anyone at all today. You could say it from time to time, but it would be a problem if you said it all the time. Why? You would be lying at times.

We are here to say that lying has an appeal today because so many are so upset inside and unable to pray, but if you lie and speak of what you think as if it were the only way, you upset another and then they might also lie today. You think that to talk the truth is upsetting and so you do not get it. You then say, "Okay, but she is fine and I really like the way she is today." And all the while you are upset about what she is doing to others or you or what you believe is right to do. Why would you lie to you?

The lie and the belief are coated in a way with a ply of envy or jealousy and may even stay, but if you remove each coat everyday and it is put away and you no longer resent whomever it was you were mad at that day, it is not misunderstood, but if you tend to coat others with a lot of ideas that you hold dearly inside you and never ever say that they are treading upon you today, you will lie once too often to them and they will decide you deceived them. Why? You must talk to each other, but you do not have to always agree. That is not what we mean when we say you must love each other.

Your life is full of wise men and women today, but you could be so wise as to just let them all advertise and decide who is the one you will remain with most of the day, or you might decide to advertise. Why? Why not? Why not speak out and say what you truly believe today?

You might decide that you would be a lightening rod and that would shock too many who now love you the way you are today, but who knows you if you are not actually speaking up about what you are or do or believe? Who would be upset if you were to speak of thee?

No friend would be upset if you said what you believed, but if you say you are able to do only so much and never ever even do that much for that other, that friend will not bend long to you. You will then have to talk to them, and will you alibi for not helping them? That is a lie.

You have to stop making so many excuses about your lives. You have no need to advance help to anyone while on this side of this life, but once you say you will do whatever, you must follow through and do it, since it is a lie to say you will help and then not deliver. You can always change whatever, but not until you learn to talk it over with us first or your own self within you, can you teach others the way to live today within you. You will find that if you lie to others, you will lie to you over time, too.

Your lies to you are very serious business. Why? They take so long to realize and they seem to be there all your life, but why are you lying to you?

Your mind often presents others as more important than you, but do you really believe that is true? Why would you think another is more important than you? If that other is very wise and lives a wonderful life and is never actually attempting to interfere in the lives of others, you might do that and be very wise. You might also see that the wise never do talk that much about themselves—even if asked by the rude.

You might think that asking questions is wise to do, but why do you do it?

You will find you are either avoiding your own life at that time, or you are wondering about the other too much to be able to wait until they favor you with an anecdote or two about them, and what they do. You might wait forever for some to ever tell you about what they do, but there are so many out there who are just wanting someone to ask them anything about what they do. Why do you always seek the one and ignore the other?

You will find that today's lesson is harder than you ever thought a lesson could be, but it is one that will make your own history better. If you never lie to you, you will in time stop lying to others about you. You will not be able to find anyone at all who is not like you if you talk about you and never ever say anything that is not like you. The work of one will attract or repulse another, but why not find out now who you are and what you love to do, and then try to find others who are more like you?

Your life will be pretty and easy and never upset by others? No, but you will find that you do not remind you over and over all this lifetime if you do not lie now about them or you or what you do together.

Old friends lie the most? No, they are not old friends because they know who the other is and why they are generally like them inside and believe in them, but if an old friend is willing to talk to you, do not ignore their advice. You have to understand that anyone who is an old man or old woman inside is inside that life all this lifetime and could seem to be a child, but not one to those who are wise. You will remember if you were old or young when you arrived. You will remember that now.

If you were wise as a child, adults often said that you were old, but now you are older and maybe you are only now thinking about being wise. Who are you in the eyes of the child who is wise?

Are you able to understand that a child who is fresh and eager and just back from the other side is wise? Are you able to see a baby is never going to cry over anything at all until at least the age of 2 or older if he is wise? You might even find a child or two who never whine, but you probably do not notice them.

You will find that if your mind is overwhelmed and an old man or an old woman sits beside you and you whine to them, they will normally not be upset with you, but you might be upset that what you say to them is not new to them. You might even whine or say a word or two that is rude, but you are who is rude and not they.

You have to understand the old and the young spend a lot of time on the other side and still like you as you are this time, so never lie to a child or an elder again.

You will find that if your mind is open and you feel fine, it is generally sunny and the weather is good in every way. Why? You are made of much water and the barometric pressure can upset the equanimity of you inside and it is open to you and available to you to check the humidity from time to time, but only the wise seem to realize that weather can affect how you feel at times.

When the old say something about the weather today, the middle-aged seem to laugh at them, but we wonder only about them.

When you lie to a newfound friend, you are dooming them to never ever be able to trust you again. You have lied at the beginning and sooner or later it is going to be known by them that you are not telling them the truth about you. If you do that, you will possibly let them like you or even love you longer than they might have otherwise done, but you doom them to finally see through you and not want to be with you.

You will find if you are easily upset by the behavior of others you are generally moral and upright by the time you are 22. If you are older when you are converted to the moral obligations of the people who are living around you, you become too strict and too moral for most people to admire you.

Who is moral? Who is legal? Not the same to you? Both are decided by you and the people who are around you. If you all decide that a law is bad for you, change it and open your eyes to what is around you and then decide why you did it the first time. Do not immediately change anything until you find out why your elders were sure it was wise. You will open your eyes. You will see if time has really changed at all at this time.

Are you aware of the time in your own life and what you are and why you are upset at times over time leaving you soon? Are you? Are you so sure it is terrible to age and go inside the mind for longer periods of time? Are you so sick at the idea of being old that you cannot see anyone old around you?

What is going to happen to you if you do not accept that you, too, will be old? You will have to die younger than you would otherwise. You will then be telling the body over and over that you do not wish to be old and the body will conform and try to find what it can do to end your life at that time. Are you aware you program the mind and the mind tells the body all the time to do whatever? Are you not able to see that if you lie and say you are sick today, before the day is over, you are sick or blue inside you?

What if you lie over and over that you are sick and do not have any money or whatever? What will happen to you? You will develop into a person who is unable to enjoy their health or wealth and you will pity them, too. You will, but you will soon learn they have both and you have none if you give them your health or wealth in order to make them happy with you.

You have to see how many people take care of others in order to appear to be nice or whatever, but why? Why not just be you and be nice? You can do it and not have to have others speak so much about you, but if you do live for you, others will advertise for you.

You will find if you are inclined to lie, you blanket everything and everyone with one line all the time. You are fine. You are not happy. You have no money. You are loaded. You are too tall, too fat, too short, too whatever all the time, but it never works most of the time. Why? Others use their eyes.

You have no money? You live in a home you are buying and it is in a nice neighborhood all the time and you are always driving anywhere you want, and you have plenty of clothing? Who is going to believe you do not have any money now?

You. You know. God will not listen to lies about you and lies that you will tell about you, but most of us do. Most of us will judge you according to what you say about you. We are not perfect and we are not God!

The work of the elders on Earth is to help others? No, but goodness is in them, too, so most of them will help you. Why? They believe in their own lives and they have been helped all the time by other people and the kindness within them and in the old times of this time, many did not have any money sometimes, so they will believe you and think you do not have any money now—we do, too. Why? We never had any money in our lives.

When you constantly talk about money and sex and whatever is never going to accompany you, are you wasting time? Are you really talking about you? Are you having a good time?

Why not speak of you? Why not talk about you and what you truly do love to do? Why? All of you immediately say that if someone would stop and talk of the truth today, you would brand them as an egotist for talking to you that way. Why? You feel uncomfortable if anyone talks to you about the way they exist. You are lying if you say you do not feel funny at times if someone talks about something that is too honest for you to take inside you.

Are you a gossip? Do you talk about others all the time? You are!! Admit it. The gossip is what makes you all exist in a society of you and what you came to do. Communication is gossip to you. You do not have to talk negatively at all about anyone and most especially about you, but if you do, it is not a mistake to talk about it, too. Why? Would you let someone whom you admired be taken advantage of by a crook who is dishonest? Would you stand by and let an old friend try to do something over and over that will never work or be accepted by others? You will? Then you will not be a friend much longer to them.

You have to be wiser than ever? Why? You have to question your motive for repeating over and over what another says to you about them or another. You do that if you are really intelligent? Why? Are you saying you have a brain and an intellect and never try to feel inside why you do what you do with others? You are lying to us or to you if you say you never do question the motive of others.

You have to question all people? Not if you are wise, but how do you become wiser and wiser as you move forward? You listen to others who are wiser than you, or you study the nature of the beast provided for you to view, or you talk about it to God and ask for advice about what to do.

If you never ever talk about anyone, you lie. You talk about everyone all the time, but usually you separate you from them when you talk negatively about them. Why? If you want them to change or be better, would it not be better to tell them? You can and you should talk it over once you are sure you really do know why you are expecting them to be perfect and not you, but once you see that this is a point upon which you cannot bend, do talk and see what you can mend.

If you are tired of working with others who are not like you, do you want them to quit and stop being around you again? Are you so sure they do not like you less than you like them? Why would you talk so much about the people whom you are tied to all day by a paycheck and do not have to talk to again once you are at home to mend? Why? You want to see why you are upset by them? You are asking the other or others to help you mend. You are trying to find a way to understand them, but if the others all say, "It's okay, you don't have any problem with them or they say they do not have a problem at all that way," are they helping you or lying to you?

What kindness is there in being a friend and letting them do themselves in, time and time again? What kind of friend would you be if you talked meanly about them? Sometimes you have to leave that friend and it makes you very upset and nervous to see it end, but if you cannot talk to a trusted friend or two, who are you? Are you without a friend? You will learn to find the best kind of people in time, but why not find them now at this time?

When you study with others and they are able to open a way for you to see inside them, are you wise to criticize them? Never. You will never ever say what you hear inside a room where it is clear and others are praying and saying what it is they are doing for God and man to exist. If you do, you will be placed in the worst position that you can be in—lying to God and others about why you are in that room with them.

If you exist to study others and pick at them, you might believe that it helps them, but a mother is the only one allowed to pick on others who are in their care or charge or required by them to help them mature, but not after the age of 22 if they are still in school. You cannot be an adult and have a mother. That is the truth and that is the fault of the mother if she is unable to adopt that rule of behavior with an adult or a neighbor or a friend or whomever is around her then. If she does it over and over and over again, you can ignore it or you must not lie about it to her again. You must sit and decide why and when you can discuss this lie with her and then do it and get it over. If you talk about your mother or father to others, they will know you will also talk about them to others.

If you never ever speak rudely of the family that grew you, you will be advisors of others, but why? You are respected for never airing the past that went before you. The Church lets you know in advance if you are in trouble, but friends seldom do. You might be warned that your behavior is going to have you scorned or shunned by the congregation around you, but friends will just abandon you.

You must remember then to have a church or two around you if you want to be without anyone again. You need friends or people who will bend to you, and the only kind of people who will do that for you are wise, old, young, or the best of those who are not at those stages of life with you. You can seek advisors, but why would you go to someone younger than you?

You could if you never were wise about what you did when you were young, but mostly you will seek those who are wise and old and discreet if you want to unload what you have done. If you are free of deceit and have no pain when you meet anyone at all, you do not need advisors much at all, but you may be proud of that today and tomorrow be needing an advisor or ten of them. You never know what is in the next bend in your road.

You will find that if your love of you is kind, you will treat most others kindly most of the time, but some will never ever be kind to anyone at all this time. Who are they? The ones who never ever love themselves and will never ever be able to believe you could ever love them. They are in abundance in these times. We trust you do not do anything that mean to you, but if you do, pray and God will show you the way. We will help you and guide you and express ways you can help you to do more today, but only God can free you from preying upon you.

You will not be a predator is the way you must see you today, but if you never were ever even interested in taking others over and telling them what to do or making them over like you, you would wonder why anyone else might try to do that to you, too. They will try? Only if you do not decide who you are and you do not tell lies.

If you ask others for help and advice only to be popular or liked or whatever this life, you will be talked about a lot more and more of this life. Why? You will not be able to do whatever you asked another to help you do, and that will disgust them with you.

If you ask, use it or tell the friend why you did not use it or it will end them befriending you. You must be wiser than you are if you intend to broaden the life you have within you. Why not be you?

This is a lesson for all of you to pursue:
You will not say a word. You will be silent within you.
As you sit and do nothing, breathe into you one word.
As you work and go inside that word, sing the word in a single note and let it float.
As it floats and rises above you, are you able to rise higher and higher?
Let your note float and just sit inside you.
As you shift from one position to another, are you able to see inside you and look for another?
Look to the left and then to the right and decide which personality is right at this time.
If you talk to you about what you do and never follow through, who is trying to take over you?
If you believe another could enter you and take over your work, why would you want them to?
If your mind is full of smoke and you have no work within you to do, will you work for you or just sit and do nothing within until the last breathe is gone from within you?
If your mind is full of you and all you do, are you really aware that no one is out there but you?
What if your mind splits in two? What will you do?
Are you able to do anything by yourself and be happy you are not with anyone else?
Are you so single minded that you cannot work with anyone now?
Are you able to split your time between being single and alone and being a partner with another?
Are you the kind of person who is not kind to you when you are at home alone?
Are you able to do kind things for others and not mind if they never understand you?
Are you fueled with energy when others admire you?
What does it mean if you are angry when another is mean?

What do you think is happening in-between the assignments when you are not asked to work on anything? Are you now ready to read? We want you to do something that you normally do not like—read between the lines and decide what we are trying to teach you.

You will return to the first paragraph and really understand why you refused to understand it when we first wrote it for you.

Once you really understand you, your mind will close and let the spirit take over and the mind will not bother you? No, but the mind will also not be able to do much for you if you never give it a day or two to rest from always working for you. You have to decide why you want to rest all the time or never take time to be you. Normally, most of the time, or whatever you say to you, you do what?

____

____

____

____

____

____

____

____

____

____

____

____

We provide you with lines when we want you to work, but you can skip these lines and just write when you have time to be you.

When do you intend to be you?

The time to unwind and bend is when you are done with your work? No, but it helps you to recommend you to others if you bend and work within you and do whatever you love to do. We want each of you to bend in this work and blend with others whom you may not see everyday, but who are here to work with you.

You will learn to enter your own mind and clean up after the work is done. You will sweep up the old and the used and clean out what you do not need to do. You will then be able to see what you still must do, but it will seem brand new because it is cleaned up by you.

You will all clean up your own life now. You will go inside you and work for you and decide why you are upset with anything you do. Once you decide why, we can then all work with you to do more and more to improve this life with you, but until you decide why you are upset with you inside, what work will eliminate the pain and fear that remains in you at this time? God will be in all you do, so why not honor that within you?

If your mind is pure and you stand up all the time for what you believe, will you be able to rise higher? Not if you put down everyone else. You must not believe that your way is the best or only way, but you must believe it is the best or you will grieve later in life that you did not clean up your own mess and left it too long in this life to be able to ascend at the end and be gone for all time from this life. Believe. See. Look. Love. You will be.

The demands you give to you are not to be upsetting you, but if they do, you must review what it is you are telling you to do. If it is not in accordance with YOU, the big YOU, you will find that your line is closed or burnt out for you. If you are doing what you know is not good, your mind will control you and worry you and confuse you and mistreat you over time, so get you in line and do what you know is wise to do and all things will flow for you—now and over time.

When you are ready, let's all get together and get time in line so we can all go to the other side together in one line.

CHAPTER 9

Without Any Idea Of Who You Are, Can You Be?

If you are able to identify within you the person you are, you can also go inside and change who you will be. But, will you achieve any difference in the being you are?

If your mind is full of regret over you and what you do, will you admire anything about you? You should be able to see within you that there is someone who is not like you trying to come through and help or be you, but it is not negativity at all. It is the other side of you.

If you talk about you and it seems to never come true, you will find in time that you learn not to talk all the time. But what if you never learn at all?

When a person begins to feel slightly ill, do you believe they should assume it is real? What would you do? Would you immediately react and do something immediately to counteract the way you feel? Would you sit and work within and see if it is just a passing phase and will soon leave you? What do you do normally when you have to change something or do something weird or new to you?

If your day is full of advice you give to others, watch out! You are likely to be asked to give up your life and not be able to take your own advice. If you take upon you the work of others, in order to be able to have them say you do such a great work for them, you will be discovered as not helping them, but maybe too late to begin again and do it better than you did when you assisted them.

If you love you, are you truly conceited and unwilling to be like others? When you question such meager demands of the higher realms again and again, we wonder why you do not get on with your life.

If you want to know about you, study the work you do. If you work at all kinds of jobs during the day, look at your dreams and see where you would rather be. If the work you do is exhausting you, you are not working at anything that inspires you. If the work you do pays you to be exhausted, you should either decide today to do it another way or get into a better work for you.

If your mind is full of you and you have no time to even look inside for you, what can you expect God to do for you? You will find God is and was and will be and so on until the end of all that you believe is time. You do not have time to whine.

What you will do and feel and believe are not as easily defined by the mind as if you had data that it can arrange and redo over and over for you, but the time the mind spends working within is helping you at times to redo what you should have done right within.

What kind of paragraph was that? Look at each line. Examine the way the words are aligned. If you have to redo any part of that work, do it for you and see what you drew. You are a line and you draw you all the time. We want all of you to redo you, but now you have to feel within you the need, too.

When the lines of a page are all the same, are you able to see inside the work you have to do? You do not see things as easily if we line up the words vertically, so we horizontally work with you, but you can read the other way, too. Practice doing more and more of what you normally do not do, so you can be open for a few new works that will be coming through to you to do.

When you feel the time fly, is it the time or you?

When you sing and dance and the world is not there for you, are you the only one who is not feeling like it is for you? What about all the others who people your world, are they there for you or are they assuming you are there to work for them, too?

What time do you want to leave? Assume you are in charge of leaving Earth and you wish to ascend with a group of old friends. Would you want them to leave at your time or would you end your life in order to go with them? Why would you worry about such things at this time?

You have to assume you have a mind to help you get things done on time, but after that, what do you do about time? You have time and you use time, but why does it exist and why does time seem to confuse you at this time?

When we talk to you and work with you, the time is always mentioned by you as not being there when you wish to meditate within you. Why?

If your heart and body are strong and you have not told any lies, what time is in the line you will miss when it is time for you to ascend from this?

That is a long line? You have time. You do not have to read another line. If you continually study and read about ascending at the end of time, you might believe you can do it when you decide, but that is not true and would be a total waste of time for you to work as if it were true. You must begin to use the mind again and analyze why you hate time and why you do not like to use time the way it is for you.

If you understood the concept of time, would you?
What is the concept of time and why are you?
What is the time of you and why are you here?
Is there anyone in the time that will disappear?
Where is the time when it is not here?

Whatever you think or do, please remember that you think of you first and then you let the mind work on it for you or you go inside and dream of what you must do. We will never work for you!

What you do and how you work, are ways you talk to you all day and why you do what is good and wise, but only if the work you do is good and wise to do. You cannot find a fool doing wise things and not growing wiser all the time, but a wise man who is inclined to do foolish things might not be wise long. Who are you?

You will find men and women blend, but we use the term men. Why is that a problem again?

The world is changing and all of you are upset some of the men have had so much power that they were not wise when they tried to civilize the world again. In the last era of women and men, the women had all the power and men were submissive to them. Will that time arrive again?

Why do you think one sex must have power over the other? The androgynous human is one who is going to be able to do a lot more than one who is polarized into two ways of seeing themselves all day. You must learn to see yourself from the other perspective before you can leave today.

Today is a term we use to infer there are periods of time in which you are enabled to do work that is along one line, but if that interferes with your sense of time, call it an era or call it an age, but move down the line. You are here to learn that you exist on another plane, but it is harder to explain than time. We wonder why you do not question the dreams you have during the day as opposed to those at night, but few of you are inclined to believe either of them is another life you visit from time to time. We wonder why?

If this lesson is a jumble to you, you need to be able to switch gears better than you do. If you cannot change the subject and remain as is within you, you are not well rounded and grounded enough to be able to work with us at this time, but will you learn enough to finish this work? You have to start someplace and here is enough.

What you need and what you see are linked on Earth, but not in the universe. If you feel you need to do anything that is real, do it now. If you are so sure you can survive in the ether and not need Earth again, you can ascend now, but why not wait until the rest of you are ready to blend, too?

The Earth is a place of heavenly births and there are many who believe they are angels, too, but that is a mistaken view of you. You are not an angel and on Earth, too, but angels do visit you.

The work you do is for You and if you are not here doing that work for You, you might have to return again to follow through and do that work for You or do it over and over until you know why you were not able to be you.

What does that mean? You have to be able to understand the basics if you want to be trained in the way of ascending today, but you do not have to fly just yet. You will be in a line at the end and you will all ascend without anyone bending the line—but you must be able to know at the end when it is time to fly.

If you have a friend who is able to fly and helps you ascend, which of you is the stronger then?

What do you want from life? A man and woman may like to bend in bed and have sex much of the time, but is that what they really like or the pleasure or the reassurance they get from each other that they are okay today? What do you do today to affirm that you are doing whatever the right way? Do you go after others and ask them to talk to you about what you do?

If your idea of being in love is to be pursued, you will never be loved for being you. You will pretend to love over and over and over and never be able to know who you were. You have to understand that love, sex, harmony, money and situations you now believe are great for you—or wonderful to feel within you do not exist anywhere else, but in this phase of your development on Earth.

You will ascend even if you do not blend, but you might decide to do it with a group and open wide the work you have yet to do inside. If your mind is bent out of shape by the time and tide and would love to know how to do the work you have inside, you will first begin by studying the water you hold inside.

What can you do to study you? Look inside the mind first and clear out the fog and the mire you collect when you hide from you. Your mind and your soul are not going to stop you, but you have to decide why you would let the mind do so much work that it is a mess when you open to the light within you. Work now to clear up the work of the mind. When the mind is confused and knows not what to do, call another and ask them what to do? Why? Who knows you? No one. Get into the moment and fully look at you from inside and see that you have to do that more than you do. Whatever you do, see in you why you need to do it before you begin to do it. What?

Go back and see why you would not do it. If you cannot understand that you must not commit to doing anything you do not want to do again, you will completely waste this life trying to do everything over twice. Do it well and right the first time and take delight in doing it that way all this life and then alight on the next step to the best of life—being with you again.

You will find there are times when you cannot bend over or you have to bend too much for you to enjoy the view you get of you, but if that happens to you, do the work and then feel within you what it was you did to you. Think of it as something you did and not what another made you do.

If you are attacked by another and do nothing to defend you, what do you think that means? Are you a friend to you? Many of you misquote the words of Jesus of the Nazarenes and say he was not wise and that he advised people to walk all over you when he said that one must turn the other cheek, but he was wise and he did nothing like that all his life. He carefully worked out a life that was wise and true to the path he had decided to walk with you, but you have to decide why you select only one or two parts of his Earthly passage to quote to you. You often lie to you about what others do, too, but this is a passage and you have to do your own work, too.

God is in the work of all the lives on Earth, so if you believe in God, you must believe in others, too. But before you rush naively to accept all that you see, you must understand what it means to believe.

To believe in you is to refuse to pull you in two whenever you have done anything that is new. You must not attack you for doing what you do not like to do or were not willing to do? You should have listened to you. For that reason, you may be wise to sit down and criticize you, but it hardly need take the rest of your life to do that to you. Why not sit down and go inside now and visualize why you are upset at any time? Can you or do you wish to collide one more time?

If you know you have the means today to survive and can do whatever you like, why are you telling all around you that you are not able to do something because another does not want you to do it? That is a lie. We have not finished that line, but we will remind you now and again why you tell more lies than you are willing to admit all day at this time.

If you admit you do not have time for the work you do, you are greatly remiss in using the time that there is inside for you to work on you. We will work with you, but sit now and see what there is to do—then do the work and be able to see you just had to do the work in the way you know is best for you. Sit.

If you are told to sit and then you do it, are you weak? Are you wiser than others? Ask you what to do and if you are following you to do whatever, you will not be upset by doing it ever. That is the way you are made and will follow everyday, but you have to tune in better than you normally do if you plan to change a way or two today.

If you decide to move away from the home where you were raised, you have to decide on another way to raise you all the rest of your days. It may be easy or it may not be as difficult as you think it will be, but one thing you cannot say is that they held you back in any way. They or them is not the way to describe the world, but it is a way of distinguishing you from others and it seldom is ever satisfactory enough to say that someone else is who you are working for today. We know of only a few who are working to do work for others and none of them are saying a word of that to you.

Are you complaining about you or others? You usually assume that what someone is doing to you is aggravating or stupid or not good to do, but it might be that you want to see if others do that, too, and you are the only one who is not wise enough to do it this life, too. If you look for others to confirm what you like to do, you will not enjoy anything you do. Why? Who likes the only things or the best things you like about you? Who knows you? Only you and the other elements of you.

The other elements of you? What kind of money do you think you need to live comfortably within you? Are you sure you need any money now? If you do, why not work for enough to provide the necessities now and plan on saving for the time when you will not be able to work for you all day? If you never plan or look at the time when you will enter it, will you ever be there or are you pretending you will live as you do forever or until you ascend? Think of the many ideas you have within you and decide what is best to do. If your idea of the best is not nearly enough for you, you will be told by others to do more and more and not to rest? No, but you will feel that you are not working hard enough to be you.

If you sit and stare into the air and then see you working with a list, are you then going to list the work you must do? Why not just watch you list the work you have to do and observe you? You could then do it without writing a thing and you might even find you know what it will bring to you—but think first. Think always before you meditate or go within you. Why? You can then clean up whatever you think and make it come to you or go away and never bother you again. That is the best way, or you can continue as you do today.

What about this group you are working with now—attracted you to them? Are you able to follow the work and do it with them? Are you tired of trying to follow them? Why are you upset with 'them' when you are not even known by them and they are not known to you, but will be when you end? Why not be you and assume that you can bend over and not break in two?

Do you think the amount of time that it takes two people to fall in love, and then divorce is a waste of time? Why? Are you so sure you could do more in the same time to learn about living with another who is not like you? What other way to consider you and see why you cannot be you if you give your life away? You will now pray for the man known as Ray and the others who are now passing through the work they do all day and have no time for themselves and finally awake one day and walk away. You will pray this is a line you do not have to learn at this time or you will know you have set it in place and will now follow that line until the end of the day. When today is over, you will walk with your new found friend Ray, into a better part of the day and be able to golf all the way through this life without a woman telling you why you are not the one to be there for her all day. Please remember that you are Ray and you will have to do this if you have no idea of what it means to be walked out on today.

Your work and your own life are not going to hurt you unless you desert you. If one attacks you and you resist, are you taking that as a risk to your divine orders not to fight back? You will remember that Jacob and other elders were attacked and fought back, but Christ was not referring to the attack of anyone on Earth. You must be able to withstand the advice you give yourself all day and not take the first idea and sit there. You have to see the first attack upon you is from you and you will do that until you learn to not take it so far back that it is not even open for you to do anything about within you. Turn your back on what is an attack from within you and do not work so hard to withstand the attacks that will follow. Why? You need to rid you of self-hatred and doubt within you.

God is not saying you have to do anything at all. If you hear the call, answer with a loud YES and follow it, but otherwise, you have no time to live the life of a liar and say you have been called to do whatever and then advise others you are not going to work for the rest of this life. That is never the way of a call today. All who are called work the hardest of their lives for others, but they could have done otherwise.

You are wise and you are rich and you have many friends who speak highly of you, are you going to ascend at the end? What do you think of you? That is the criteria that will take you over to the other side of life and help you ascend at the end. It does not matter what another may do to you? It does if you let them do it because you do not think well or wisely enough of you.

Betraying your own life to others is not the prize that gossips want to use and abuse when you are not with them to talk about you, but if you generally run you down and do not like you, most will gladly prolong the time you are upset with you by talking down about you to others. Why not get it together and stop sitting and making others mad they ever met you?

Now we have attacked you and your care for others who are not you, but are of God, too, but we are not saying anything mean or negative about you at all. If you feel that, you are too high or positive about you. You need to seek a balance within you. Negativity is misunderstood by many of you, but the idea is okay today since you will work harder to balance you than you would if you never realized that moods are there inside you for you to work through.

If you try to drink and gamble and raise your spirit with other means of spending money unwisely, you will end your days with a lot of bills unpaid, but you know that is the way now. Why do you tempt you and reduce you to such a bad end when you could be preparing you for the best of all ends, too?

If you cannot rest, you will now sit and zoom into the work you have inside you and we will work with you to reduce the worry you feel within you.

This is your life and you will do this life for you. If you do not live for you, you are wasting this time for you, but it will be practice and you will have to redo it in time for you, so get the best mood you can within you and practice to do nothing for anyone who is not going to love you. That is not exclusive of the universe, you see, because the universe is love and you are going to be a part of it, so get used to being in love with you.

You will find the Earth is a time of patience and the practice of working for you and the enemies of you, but the enemies for the most part reside inside you. You are the daily means of you being as you are and will be, but you try to find others all this lifetime to blame for who you are. Why are you lying to you and why do you think it is wrong to do? Now think. We ask you to think of why it is wrong to lie to you, but now we want you to meditate within you.

The time to end this work is when you are hurried and cannot do the work, but today work anyway. You will not hurry or go out immediately to work for another who is not going to want you to do anything that is not good for you. You can blame another for hurting you or advising you to do something not wise to do, but you had to do it if it actually was done by you. You committed to it, so you are the major role player within it and not anyone else who may have inspired you or told you what to do or even persuaded you to try to do it. You have the mind to decide, but you often take pride in saying to others that you work for others first and then you take time to work for you, but that is not true. You always work for you first. Admit it and do not lie about it.

You will find you may be able to be persuaded by those who are lazy to do work all day for them and not be at all paid in any way to do that work today, but God is in the work and you are paid in so many different ways, you will only learn later what kind of day you built that way for no pay. You will find that payment of money takes the other off the ropes and makes you the one to do all the work. You are who is paying you to stay and do whatever you accept for pay. You could work everyday in some other way, but you choose to do that for you, so gather what you may and try to understand why you are there at that time and why you wish to set it aside. You will move immediately upon the day you are done with all you want to do in that one job for you, or you will continue to work over and over until it is done.

You are to decide why you have so much pride in you that you would even try to work all day for someone who is not going to be there for you. You have to figure out why you would stay with anyone who is not going to help you in anyway. You would also have to understand and decide why you plan so many things with people who are not like you. Why?

You are who is here and now and doing this for you, so who else can enter into this world within you?

Not one human being can enter you or do unto you anything you do not like to have done to you. It is reasonable to assume there could be a person who is so forceful to you that you give up your life for them, but it is not a rapist who is so often the one who takes a woman's life from her, but one whom she is supposing will always take care of her and her home. You are who is here and now—and you will find that you alone can take your home and make it there within you where it will never burn.

You can see that your home is a family of one or you add others at times in order to find ways to be more and more within you and your own world, but you never own anyone of them—and should never prevent them from leaving the home you have made for them. You are free and you should see others may not always agree, but if you always agree in order to provide peace and harmony, you lie.

You will also see if you never believe in anyone at all, you cannot be you all the way through to You. You could be all you are and still not see that you live very comfortably, but that is not a problem to us. You will find comfort is not kind if it never brings changes you want to be within and around you now.

You will change if the pain is so intense that you are extremely nervous or upset by others, but normally you remove that one pain and let the next remain until it commences to do so much more to you that you must move. We would then say the wise leave, but some remain. Why? You ask them. We are not on Earth to talk to wise men? We are, but we generally provide them with the means to be even wiser men.

You will see we release energy at times and then we say men and women rise in their minds. Why? Are you all so angry within? Some men are angry again, but most of them are so old within them that there is no time left for you to worry about what to do with them, but what about the young women who are so violently opposed to men? We want you to think of you and then of another who is violently opposed to you.

Who did you suppose was violently opposed to you now?

Did you see you and a vision of the darkest soul you know approaching you and saying you cannot do it all? Are you aware you compare that dark soul to anyone who is not known to you? You do. You reveal to you and others who are around you what you feel by talking of the worry that comes out of you, but that is why you are supposed to talk to others about you.

You learn if you talk about what you do to you, but not if you talk about what another did for you. That is not the way to see through to YOU, but if You and you decide to work today on you, what way would be the best way?

Will one person in the group speak of what they would do?

Group response:

(I would do things at my own pace).

We agree completely with you. We would never ever tell you how to work, where to do it, or compare you to others, but you do.

You will now see there is a point of agreement with us. We can work as a group of teachers, but it took us about a month of your time to arrive at that place in time where we could meet with you and talk to you and still remain the same inside and not be upset by the profane, but what about you? Are you all able to sit and meditate and still feel the same?

No response at this time.

GOOD. THAT CONFIRMS THAT YOU ARE ALL WORKING THE SAME WAY AND HAVE NO CLAIM TO PAIN OR SORROW THAT YOU CHOSE TO REMAIN.

The capital letters refer to the Saint who is always so complacent when it comes to matters of the work of others who are not on this plane, but is upset when anyone complains about this plane to others. You will find that we still complain about others, even if we are not on your plane. Why? You are not perfect even when you die.

You will find there is a measure of perfection you choose everyday to find, but do not refine you so much that you do nothing that day.

You will find humor or wisdom with a bite is so much more delightful than a dry lesson today, but who is believed? Not the comic or the relief that comes that way. Why? Today most people are so sad inside, but say they are happy, so they do not believe that anyone is happy today or is able to make them laugh in any way. How sad for you all, but it is your day and you all are granting that to everyone except to you, so say to you, "Hey! Why are you so sad today when you have it all"?

Repeat that over and over until you can see you do it to you and you are the only one who is a fool to do that, too. You are who is damaging you, but you could be leading others, too. If you stand up in a group or out at a party and seem to be sure of you, all will notice you and pretend to be like you, but are you having fun or making fun of them? You need to be sure you can make fun of you, but that is not the best way to be you in a public area today. We see many agree to crucify someone who is not like them each and everyday. We see it on TV and we watch to see what everyone does about it that day, but some of you do not agree. You see, but you do not believe. You act upon the act and do not see anyone doing anything wrong unless you know you are on the way home and it happens to you and then you see it on TV, too. Why do you all disbelieve the TV and then sit and read and study within it?

You will find that seven different beings are not likely to lie all the time, but one or two will see you do not like to talk about you all the time and will prod you to do what you do not like to do—be.

If you can be and see and feel, which are you? The part you are. You are not a hand that feels and you are not an eye that reveals, but you are you all the way through to the next view of you and that view extends into You and then all the way back to YOU.

YOU are connected to the God of All within you and are you and can take you at any moment, too, so be true to you.

If you feel certain you know so much about God, then say when you will go and let us know. We will all wait for you. The lamas of Tibet long ago knew for sure when they would go, but did they know that China would come and take them away from that day? No. If you know so much, why are you still on this Earth working like us?

You are not doomed to work over and over and over again on Earth, but you do not trust that you would be able to move up, so you ask at the last day to come back again and work for Earth. This time, ask to move up.

You will find that your day on Earth is a time you will never ever live again, so live it up. You deserve to know this is a time when all things will be revealed to those who are willing to study and do the work within and then reveal that work to the rest of the world, but are you able to study and study and study to reveal you to others who will say you are not telling the truth today? You must be able to be reviled by others or you will lie. You will lie if you are not stronger than the mind of another.

You have seen a child squirm and tell a lie time and time again in order not to be reviled by you or others, but do you see you cannot help them if you do not strengthen them and help them to rise above it?

You must not covet what another brings to Earth with them!

You brought a lot of presents for others with you then, but many did not like the way others looked at them or said a word about them and lost those gifts and refuse to use them now. We will not point out to you whom you are and what you refuse to use, but you are a fool and all will know it when you never use what God gave you and you refuse to admit it is a gift to you.

You will admit you can do work and you can study a bit and you will even say you are stronger than most others, but you will not say you commit to you everyday or so and work with God inside you. Why?

The time is over for people to sit and do their own work as a single unit? No, but it is harder to be admitted to any new work within you if you have no one at all who is there to show you what to do. In a group of folks on Earth, there are many who are there to tell you whatever and they seldom do know what it is they pretend to do over and over, but you will know it. Judge not, but watch the way they live today.

You will find that the gracious and kind with a sharp tongue today will in time have no good times offered to them. You will find the tolerant bigot is not going to be asked by others to attend some class if the class is run by one whom they cannot tolerate today. You will find that minorities are all inclined to be paranoiac about others.

Think of the largest minority of all time—women today, and then see why they all whine that men have all the good times. You will want to strangle them? No, but you will wonder why they want so much more when they cannot handle what they have.

You will find if you are inclined to want more, you seldom even notice the increase of money, time, friends, or presents if you are greedy inside you, but if you truly admire and it is easy for you to buy it for you, why not do it for you? You can buy things for you, but it is unwise to load up on things that will not be there when you die.

You will find if your car is a mess and cannot run well, you go and see someone about it, but if your mind is a mess and cannot run well, do you go and yell about it to someone else? Why? You did it and you alone know what is wrong, so if you have to go and talk to someone all about you, make sure you have enough friends to spread it all about you. You can, but you then have to listen to them.

You will find whatever you are doing at this time is fun. Why not? If you are not having a good time, why live within you and do nothing you love to do? Your mind is what is always jumping ahead in time.

You leap and you fear others and you jump into the arms of anyone who is willing to say "I love you," but is that wise? You are who loves you and if you cannot see that is why you get so upset with others, you will find you are not going to prize you all the days of your life, too.

When this work is done, and all of the readers combine in a long line, will the readers and the greeters from the other side work alone or in a line at that time? You are all working in time and you all are in a line, but today as the machine writes away in time the machine is alive to the way it will be for you in another time. You have to be able to visualize today the machine, the Scribe, the gathering in the room, and you sitting there in the same view doing the same work, as you love to do.

Now, are you able to smile at the group gathered around you?
Are you aware the Scribe just more or less smiled at you?

You will find your mind is open to the day and you close the mind to it, but if you begin to open within, be sure you know the climate of the group you are in.

You will find many are inclined to seek power, and many envy all who are in that way again. You have all had your turn on Earth to do this work and do whatever you are trying to win, but now it is you who has to do the work. You will learn in another experience or view of you what you did to do this for you, but then it will be done for you.

You are here to learn to manifest and deliver and follow you and do what you intended to do when you arrived on Earth, but some of you are all the way through and still do not know what time it is to you.

What are you trying to do? Are you still unsure of you? You are still not doing work inside you if you are still unable to see you are doing what you came to do. You came to be you and follow you all the way through to you. Do it.

When this day is over and the class or two you try to do over and over are all done and you are given credit for being able to pass over into the next work you must do, you will remember that this group gathered in this room and worked with you. Why? You are all in the same line, but some of you are now only finding out what to do for you.

When the room is warmer and warmer and then it grows cool, is the room changing or are you?

You will find many people do not like to heat up an argument if it is going to mean they might stand out too much and be seen, but is that a wise thing to do? Maybe for you and maybe not, but you have a mind and you can speak up a lot more about the way to run today than you do.

The wise sit and complain today too much about the way the others are trying to ruin the world, but who is wise? The ones who just complain or the ones who steal the scene and make everyone else look nervous inside.

You will find some of you are upset at this time, but it is your time to be you and we have loaded so many questions in your mind and you still chose to concentrate on negative issues you do not like about you at this time. It is your mind and your decisions that make you do whatever you do at this time, so wisely choose to be you and enjoy all the many aspects of you.

Anger is not the best one to choose, but we choose it because so many of you are consumed by it. Today's lesson is to learn to chew on your food and not be upset by anyone around you. Does that upset you? Are you now saying, what is this all about?

You will find if you are upset and unwise, you get into others' lives and you begin to make trouble within, but you do not have to ever say it again. You can pardon your sin and work from within together to improve your own lives, but why lie so much in order to get together?

Most of the events in modern life are now arranged so people do not have to talk to each other, and if they do, they can run down a few and feel better. If that is the type of life you now provide you, smile. Think of it and then try to stop the gambler inside and say, "Hi, I'm lonely, too, so why don't we sit beside each other and talk about you"? The way to absolve loneliness within you is to be you—and then seek others who are also being true to their own beliefs, too. You will argue. You will get upset at times over their views, but it will enlarge you.

When you refuse to actually talk to each other, you burn up so much of your own stomach lining and intestinal fortitude that you never eat food that does agree with you. Why not eat food you like and that likes you?

You will not abuse the body if you truly see that the body is you. You might believe that your idea of loveliness is not accepted by everybody, but your body is. You are humans and you will have the same bodies as others, unless you are a freak of nature and that is seldom the case.

If your own decisions for you are other than you are, you will be insecure and lonely if you are too far from those who are like you. Why not try to accept you, too?

What a woman will do to meet a man is not very good to talk about to you? Why not? Most of it is very funny and seems to be of help to all of you to see why you are so angry at what you say you want today. You do not see that you just want to be believed. That is all. If a man has a wife who listens to him all day, he is very inclined to believe he is very wise, too, even if all others brand him a fool. You will find if the wise are able to withstand the attacks of enemies and fools, they will then be able to help you to withstand your friends and family, too.

You will find enemies are not that unkind if what they say to you is true. If they tell you what you do that is irritating to them, you will be able to do it better for you. If you are able to clear up your own view of you, that is the way to perfection today, but few of you choose to do it that way. Introspection is the best way.

You will look inside you and do not throw you away. Just inspect and look up a way to do it better the next day.

When this group of friends is able to write and pray and meditate all day, we will have such a wonderful lesson plan, but today we leave you all this way—peace and humility are the ways to pray.

Today is the day you are awake to the life you have inside. We will not stay long in the day of this life that you use unwisely and scatter around you with fools who are not even aware you exist or that God is in their lives at this time, but if you do, you can take credit if you can ascend at the end with us and the others in this group. You will have had to do a lot of work within you and that will require a lot of credit from all of us, so you will be like the lost sheep who returns to the flock in time for the shepherd to count him among the group, but why wander away? Why not have a great time today and know that you will fly away? You will decide what to do, but whatever it is, you alone can be you and follow you through to the other stage of you.

What stage? You have to realize first that there are many beings within you who are you and are trying to exist within this one being you call you. If you have not one idea of who you dream of and scheme with to do things to others, you are not really interested in you. We cannot expect you then to do anything for you, but if you decide you would like to join us at the end, you will not be welcome by us, but God may want you to go then. God is the only one who is not going to ever be able to say what you do is not wrong or right or be admired by you? You will find you are human until this time of you ends, so why not lighten up and admire whomever you like, but remember this is a time that decides how you will end.

We will have a brief time in which to offer suggestions to the group gathered around the Scribe, and we will share with you what they do to get through to you that they are working today to pass through with you one day.

What happens outside the body and the mind is often upsetting to you because you are too kind. You try to do for another what you would never ever accept for you, but you do not see God is kinder than you. You will be over the worst of your own worry and you will find many are not that unkind who are trying to say you are right, but you know what to do inside. You will not comment to others if you do not wish for them to make comments around you or about you to others. The gossip is what you are so afraid of today, but that is because you often succumb to it as if it were prey. You will pray now to never again succumb to the worry of others who are too young or too mischievous within to know they will one day walk the same way as you today.

Group comment:

(I saw a large group behind this group and layers behind this group and it kept expanding. Although you are reading this now, I know you were here. It was a huge Woodstock type of crowd gathered around this group.)

We wish to take time to include all who are in the room and able to zoom and know all about the ways of the world today and still remain unsure of what they may do in the next view, but will work hard regardless of what they do today. You will remember that Ray was the one who was asked to be you, so who else would you be able to see now if you were always in that room, too? Look for Ray. He's going to zoom into you today.

Group comment:

(The room is now cooling off for me and I noticed how hot I was when the message spoke of it tonight.)

The heat of the body is capable of elevating and dropping within a range that remains normal and now gives you pain, but what about the mind? Are you able to elevate the mind without pain? Obviously you are able to sit and study and meditate and walk and talk and argue if you care to and never be abnormal, so why not do more of that for you?

There is nothing we can talk about now, but we will ask all of these people who are in this gathering to speak of other things, too. We want to hear from the group and know you do, too, but it cannot be included in a book, which is flat, and people in this group are well rounded and certainly have too much fat to be called flat.

We do notice that you all eat a lot and you all laugh a bit, so why not eat a bit and laugh a lot and keep the fat off the butt. You will find we are very tough, but we are not in your pants or skirts, so we are inclined to kibitz too much.

You will find we are never so dense to you and your cleverness, but we do laugh at you, too. We do not commit to you because we dislike you, but because you are so much like you and able to commit to working in this group for you.

CHAPTER 10

The Work Of The Will

When you are full of power, are you?

When you feel like you are able to do whatever you want, do you?

Why do you feel powerful and not do what you want?

Write in this book now why you would not want to do something for you.

What would you like to do? Are you free to be you? Why would God provide a will for you if you were then to do only what God told you to do?

When you feel that you are a fool, are you?
If your mind is full of being you, are you foolish? Why?
What if you could see inside?

You are wise. You have two eyes in most cases that see inside the work of today, but seldom do you look inside to see why you behave as you do today. Why?

You will now draw up a list of the things you can do to be you and find out what you would like to do now. If you cannot do anything at all for you and you have no time to be you, who are you?

Fill in the line.

____

Did you?

What if you were told to live, would you do it or survive and do whatever you choose to do? You always choose! You live as you choose. Only a very young child cannot choose to be whoever they are. You will now decide why you are alive and why you would not like to be you.

If you sit and look at you, what do you think of the things you like to do for you?
If you stare at the sky and wonder why God is not there, look inside; but if you look at the stars and see that God is there, look for you there.
Why would this Earth of yours be any different from the planet where you were birthed before you came to Earth?
What? You think this is it? You believe you begin, exist, and then leave this Earth? Why?

When you decide to accept what everyone else tells you to do or believe in, you let your own mind decide why you are alive, but is it helpful this time to live as your mind divides time?

Your mind is a kind of machine that counts time. If you want to know what time to do anything, go inside the lid of one eye and look at the time, but if you want to see the power inside of you, look at the middle of your forehead and see the biggest eye—You. Look inside, decide why you would listen to anyone but you and then decide why you do.

When today is over, the group gathered with you will do a bit of eating and drinking and consuming what each other brings to the group. Some of it will be food and some will be the work you are about to use, but what if you never consume anything you need to do and just view the meaning of it? Food not consumed means little to you and the body does not even think of it, but we use food for you to digest and understand that words are food for the mind, too.

You need to read and write and divide your time more and more as you age or the time will not work in its best way over time. If you just sit and work and do nothing inside, you leave the mind behind, but if you let the mind work as you divide the work inside the mind, you can arrive ahead of time at all you have to do. Why? You will then have time to work on what you have not had time to do—be you.

Your work will grow and develop and reside within you only if you cherish what you do. If you hate the work you do or desire to do more than you do, you will not be so easy to live with or be around when it is through. You will not know why you feel so upset inside and cry at others who are just working to do what they came to be, but not do it for you.

You will find one of the people inside you is always aware of the work you do, but at least three others inside you do not even see or care what you do. Why? You have to know you are a complex being who is not just here to breathe and then leave, but do you understand that concept in the best way today?

What if you were told to explore the Earth today? What if you were told to go inside the next boat you see and work to go to another shore? Would you be able to fly in a plane all the way to the other side of your world? You can do whatever you decide to do even if it means you have to work for a year or two to save money for it, but do you?

Your work is not going to stop you from doing what you want to do, but you will do that to you and not even realize why you are so unable to see you. Why? Write now what you will do when you have time to do all the things you truly believe you want to do.

____

____

____

____

____

____

____

____

____

If you have a long list, you have prevented you from doing more and more as you grow older, so go inside your mind and release the wish to stay as is. You must not do that again or you will be unable to move up to the next plane. Remember, we are all here to do this work and exist and then leave this plane with a group who are working as is to free the Earth of the pain of too many souls remaining upon it.

When you read the Teachers of the Higher Planes' work, do you feel that they cannot exist? What is so real that you cannot feel it exists and is real? You will feel only what the mind will explain to you and releases to you to feel. You cannot exist? You do! You are 'real' and very much able to reveal what you do to exist within you, but you refuse to adjust to this reel—this movie of you. Why not let the reel move within you and reveal what you will be and want to have happen to you? You cannot decide what way to move inside.

If you never do anything at all for you, you will not be able to decide what to do, so why does the will exist if you never reveal to it what you wish to do?

Your mind is a machine and you are the one who decides how to use this tool for you, but do you like to decide what to do with your own life this time? We ask a new member or two of every group to always use the tools of the work we do, but each time a new face looks inside, the work grows by a group. We want all of you to collide this time inside and meet each one in the next life, but will you?

You have to decide what to do this life or it will never be able to join with others and enlarge this life for you. Why do you hide? Why do you sit and fret all day to be you when it is what you do that makes you, you?

What do you think of this day and the people who normally are with you all day? Are you able to see anyone now who is usually not with you? What would you do if you had all your family now gathered around you? You are the same every day? You cannot remain stagnate and still gather a lot of energy. The result of stagnation is death and decay, and rot does not become you.

What we will now do is read to you a list of things, and we will tell you what you need to do. If you cannot accept what we tell you to do, fully develop another list and do what you tell you to do.

1. I will not smoke or drink to any degree within the next week, and if I see anyone who is not well because of smoking and drinking, I will not say a word to them. I will expel all my will power to see that I do what I believe another should be doing to be well.
2. I will not do a thing that hurts the will of another. I will not try to make anyone look unwell or unpopular to another. I

will sell whoever is around me or leave them to be. I will not try to run over anyone who is not like me. I will be me and let all others excel.

3. What I see and what I believe will remain within me and I will ask others only what they wish to share with me. I will not probe or question another.
4. When the day is over, I will quote only the most positive stories to others. I will not try to exaggerate what I did all day, but might poke a bit of fun at me to show that I do know why I am not doing as good today as I will be able to do tomorrow. I will not laugh at others if I cannot laugh and enjoy me. I will be as I am. I will grow and become the strongest one within me.
5. I will not work on another to make them superior to me.
6. I will not work for anyone who is going to then use me to predominate over the work I have to be. I will work for me and do whatever comes through the inner way to me.
7. I have work I must do everyday to be me. I will finish whatever I promise another, but I will also work for me.

Write up a list now of what you would do if you had nothing to do on the work previously listed for you to be.

____

____

____

____

____

____

____

____

____

Which list is the most difficult for you to achieve? You ask too much if your list is harder than what the universe would expect you to be, but it might work. It might be that you are here on Earth to work for the Earth or to be what you are to be, but usually you seek the work inside that is easiest for you to feel works for you. Be!

When another person sits and complains and cries all day, who is to blame? You will not know if you have never felt pain, so days can exist in which you are shown why others cry, but why not empathize now and not ever have to go inside and feel that pain? Why not cry for you? You will remain and be you all the time you are on Earth, but the best way is to remain inside exactly as you were when you arrived. Can you achieve that now? You would have learned very little from the world if you arrived as a child and never grew, but most of you are old from the moment of birth. Realize that now and go out and grow up inside and live the way you arrived. Work on the way you were and then thrive.

If you can drive a car or a car is available for you to go about and visit the sick, do you? Are you so sure you do not have to? Why would Christ have raised Lazarus from the dead if you were to not know that the dead are still alive—just waiting for the hand of God to arrive?

When you thrive and then go forth into the work you do and drive out whatever stops you inside, are you successful at what you do?

If you had to decide today to end a few old ways, what would you do?

Look for the old you. Go inside the way you once looked at you.

Now for the next few minutes, do nothing at all and see who is there inside you.

What if your mind is upset with the view you just got of you? Do you have the will to provide you with the time to go inside and erase whatever is upsetting you?

When you feel your mind is not going to be able to grow and divide time, do you say you have no time today?

Look for the top of your crown by going inside your mind. Did you? Did you feel that you would do it later on and now you would just sit and go on? Your mind is going to do whatever you normally do, so you will have to develop your will if you expect to enlarge what you do now.

Discipline is not the way to excel if you have no time to be you, but if you are top of the line and moving forward, you need the discipline of the disciple to be able to follow You to the top and not topple over when the next plane arrives to take you inside.

Your mind saw a plane? Your mind cannot remember who you are when you are not on Earth most of the time, so you must decide now to practice a lot if you wish to remember what the next plane is for and why you would want to move before this time is up. You could decide to ascend for a short time and end this life, but when would you be able to do it? You have to live in this time. You have to breathe for the body to be able to store energy within you. You work on the will all the time and descend into the spine whenever you cannot find time, so you must not let anyone blend with you until you know if they will ascend again in time with you.

What? You cannot ascend if you blend with one who is not going to go with you through time? Why would you want to?

If you feel within you a collision when you meet another who is not like you, do you bend? Do you want to? Are you free of the cold morning air when you see the sun ascend around you? If you cannot bend or come to any decision when you are in front of a friend, are you just blending with them or trying to make them take power over you—again? You must not blend with anyone who is not like you if you do not even know who you are and what you have inside your will, but if you do, remember to unbend before you get back inside you. Your will, won't like to be inside anyone ever, so it is what reminds you to be back and not get too clever with another who is not going to like you forever.

When you are told by the mind to be clever, are you willing to study and devote time to promote that kind of training inside for your mind? You do? Good for You! You will find that the you of the next plane is working always to help you, but the ascent can be harder for you than you will admit to, if you never ask for help from you. You can ascend into you most anytime you will, but it is not easy to do.

Your will is now open for the next session and we will work with you. Please remove all obstacles now from in front of you. The Teachers of the Higher Planes are always around you when you call out and ask for them, but the Teachers of the Planes Within You are unable to find you if you never reach within you. We will now blend the two and meet you—with you.

The year of this meeting is not important if you are not breathing and living in this meeting? Why would it matter to you? You are who is reading or working for you, and if your mind cannot conjure a meaning of life within you, whom do you think will arrive at the other side of life alive?

You have to see that love and character are two kinds of ways to be within and see you all over again, but if you never develop them, what does it mean? You are not here to do work for others who are not willing to work with you, but if you do, you learn to do things you never would have admitted before that you could do, so they bring things and take away much of you that way, but what builds you? The character of a play or a drama or a comedy may be able to learn a few things, but the writer and director of that play is who is telling them what to do. You may see yourself, as being directed by God, but is that true today? You may if you do things for others in order to be able to ascend one day, but are you going to help you to find you and do what you wants you to do all day? You have to secure a path in some way if you wish to be able to wander about and learn about others. If you do not secure a path to your own source or feel secure, you will not learn much today. We want you to be able to respect and deny no one who is alive, but if they try to take your life today and put you outside of the way you are here to be today, it is your choice. You let others decide.

You will find even a few children are able to direct the way for many today.

Why? The adult population is at play and does not really think it should be any other way. Why? All are sick inside of the worry over the means of making life better for themselves over others it seems today.

Why would you strive to not thrive? Why would you hold you back inside? You do when you refuse to enjoy you and do what you love to do for you. You might like to bake and eat a few cookies when you do, but because your friends are all so thin and you wish to be like them, you never do. Is that not a tragedy, too? You could be thin or fat and not be happy within, but why would you deny you a cookie or two?

You would be able to sit at any table and smile and be happy if you had not eaten for two. You have to see that gluttony is the worst sin in this life when you have too much to use for you and do not let others even win enough to be themselves, too. You are here on Earth demeaning you? No, you came to Earth to breathe into your own soul a new way to be you today. What are you doing today?

Are you here and there and everywhere? You may see that as a larger picture of you than you can view, but take time and relax inside the mind and view you from time to time. It takes energy to be you, so do not overfeed you, but do feed you enough to enjoy you as you are and not try to imagine God would prefer you in another lifetime to the one you have inside.

You have seen many remain as is all the time they exist on Earth this time. Why? Why do you think an adult would imagine other adults should feed them or treat them or take care of them? You might wonder why, but you will not know until you die.

You are here to provide love and life and have a great time, but why not share it with you and the others who say they love you. You might even believe they do, but that is not why you are here on Earth to be you.

You may try to envy another in order to get you to move and do what you came to Earth to do, but you will seldom ever want what they are inside. You are who is here to be you, so do not envy another his or her life or it will end you.

You will find whenever it is time to help others, some remove themselves from the room in order not to be talked about by themselves again. Why? They criticize themselves all this life in order to pretend that God is inside them telling them what to do, and you are not able to know. That pretense is what will happen to them, but not to you if you work inside for the good of what you came to do.

You are here today and you will strive to stay in your own path today, but if you do not, you will sway and lose your own way. No one else can tell you to stop being you. You might say they do, but who believes you? You will be exactly as you are and agree and disagree and achieve a lot of what you came to be only if you use the will within you to discipline the lies the mind prepares for you all the time. You lie and then you follow into that line over and over again? You do if you believe you cannot tell the truth and others will like you.

Is that not the most pathetic idea that you could have within you?
Is that not the saddest story you could write about you?
Is that not how you get upset with you?

Why does it take so many hours of meditation to restore you? You get into a rut and explore? No, you start to listen to others who would normally bore you, but you do not like to say they are not like you. What if others like them more than they like you?

You have to see how immature that sounds today in order to be able to change a way or two about you, but will you?

When you explore the different people who adore you, are you placing them on the floor and looking down upon them? You might decide that if they like you as you are they cannot be good inside, but that is not the way to excite you today. Explore you and find out more about you and then see if there is any sign of such life around you. If you find that you discovered within you today a new you, would that one within you feel proud of the crowd around you today?

Are you going to be able to say to relatives that your crowd is so popular that they love you? Not if you know most relatives around you. You would know you would offend them to mention too often to them that you do have many others who love you. You would open your mind only so wide if you thought it would offend them? You do. We watch you, so watch yourself when you are around others.

You are who is disciplining you. You are who is striving to do what you came to do, but others will indeed help you. You only have to see that this Scribe is alive to help you to see inside and when she is over and done with this work inside, is she still alive? You are, but is she inside working still within the work and doing what she is trained and willing to do for you? You have to agree you do not even see the Scribe and she is not alive at all today in this time if you cannot see what she has written for you.

You will be alive to time only when you see time is definitely not inside you, but a concept that you grew and you knew was not for you. You stood on the other side and you looked at this version of you and said it would be easy to be on time on this side, so why aren't you?

When we talk to you about being on time, we are talking about getting all your work together and in line so you can ascend at the end, but you all pretend you have much more time than you do at this time. Why?

You are not to be afraid of what is to end this time, but if you are a friend and you have the means to help another end this time, would you? You cannot. You cannot end another ever at this time and not assume for them the work they did not do. You have then both of you to take care of—you and the aspect of you that took you inside them and helped you to pretend you ended them. You cannot end. You cannot pretend to be anyone else, too.

Your mind and will are still inside you? Are you? Are you still inside you when you sit and read and meditate for you?

What if today was such a great day you never feared anyone at all? Would you? Would you still want to do what you now do? Are you so afraid God is going to let you starve or not be safe in anyway that you would be pressured to do what you know is not wise to do? Are you trying to take away a day or two from someone who is good to you? Are you taking them by the hand as a friend and leading them astray today?

What do you think the world would say if you told the world all about you today? It would be obvious to us, but what about you? You cannot take that much time today. The world will not listen all day. You are here and your work speaks of the way you live today. If you are not able to save you and do work within you, you would not have the best of lives and you would not thrive? What do you think when you think of you today?

What the will does is save you from beheading you and not listening to you. If you could always be logical and truthful and never ever say anything that is disrespectful of you, you would not be able to say a word—you say today, but you are here to be you and end all this work on yesterday—today.

You are all trying to remove you from the other side of you? Who among you still talks about what you once did when you were a child? Who still talks as if they had a mother to blame when it is not going well for them today and they will never ever see 29 again in May? You will find many people are unkind to parents and children are not treated well by many today, but what does that say? What does that mean? Why are you here? Why is that important to you?

You will find that all times have mistreated and deleted people in terrible ways, but today you do not see anything that is not written or televised before your eyes. Why? You are preparing you today to end all the old ways.

You will find many old people today are buying computers and connecting with others in so many different ways than when they arrived on Earth for a short stay, but are you able to do that, too? They arrived at a time when Earth was striving to stay alive and they changed the way money was made so the Earth could be alive and not die. You are late if you do not see you have achieved only what you have seen the older people be. You are not you if you do what you are told to do. You are asking too many people today to tell you what to say and believe and then you say they are wrong for helping you.

You gossip about those who do know what to do today. We see many strong leaders are talked about in order to stop them from growing into dictators today. Why such a fear of strength is here is because you in the smaller occasions do not use your own will power to decide what you will do today. You let another talk to you and you then tell others you decided what to do today. Is that a lie? You can believe what you might, but God is still there and inside and knows when you lie. We don't.

With this class and the next combined into one, we want you to begin to see why you have no fun. You do? Good for You! If you do not have much fun doing what you came to do, look inside you.

Did you?

Are you able to look inside you and see why you have no way of being anyone other than you? Are you full of ideas about you that do not compliment what you do? Are you unable to believe in you and accept you as you are today? If so—do nothing now. Dream of the way to be you all day. We will all help you.

This work is going to be short, and you will know what to do only when you get into the work you have to do, but it requires a strong will to get you to work if you never have wanted to be you.

Think of your own desire for someone who is 'close' to you. Think now of how much of that dream is about you.

What do you think of others who do not do what they want to do? Are you disgusted and disoriented when you come away from working within that group? You will be dizzy for a month or two if you let the dependency of anyone get to you. You need to drop all who receive a degree and then try to preach to you, yet never do anything they truly want to do today. Be yourself. Do what you want for your own life to flower and then die a perfect way today. Do what you want, but make it the best for everyone who is now on Earth. We will help and you will flower if the day is over and your mind is not in your way. Do all you have to inside you to be able to put away today.

The day is over.

CHAPTER 11

The Work Of Being You Goes Forward Into The Being Of You, So Does The Work For You To Be You Before You Go

If a title is long and very distinguished, do you believe that person is smarter or older or wiser than you? You are wrong if you believe in another being stronger inside or wiser than you are by the lines behind the name they have arrived with at this time. You have to do what you know is best for you to do to earn a living this time, but otherwise, why lie to others about you?

You lie about you and talk badly about others all the time in order to make more money in order to be thought better of by others, but do you arrive there anyway if you are just honest and law abiding this time?

What did you think of just now? Did you arrive at the same decision as you might have a moment before you began to read this session about being you? Are you able to see now that this book is about taking care of you and striving to arrive within you at the place where you and others within you can ascend and be you? Are you still looking for another to be you? Look inside. Go inside and be you.

What did you just do? Are you sure you understand what we are all trying to help you do? If you are tired of the being you call you, who cares what you do?

If you do not care about you, what do you think anyone else will do for you? You must not look to others to take care of you unless you wish to be reduced to poverty by the next moment or two of this life for you. You cannot let anyone tell you what to do and let them run you or you will have nothing left to become. You will be a person who does not like you or believe in you or want to care for you, so do more for you now that is wise and full of energy for the best years to come for you.

The future is always within you. You have only to look inside and see if you have anything there that is undone, and then finish it and do whatever else you have promised to do and move on. It is not hard to do, but so many of you refuse to listen to you or do the work you have asked to do. Do you want to just sit? Why not exist in a vacuum then and do nothing within?

You are here and now moving in a direction which is not going to change unless you do, but do you express which direction you want or do you just crash into anyone around you who is also moving at the same time or place with you? You can align your spine and channel to all around you what to do when you want to move into the next plane and be you, but you could also remain as you are within you. Why move?

You are here to decide what to do and then follow you to the end of the work you asked to do. That is all you ever have to do, but some of you refuse to listen to you or do what you came to do. We will help only those who are able to direct themselves to survive the falls from grace that they have provided in order to teach themselves how to live and dwell within and be you.

You will find that You is not the collective being YOU, but a portion of the being known as YOU and that portion is well able to do whatever the smaller self of you wants to do, but you have to let it come forward and work within you, too.

You will know more and more about the work you do by using the tools you are helped to provide you. If you want to write, you must learn to use the tools of that particular society and do the work of a scribe to help another decide what they might like to do only if you are not ready to write the way you have always written inside you. The Scribe writes now for others in order to pay for the time to work at the writing she is able to do from inside, but she always could. Why did you want to work with this Scribe? You are all here because you all knew the tools would be provided and others would arrive when you asked them to. The Scribe is here to help you find the tools you have provided you, but the Scribe is not here to work inside on you.

You may not see that some channel the work of others in order to help you to grow inside, but you might decide the one who channels is wiser than you and provide them with work you must learn to do for You. You have to work for you or do what you came to do. If not, why not leave Earth?

That shocked you?

You will find suicide is a time when a soul arrives at the false and unwise decision that this life cannot provide anything more to do or is not able to do this work before it is time to cross over and close the door. What do you think of the soul that is so unwise as to choose to die? Are you able to decide such a way is not good or God would refuse to accept that soul when you are able to go, too? You are not to know if that soul is good or not, but you must assume God is in control of all you do. Why? You have to decide why you are, and that could take one life or two. Why not assume you wisely chose this world and the work you came to do—be you, and move on with the world?

The world moves up and down and forward as you all learn the lessons of the society and time within, but do you gain from it again?

You either help a friend and gain, whatever is in the work you do or you resent that your friend is unable to see why you helped. You have to do nothing for anyone now or then, but if you ever do or did, you must assume you will be paid well for whatever you do or did then. Why? You could cry yourself away from this life and gain nothing for it. Be good to you and decide today to be you and not cry.

If you see a dog and cat fight, do you run to the cat and protect it from the dog? Do you sic the dog on a cat ever? Do you want them to be friends? What did you think when you saw them fight? Why do you mismatch friends then?

You can find many friends who are like you, but you often choose those who are most unlike you. Is that wise to do? You could also help you by never talking about your own life to anyone but a friend, but will you be able to mend anything if the friend unwisely tells you nothing ever that you are doing that is not good for you? You cannot love and never talk to a good friend about what is not good for them. But why would you have to tell a friend anything they should be able to know about them?

The sense of a sentence is not in the way it is written today but the way it turns into a friend or enemy within you. You must not be upset over the unseemly degree of disloyalty among the friends you want to love? You would be unfriendly if you let one friend constantly talk about one who is not an enemy to anyone, but if the one talked about is a woman or man of great animosity and could hurt someone, are you a friend to anyone if you never warn them of that one?

Think and then do what you believe within you.

If you cannot think or be you, what will come through from you? Wisdom and the best of you will come into you and be you if you cannot do it now for you. Work now to open within you.

If you constantly work against you, are you going to ever find your own way back to Earth and redo this work for you? No, but you will be reversed in the same degree as you worked on Earth and have no one there who is going to help you to undo whatever you have to do. If you are a patient person and have no problems today, you are blessed by the Earth and have a place where you will always be able to stay, but if you are the impatient sort who is unable to work and save and put anything away for the days when you must not work, you will not like the Earth and will not want to return for even another day. Sadly, you will be sent back anyway.

You will not have time to decide why you did what you did in another life if you are as busy today as you should be working on this life, but if you backtrack and redo that work, will you? No. You study the past in order to save you work, but it seldom leaves you time to unwind and do the work you have to do this time. Do the work you came to do and leave Earth. Do this life and forget you ever had nine or ninety-nine lives. No one will ever believe you did anyway, so forget to ask for that kind of advice.

You can dedicate that life to no one until this life is over; so do not write autobiographies about you. You do not know you well enough to write about you. If another wants to write about you, say 'no' because it will then become who you are for the rest of this life. Relatives are not known as well as friends are because you do not like to be told from birth who to like, but if one of those relatives is alive to you always and helps you to arrive at the other side ahead of time this time, you will always take care of them regardless of where you have been. Thank all who are here with you, but be a brother to no one who is not going to be of relative value to you, too.

You could help your enemies destroy you, but better to love those who always love you. Why stand in a crowd and yell at others who are not like you? Work now to see why you do.

If your mind is not going to be open wide and flowing within you, what do you want others to do for you? Look for the time to be you and decide why you would never be able to do that for you. If you cannot understand a way is opening for you, do not say a word to anyone else about what you do. If you do, they will all know you better than you do and kill some of you off in order to control where you will go. Why? You have told others what you do in order to make a lot of trouble for you or you want them to think better of you than they think of themselves. You cannot win that way, but if you do, you will not hold onto it long.

What you do today is full of the future of you, but it may not be apparent to you. Look at the hands of the women and men around you. Are your hands harder or softer than the hands of those around you? You will generally know who is working and helping others by the way they shake hands with you, but do you know what they do to be themselves, too?

Your day is over. You will stay inside you and do whatever you have to do in order not to delay you at the last day, but otherwise, you should be able to end this day or era within you. Why?

You grow and blend within in time in order to be alive and able to thrive or move beyond you. Whatever time it is inside your body is not the same as the time within you and the work you came to do, but it is best to always have the body able to take on the work you came to do and not go before you do.

You will find some people fly into a rage over the idea of another having more or less than they do. Why? You will find you are inclined to do more and more for another if you do not ask them to help you, but if you do, please remember you must redo whatever they did for you. You can pay others to accompany you, but then you do their work and yours, too. Why not move and do whatever you want to do?

You will find that today is a tough lesson if you have not loved you, but if you have and do, you will fly through the lesson and be you.

We will now teach as a group and see what is going on inside this group, too. We want all of you to know that the ones who come into being in a group are not being deceived into believing, but you might deceive you into believing they do not work for you. You are a part of the way they see today and will be on another day, but now they are working this way in order to be able to earn the way through in their old days, too.

You will find one or two of this original crew is not going to teach anyone who is not able to do things inside as we do, but most will emerge into another version of you and help you to decide what to do. If you cannot understand what we do, think of what another human in a similar view as you—might do. This is what we do with this group. Why don't you?

Now think. See inside you.
What does this group look like to you?
Are you going to want to see a picture, too?

We want you all to decide first why you are in need of a prop until you die? You know why you marry or desert those around you, but do you understand they need to know if that is what you intend to do? You cannot desert an old friend and be like you were and feel great about you. That is the way to be you? You will find you will not like anyone who is not able to let you be, but be you and see if they cannot agree you are better that way. Work and see! Wait for others to see you and then drop those who cannot let you be. Do not work to rid yourself of others, just let them be and see if they agree to let you be. If not, you can then move to a more perfect spot. We agree, but you will feel upset as long as you are not willing to let another be.

If you intentionally drop a friend in order to impress another, who is going to win? You will not have either one again. The one changes you so much and the other will not like you for dropping anyone again. You have to let others bend and go within if you want them, but why not go inside and let them see what you are and will do for them first? You can decide to just let anyone die in this life and they need not ever go, but you do. Go and see how many will run after you. None will come for you if you truly do not want them. When you are able, we will go inside and blend.

The day is now beginning and beaming a message to you from within. Do you feel anyone in? In? Yes, do you feel anyone is inside you and wants you to do anything at all to you?

If you do, that is the mind instructing you. The mind is a perfect example of a tool that can be used in so many different ways and most of them can be ways that are helpful or ways that are capable of harming you today. You must control and discipline the mind if you want to be able to ascend at any time.

If you cannot do your own mind work, too, who will do that work for you? No one is able to speak of the work they do without assuming another is interested, too, but so many are misguided into believing and accepting that others are not as interested in them as they may be today. Why? You lie. You lie in order to be able to say you are confident of your life and what you have today. You lie in order to appear superior to others who are honest in all ways. You lie to another if you do not want them in your way, but are you delaying you that way?

What if you and your own family were in a ship and it had no crew, what would you be; the captain, the mate, the crew, the cook or all of them for all the rest to use?

You have to designate from day to day what you want to do for you? No, but if you are not complete, you might want to do discreet and concrete ways of being you today that will not meet the approval of some you once knew yesterday. Why not move if you do not love you? You would simply take you with you and then have to do a lot more on you by having to perform in a new way, but the new way could be better than the way you are today and thus you would learn a better way to be you today.

The long and the short are all the same today, but one takes you a moment or two and the other takes the long way home into you. What do you want to do? Are you able to be you? If you could sit and sit and not do anything at all for you, would you?

What if you had nothing in you, would you feel like you do?
What if this is the best there is for you?
Would you want to be new?
Are you able to sit and stand and walk and plan? If not, why are you?

The only one who is unable to have fun is the one who has to do all the work and not be able to sense within that they are the work and are doing it in order to have fun—but later. You will often work hard in order to permit you to do something later, but now that is not the way most live today. You are inclined to want it all today and think of later never, but if you do, you could save a lot of work for you.

You learn new ways to be today in order to flow and flower and gain a better way of being you today, but if you never ever ask you for a thing to do, you will find your mind has many things for you to do anyway.

If your mind is so solitary that it never minds anyone being around you, you can do a lot and not stop to think about what you bought, need, have, or would like to do, but most of you are not solitary inside you and have to be like others in order to feel you are here and are real. We are not like that, but we have had a lot of lives that do seem to you to be like that. The Teachers who never had a life on Earth are truly unique and will be available from birth, but not until you know this is the time to go.

If you never see and hear anyone in your own mind, are you alone?
Are you there? Are you ever out of air?
Up until today, what did you do for pay?

If you think like that, all days become the past and you have to recommit in so many different ways. We always suggest you get a career that pays and then do it for raises and then go on your own way, but today you must see many refuse to be and will only work for pay. You could see it as a way of making sure there is nothing in the world they want to have today.

The world does not miss anyone who is just there for the pay, but misses anyone who is able to do things and make you feel okay. You will not be upset or bothered by anyone who is not like you, but if you delay you, you will be unable to save you. Only God can help you to ascend once you bend into too many who are not like you.

You may or may not hear of people who are saved by the grace of God today, but if you believe only God can save you, that is what it will take to make you follow you today. You might say all others are not saved because they do see that they know within a way and can follow it without delay. Who knows? YOU! You are the biggest source of power within you today.

You might believe you talk directly to God all day, but why do you think all others would then be inferior to you always? You have to see you are connected to all others and in some inferior way you are all in this work today—regardless of what you say.

You might not like to see people fight, but they are saying they care enough to fight until they are able to find a better way. You might not like to find a fellow who is not like you taking credit for what you do, but if you are not willing to speak up for you, who is going to think you are right if you do? You have to stick up for you.

Your own mind is a tool that is capable of making you a fool. Remember that.

You can also see you have a degree of competency within that matches whatever else you would like to do this life, but do not feel you must get a degree in order to impress that your beliefs are right at this time in your life.

Many who are doctors of this life are not able to think of themselves as wise. Are you wise then to listen to them? You have many things you like within you and return to them and listen when they tune into you today, but what is it that makes you often ignore the right and follow the left into the night?

You want to know more? You want to see what is in the other door? What are you for? Are you not to know what is right or what you should have left before you went out the door of this life? If you never check and never see for yourself, what are you going to do?

You may decide that the profligate is high on the roster at times and not liked at all by the righteous at this time, but why would that be? You have to know that the right has to be able to see the left or it knows not how to be.

If you are right and never fight, are you sure all others say the same to you and about you, too? You have to be wrong, but you must be right more times in this life or you will not like what happens before you end this life. The life pays you back? Yes and no, but you have to know why you are who is making the decisions not to do more of your own life.

If you experience a problem and it is not good for you, do you repeat it once or twice just to make sure? Why not redo the pleasant things more? You could, but why not do what you are afraid to do and see if it is not more pleasant than before?

You have fear and envy and greed and gluttony inside the work of this world, but do you agree that fear and envy and greed and gluttony are only degrees above what is liked by the world? You can see? Good, we will grant you a degree and you will be able to talk to others all day about it. Well? What did you think of you then?

You either think better or worse of you if you believe others can grant you a diploma and let you do what you already knew to do. If you have never been taught a thing, why would you take that diploma now? You all rush about studying with a guru or two in order to brag to everyone who is new? No, but if you are a fool you will do that to you.

You must know only the gifted show anyone where to go. The work you do is not necessarily good for you to do, but if you do work for you and it does help you, why not do it for others, too?

When this day is over and the host and all the folks who ate with you go, too, are you able to remember what it was you said to one another that was true? You will remember because you knew. If you talked to anyone at all and said anything that was new, you would have to assume that it might not be true of them, too. You only begin to understand another by the time you are through with you, so get off the record and begin to talk inside to you.

You will find that music is not upsetting you, but if you find a kind of personality does that to you, you will not be upset if they move from you. You will find if your own kind of personality is open to others to talk about and they say you are great as you are, you will be able to know more and more what to do, but why not listen to those who tell you what you do that is not as good for you?

You could observe you and then suppose one or two others are just like you, but the personality traits are repeated within this race and so why you do not know you and others like you, is a mystery to us, too.

When you find another and another and another who is so much like you, do you assume you must marry them? You do. We listen to such beliefs time and time again, but you are not aware that the other is not there. You are looking at you.

You will need to succeed in order to know what disbelief can be. If you succeed, you begin to believe you alone know what to do and are strong and able to do what others cannot do. You will begin to succeed and disagree at times and not wonder why, but if you decide to never win or succeed, you never go within and find out why you lost that path one day and found it or lost it again that way.

You have to do things over and over to bring them into the view you have of you or you could just disappear and let them come into you and bring through from You what you need to do.

What if you never felt anyone else within you?
What if you had nothing you wanted to do?
What did you do when we said that to you?
What is the day and the means for you to feel good about you?
Are you sure you know what you mean when you say you will be you all day?
What is today and why do you need to be you?

If you know, you can show the rest and follow the path to the end of this day. We know, but do you?

Today, a class and a half are here to work with you, but you have to see this class is in harmony and able to know who is about to go and who is not going to be able to flow, but do you know what they do? No. You do not need to be aware of the cares of another in order to share, but if you know, share that which is positive and not dangerous to their own perception anywhere. You are who is going to be you, so do what you dare and see what you can be.

Today we have a list of people who are trying to follow the class and know what it is they must do to pass, but do you ask for that class or does the class simply last until you are able to pass?

What if you never do anything at all for you? Are you able now to sit and stare within you?

The people who are here and able to do this for you are aware of nothing at all going forward from this class, but we do. We know you. We are connected to the same flow within you. What did you do to deserve to be in this group, too? You were asked and helped and decided to follow you.

The group who is here today is not the same as always, but it is close to the point where only one needs to be here in order to be there with you. You could see that some people are able to do a lot of work that helps you, too, but most are sitting and watching to see if you do any better than they do and they do not have to work, too.

You will find whatever you do is good for you only if you feel kind and generous within at times and can begin to think of others who are not like you. You learn by contrast and you accept what you have inside you only after you learn to know you. We will help you and bless the day you set aside to work this way, but it is your own work that will pave the path to the next life today. You alone do your own work, but if you never sit alone, you can still work for you at home. You do not have time to let all others pass over you and not learn from the work you do.

Your home and your own work will sustain you in the end of the time of Earth for you only if you maintain what you have to do. You could turn over your entire life to others and let them tell you what to do, but why live then? You have no reason to give up on you, so why do you?

You will find there is a time for others to go, seek and find, then return and work within on it together with you, but do you ever work within and ask others to help you mend what you cannot do over? You might find help is not the way you thought it would be today, but help is in the way you see yourself everyday.

You will find that the helpless and the blind have nothing in common at all, but one is seen by many as unkind if they do not help the blind. You may find the blind are sightless and the sighted are blind to others in so many different ways, but is it unkind to help them? You might not think the rich need help within, but why would they not be able to seek what they need today—is what you say? Why? You have all you need within, but how many go there today?

Whatever you say, you talk about you all day. You talk about you and you mention to others what you do, but if you direct them to be like you, you will end all friendship that way. You can be you. You can do what you wish, but you can only talk about you. If you move into the lives of others all the time and talk about them to those around you, you will lie. You do not know what lives within them, but you can assume they believe as you if you talk to them and they agree with you.

You have to see that talking and gossiping are two ways to be you, but one is not liked by the many within them. You have to be aware of what is going on inside your own mind most of the time or you will not know who is gossiping about you. You will find that most people who are apt to talk about another are not willing to ask a question of the most important way to be today. What question is that you ask? The question is one of integrity and honesty and good breeding and being okay inside today. Why not check and see if they know the way? You could solve a lot of your own problems that way.

You could also ask others to explain for you a way to be better at what you do, but do not seem to agree when you do not see. If you are able to nod your head and exclaim over and over again that you understand and they continue to talk about it again, leave. You have a brain. Use it today. Use the mind to compute time and get you to the next gate. We will sit within you and let you do? No, but we are not here to live with you. We are here to work and do what God has wished us to do—help you.

If you do not want our help, that is okay for you and we will never bother you, but if you do need and wish to succeed in ways beyond your own belief, we can help. We know of many ways to help you to grow outside this decay, but do you?

You must not see inside the rest of your life at this time? Why? You have the entire day today to rest and look inside and find out why you are blessed, but most of you will fly and do nothing today once this book is put away. Why?

When this day is over, we will do our own work and that work is to help you and the rest of the work you do to pass into the next class. Do you prepare for work that way, too? Are you doing homework for you?

We will ask this group and others who are working here with you to develop a better way today to see themselves and help others to know who they are and why they are put in this way. You will have to pray. You will only have to look inside and then speak of what you see, but this class will have to write and present what they have inside. Please pray tonight that your class is in the same way.

You will find in time another class will come forward that is not as great as this is today, but will it decline or will you assume it is time to teach a class of your own today?

You will tire of hearing about others' opinions and decisions and whatever if you are above that class today, but many are not above talking about those who are above them today, too. We want you to be sure you know why you are doing whatever you do, so talk only if you can listen to you and work on what you suggest another should do.

Do not talk about you unless you know you.

Today and forever are the same to us and to YOU, but are you the small incremental being that is now working on this Earth above doing work for You? You might decide that is what you did for you, but it is okay, too. We will help you.

Now class, you will remember you have to write up a letter that states what you would be like if you had to be another personality now. You will talk about it and write as if you had a lot of fire within you and must be put out of this life. You will talk to you. You will ask for help within you. Do you know what to do?

Not one person asked for help now, but once the class is dismissed, all will want to know what to do now. Why work on work that you do not know what to do? You have too much pride to ask for help inside? Why? We know you. We can be reached on either avenue or street you keep open wide, so open to the new you and go inside.

This is the class and you will work for you, but those in the world will not be able to understand you unless you can also talk and write and express what you like, so write today and get it back by Tuesday night what you want to do with your life.

We will now go onto the next flight, but if anyone in this crew wants to go forward and do things with You, tell them to listen next Tuesday and it will be you.

This is the end of a long session and it was not the best one for many who were unable to bend or blend within them to accept that another was superior or inferior to them, but if you can accept and reject and do whatever work there is for you, you will know within a moment why you cannot go. You cannot end what is not going to take you to the next episode until this one is over for you.

Read now and see what you think is going to happen next to you. See why you hold up the episode you now have in order to take time and bend it inside you so another will help you. Look out for your own work and it will not upset you, but do what you expect you should do or what a friend expects you to do and it will never end.

We will now go inside the one we ask to write for you and bend into the time to come and see if you can write this way with what comes to you.

The Scribe:

(I am not alone and what I have comes from the mind and home that was produced by me alone. I have not one person who is not of help to me, but at times I am not able to know why each one comes to my side and goes from me. I have a time to write and I decide why I live alone, but do you see me as a lonely being inside?

You will never cry for me! I live and breathe better than at any time in this life, but I still have much to do to enjoy the work I have to do inside in order to free me for another life that is also living within me. I work in my mind and let the fingers fly, but the work is a wonder to me. What do you do that makes you wonder about why you are and where you go when you are not in this world?

This is my life and I have always known it was not the life I was supposed to have inside, but what kind of life does this one within me want this life? This is the question I want answered when I leave this life and begin the next life for me.)

Write a letter to you and talk about what you do when you write and talk to you.

____

____

____

____

____

____

____

____

When you decide to write, write. Do not start to look at anyone else who may be writing or wanting to work inside and wonder what they are like.

We often watch the Scribe and others who write as a way of making their life the best it can be this way, but we see others standing there and wondering what they believe. Why? Why do you care about what the Scribe may believe or write today? You can read and write and follow your own path today. Listen to you and follow what you tell you to do and you will also know the way, but you still have no time within you today to wonder about the Scribe. We will take her for the last day and will show you what you do not know when that day arrives for you, but today, write about you.

You can decide to work inside your own life again, but some of you will not be able to understand why the Scribe is paid to write and they will never be asked to do work that way, too. Why?

Jobs are given out by the way you pursue what work is given to you. Do you work in the school the way you can or the way you wish to let another see is you? Are you doing whatever you can to help others when they need a helping hand? Are you full of hate for anyone who is unable to seemingly make a huge mistake? Are you always upset that another has made more than you with the same hand? You are then not serious enough to be given a gift to help the land.

You need to be able to do whatever you can to help you advance. If you cannot work for you, who else will want you to work? Not YOU. You have to advance as far as you can, then it will be easy for you to leap over to the 'promised land.' You will also be able to land on your feet if you strengthen the back and proceed to believe as you alone can. You are not helping you by always following what another might tell you to do, but the beginner who wisely observes a wise elder can often leap ahead of the pack that are unwilling to acknowledge they cannot work. You can! You are! I am! I can! The way you write or talk today will be you tomorrow.

The class is dismissed, except we want to correct the margins of the letters and the arrows that we add will be like no others. We want you to see what two people in this class do to get inside the work of this world and do the work they came to do. Can you?

The three letters we want you to see are not from anyone who is in your life, but once you have learned the lessons they are writing to you about this life, your life will increase and you will know surcease of pain and sorrow over not being as you are and will be in this life.

We want this time to be used by you as a means to feel within you that you do not seem to be a fool unless you are willing to let another work and do their work and not be able to help you. You would fool you if you never ever thought to use what another has learned, too. You may find that too much of anything is not good for you, but wisdom is not like that, too.

The letter from Maggie is to be used as a way of settling your mind on a hard, cold day. You will remind you to do this for you and perhaps bathe that day in a warm water or spring that you may prepare this day.

Group response:

(What I do when I write or talk to myself is to focus on keeping a clear mind so that I may write or think honest thoughts. These thoughts would hopefully be without ego. I usually light candles around and dim the lights so I surround myself with white light and ask for my Higher Self to be with me. I will ask for any help or assistance with a problem or situation, allowing my Self to go free, to relax and let go. I will just write what comes to me.)

The letter from Maggie is not perfect and she wrote it in a hurry, but if you say that she is not on her way, where are you? Are you in such a hurry today that you cannot do anything that way? Why not try her way?

Now Ray is here and able to talk in his own way about the mind interfering all the time in the emotional process of working on time. He repeats it for you because he knows you are not like him and will not be like him ever, but he is going to help you succeed now by being able to know all who are like him. You need to know them before you go.

Group response:

(What goes on inside of me when I write?)

(I hear the words become sentence fragments and then complete thoughts. I listen for changes and then write the best version. It is the same when I read. It is the same when I listen. I have to repeat everything to myself and have only recently realized that not everyone does this. Wish you were hear. (Not a misspell.)

This letter to you is not anything you ever have to hear over, but you will find out that Raymond is not the clown he tries to make out that he is inside and out for you. He is not that kind of guy, you say. What about that Ray? Are you indeed able to laugh at you and then pray for you today?

Group response:

(Yes, I think so.)

We do, but no one else will, so we move into the context of that message you wrote up for others to discover for themselves that they may also have to restate today what they know to do and don't. You can go on and on, but you need only write what comes out at first. If you do it over, you will not always reduce the facts to a coherent statement anyway, and normally, you lose the spirit of your views doing it over and over to improve the way it sounds to others today.

Group response:

(Whenever I go inside myself to seek my inner wisdom, my Higher Self takes me along the path of my life plan, it is a struggle to get down that path, but it will be a journey that will end at my Highest Self. The road that leads me home has been long, and I want to use the word strange, but that is too harsh, I enjoy the world inside. It brings a peace that I never had before and I look forward to all the wonders this work will bring.)

Jack

Now Jack is not sure of the way to state what he has to say today, but he takes the path of the one who is loose in some ways. He is not, so he practices that. You can find a discipline within his lines, but he is not trying to make you stop and wonder about him at this time. You will also see that his marking of the paper is not the same as it was when he started out.

If your letter to you is hard to read and you have to review it in order to believe you wrote it about you, you are now headed into the proper hearing of you. You can do more and more within you once you learn to just roll within you. You will find there is no time to do more, but once you have time within you, you can go forward and be you. We work for that end and we pray with you today that this is the end of all the days in which you bend to be someone other than you are today.

CHAPTER 12

There Are More Works Than You Know Going Forward

If you are able to sit and stand and not drop anything ever, are you agile? Are you fragile if you break a bone and it does not mend? Why pretend to be physically or emotionally strong when you are dry to the bone?

You have no meat upon the bone if you are starving from within, but if you overeat to compensate for the lack of love or whatever you want, you will look full or sated, but not have enough inside to survive. You must regulate the way you eat every day if you are to survive. If you regulate the food and the vitamins and exercise and are wiry inside, will you survive better than someone who is all alone and has a lot of pain to overcome? Who knows?

You will find there are many people who are willing to take up a game and stop halfway through it, but most are not. You should be willing to do whatever you pursue and do it for you, but if it no longer interests you, stop. Do no more on it until you know why you no longer want to work as you do.

If you were heading a group who were confused and unwilling to go with you, would you continue? Would you decide what is best for all of them to do?

Now, let us all go inside and look at the group of individuals who are writing this book with you.

The Scribe is not paid and is a woman of high moral fiber, but what if she were hired and had no need to be of the highest level of integrity? What kind of book would you be reading if the Scribe was not here to do this work for you inside? Why would you buy such a book?

You are tired? You feel brand new today and want to excel in all ways? Are you willing to try anything new for you? What do you say?

If you hate to be questioned by you, who do you want to listen to all day?

The mind will never stop and rescue you from pain or sorrow, but the Spirit will do whatever it is you need to help you over the bump in your own mind that sprains your time and makes it go out of line. You can sprain a limb and it will be out of line for a time, but the mind is easily sprained by time. You must not overload the mind all the time. If you do, you will find you do not like anything that you do or you are so lazy that you do nothing at all for you.

What do you need? You need pain and sorrow to help you sense within you why you are human and why you are not going to do anything new, but other than that lesson or two, why would you do that to you? You do that to you!

Your mind cannot sense the direction of your life most of the time. If you suspend judgment until the end of this lesson on time you will find your mind is not happy within to know not what you do, but we will work within to make the mind confess it does not know anything about time and let you unwind. Work now in a new frame of mind. Erase the old line.

Erase a line? How can you erase a line and not remember the time? You will. You will begin by never referring to the time and place or person(s) who was there when it first took place. You erase them and the time then. You begin to erase all over the place and may not have any sense of what took place, but better to just erase one person at a time.

If you erase a man from your life and it hurts you much more than you ever thought it could before, you have done something premature. It is that simple, but most of you do not seem to think you could do anything yourself that would hurt you more than what another seems to do to you. That is not true.

You cause the hurt and harm within to you. You could shut out anyone at the beginning and end whatever is going to harm you, but most of you go to the bitter end in order to say you win. Why risk losing you again?

You have no one in your own home with you who is happy that you both are there and able to live in that home? Why are you there?

If you live alone and have no one at all who cares about you, whom could you add to the home there that would care about you? No dog or cat can stay like that, but one may open you to taking a risk on a human again. Why not start out small and go from there to one who is all?

You would not like to take men and women into you life again if you never had any life with one of them, but you might decide late in life to share your life with a man or woman who is more and more like you than you would have ever thought could happen in one life. Why do you wish to increase the time you spend with someone who is not like you again? You cannot find anyone more and more like you as you mature. It is the way of human beings to advise others about love and exercise and not take credit for what they do themselves all this life, so you can survive and die and do whatever you like, but it will all come back to being yourself.

You are a person on this planet and you have a life that you design and may or may not like the process of birth and death and taking a few people along with you most of the time, but it is a process you learn and adjust to at home. You will go back to the home where you learned to do the work you now do.

Sit still and enter your own mind again, and this time, work on time as a means to enter a new life you have known. You will be at home.

You are sitting still and your mother or whomever fills that role in this home is talking to you about the subject of stealing and what the ramifications can be if you take anything that is not your own and use it unwisely.

Did you see a calm and even exchange of agreement of the principle that she is teaching you? Are you calm now? Did you accept that she was wiser than you? Are you now any different in your own assessment of the act of theft that you were taught then?

Now, go inside your own mind and see when you tried to do something she told you would not work out well. Look inside and go around and tidy up whatever is not going to go well now. You are in there and cleaning up your own mind. Do it now.

When you left the door open to the past and recovered from a bit of the timing you mistook as leaving this time, you were unable to close the door if you still walk back. Close the door on the past. How did you close the door? Did you advise you what to do or did you slam it? Go back and see if the door is shut and if there is a light shining through any crack. You will be back if you leave a crack. Now that the door is shut and you have no other alternative but to head out into the future path, what do you see? You will see no bitterness or reproach now. You are who is clearing the work in front of you so you may go forward and not be upset by anyone who is not there to work on your life, too. You have no one who will work on your life once you are above the age of twenty-two that is not trying to parent you. Do not let anyone be a mother or father to you. Why? You will then stop working as an adult and regret later if you do.

Why does regret hurt you? It takes a lot of energy to subsist in a limited space, and you limit you when you regret anything you do. You make you sit and not do your own life for you. You let another tell you what to do only if you are unable to decide for yourself what kind of life is best for you. You will be depressed if you do. You cannot limit you if you wish to successfully pass the life of tests before you.

You will find that tests are fun to do if you are prepared and ready to go forward into the new you. If you have no fun passing out the paper and the pencils now, you will not enjoy the results of the final review. You must assess you all the way through if you want to be able to do what you came to Earth to do and still have a lot of fun being you.

What if your assessment of you is greater than what others think of you?
What if you always limit you in order to be able to fit in with those around you?
Are you still here?

What if you limit and do nothing for you and it cramps you inside so much that you limit the work of the bowel for you? You will get cancer in time or your bowel will bleed all the time, but it is not you who is upset with you. It is You being eager to enter the work of you that makes you feel so superior or blue. You have to regulate your work inside you enough to view You and what you want to do.

If your book is crowded with notes and you have written whenever we asked you to, do you think you will pass? You will if you have worked inside you, too. You can write and write and never do.

Your life as a scribe of your own life is polite and new only when you first learn to do this work inside you, but later as you gain proficiency and lose all aim, you might begin to do nothing on the work you have seen coming from you. Now, if you do, begin to say that it is what you do.

You will then be able to see you have gained immeasurably more than those who say they worked and did all they were supposed to do. Why? No one on Earth is alive to all the tests going on all the time.

You will find that tests and examinations are there for you to know where you stand and why, but if you never stand for examination, when will you know what to do with your own life this time?

If your mind resents talking about you and asking for help from others to do what someone else can do, you will stay as is. You will never find time to develop into the next phase of being you. We want you to confuse you now by assuming you are in this life to succeed and be the greatest there is at this time and what you need to be such a success is there inside. Can you do that for you? No, but if you are attuned to You, you will do what you want.

If your mind is open and the air is not good, what do you have to do? You will not be able to deeply breathe oxygen you need to heal you inside. You will drink of water instead and if the water is not good, how can you get enough oxygen inside you?

If the Earth is unhealthy and you are not good inside from a life of living for you, are you going to leave with a lot you could have done? Probably, but it might already be done inside you.

What if you sense a man or woman is dying and no one else is around? Would you sit down and talk to them about the time of the day and the weather and never mention their pain? Why do you do that all day? You all are dying and the day is not known to anyone at all until the pain is so great or they are swept away, but you all will die one day. Speak of your own life and open up to those who are around you. If not one of the people who are there with you is interested in you, walk away. Find another game to play.

You will find some people constantly move in order to never get beyond today and what they do to others that day. You might think that is unwise to do, but they are there and then advising them to move along and not delay the time in any way. What do you do to advise you of your own time on Earth today?

If your mind is full of time and miracles and what others say, are you able to sit in your own work and not slip away? If you have no time to be you and you are not able to sit for a day or two, are you happy to be you?

When you are too tired to listen to You, you will not do anything anyway for you, so listen to You and then rest inside you. If you have work to do that does not distress you, please work in that way. If what you have to do is demanding of You and your own mind is tired of doing it all for the few who will never remember what you do, sit and do nothing for a day or two. It will then come through to you that you have time and will be able to do whatever you wish to do.

You will not be upset by anyone who is not like you? You are not like anyone else on Earth and if you think you are, you will upset you. Do not upset the inner clock if you wish to be on time and leave this Earth and do the work you have yet to see and must be and do.

Your life is you. Treat yourself to the best within you. Do your own work and seek only what is there for you to do.

If your timing is off and others are ahead of you, look inside and adjust what you do, but do not ask anyone else to do it for you.

You might have missed that sentence before this, but go back one line and redo that one for you. You must know how to reframe a line and remind you that time is moving always from you. You exist, but time is there as an issue of your own mind. Why not exist inside you?

You will find the time you have inside you is not full of anyone else but you. Why? You are here to do this work on time inside your own life and your mind is what regulates time. If you never listen to the mind, you will be behind all the time.

If your mind is so completely ruling you all the time, you worry about what is done and what will be coming and do nothing much at this time. Why? You are not willing to do anything you need to do to have fun. You want to be upset and overrun your own work in order to have no fun. Fun and ambition are not the same in everyone, but one without the other is no way to live today.

You will find many who are happy today are so busy they do not see anyone long. Will that help them to cross over one day? You may think so, but we agree that you all have not built harmony into the framework of your own life today and it will in time erode into the prime time of each life and take the vitality away from your own way of life. Think of another now and see if you can smile and laugh at them in the most wondrous of ways—with love for them that is at times great enough to be compared to loving you all alone all the time.

You will find only one face at a time can come into your mind if you are able to love anyone at all almost as much as you love you now. You cannot love anyone at all? You have no love inside you now.

The worry of most is that others will not recognize they are great or wondrous at all. Why not profess that you are like the rest and enjoy one and all now? You will find if you are able to laugh and help others exist on a higher level than now, most of them will reach back, but not up to help you to move higher now. You cannot help them? You will not have anyone reaching to help you again.

When your life is full of advice you give to others about what to do and how to live, you seldom live for you. You are so full of looking at them and what they do that you forget all about you. That is bad advice you will not give to anyone else—but how will you know unless you find out for yourself?

You will in time find you have a lot of time to do work on others only if all you have to do for you is done. You might even think one or two of those who work around you are not like you, but why would you stick around?

You are who is moveable and able to do whatever you are equipped to do, but only you can discipline the mind and make you do it all the time. If you do only a few of the many talents within you, you normally prosper more than if you do all of them and then decide later in life to divide them in two, but if you do, do not worry since you have learned to develop you.

You will also see the greater the degree of intelligence within you at this time the greater the time differential you may find between you and others in the same line. You might be so slow and upset that they want you to move more and more in this time or you might be so advanced few will ever know who you are until you go. We want you to slow or speed up enough to enjoy the world around you and let them know you are here to enjoy what you do and then go. Why would you want to do less on you?

When a lesson is going too fast or too slow, what do you do?
We know, but do you?

What if your mind is too slow or too fast for anyone to know you? Go inside and regulate you at times to agree with them and not be upset by anyone who is not helping you to pretend this life is the only one you have to mend from inside.

If you pretend this life is perfect and new all the way through, you get into the best part of you. If you do not like this life and attempt all the time to disguise your dislike of you, you will not be able to maintain a friendship within an hour or two. You will talk beyond the time you are together and it will end. You can measure your love of another by the time you spend together. Look at those around you and see who they are.

If your mind is upset and you have nothing inside you can lend you, who will give you more for you to use? You! You and the outer part of this work on you will help you maintain a lot of work inside you, but you will also have to remember that you are who is telling you to do all this work inside you.

Did you follow that line or two? Go back and reread whatever you have not had time to consume.

You will find that listening is harder to do than reading and it requires that you confuse the mind into being you all the time, but it helps you to develop into the highest ability within you—to excel at following you well.

You listen to others who talk like you very well, but most of you have trouble listening to anyone who accents other ideas different from you. You will help you more by listening to them, too, but it might take a bit more work from you.

You will also learn to do more for you if the others around you do not like you that much or want you to excel. You could try to be lazy and work around others as well and not do much for you, but it generally will not work at all for you. You will only be able to work as hard as you are training you to work for you. If you cannot work for you, you will not be able to do much for others, too. You might believe you work for them, that you are underpaid or annoyed too much today, but it is always you who is working inside to do this work for you. Remember that and do the work within you as well as you would want someone outside of you to see it done by you.

We will now sit and admire the work we did? No, but many of you do. Why do you congratulate you when the work is still not done and others are not admiring what you did? You fool you into believing you are done on Earth, too. You will find you have to work all the days you are alive, so sit and admire not what you do.

Your day is now to be handled in a different way, but we will sit and talk within to you. Do you know the work you do and why it is different from the view we have of you? Try now to sit and look inside. We will now try to work with you in a totally new view of the work you do.

There is nothing in the world! You are here to do only what you want to do, but so many of you think that this is the work. Why?

The work is not in the world, but the world is work for you to do and admire and feel within and outside of you that it is hard to do and others have more than you, but you must strive to remain alive and be you. If you do not strive and you drive only the parts of you that you can rule and command and never control or do more for, you will ruin a part of the body long before the rest of the body is done working for you. Look now and decide what part of your body you try to hide.

If you work and work and strive inside to live everyday as God would pray and ask today that you do your own way, what would you be? You would be you. You are the creation of the God of All and you are connected to all, so be and ask not why.

The side of you that is the best view is seldom exposed to the view of those around you. Why? You have little time today to be wise. You have little time to sit and understand and begin to pray inside before you talk again. You all talk too fast at this time.

Your own mind cannot comprehend all the facts that you bring inside? No and yes, but you are who is controlling what you do and how you use that smile within you. If you hate you and you control all you do with the intensity of it, you are a fool, but you might commit no crime or be seen as a fool by anyone else on Earth, but You—and that is when you are in trouble with YOU.

If you have to be told over and over that you are out of control, are you able to understand that you did it to you?

If you are sick and disabled and pretend it is not a problem ever to you, are you lying or trying to help others understand you? We seldom see many today not grumble or complain about simple life things and yet the ill never complain much today. Why? You may decide the world has spoiled so many now that they do not smile, but why would you assume the world spoiled you?

You are not you if you have so many possessions that you seldom know what to do with any one of them let alone use all of them in a given day or two, but you all want more. You could design a better day by not having so many things you often have to give away, but you are who is deciding what to do with the work you choose to do.

If you work harder than anyone else and you have nothing today, what does that say? Are you working for you or for pay? Do you have a great day? Do you feel like Ray? Are you able to sit and stand and enjoy your own mind all day? That is why we refer to our friend Ray. He is now going to take you and his own crew on a picnic so that you will have time to do all the things you never get to do.

Ray, we want you to design a picnic for next time that all can enjoy one day. We want you to do that so that you can have a picnic today. Your mind will take care of it, but you will also be able to share it with you and You and YOU and if it is so happy and wonderful and fruitful for you, the genius of You will follow it up and bring it to you.

Now, Sharon is a friend of ours, too, but she is upset in the area of the uterus and is not able to sit as long as others do. We will tell you all and let you all grow a bit, too. Sharon will be a mother who is able to take care of you, but why should you give your troubles to her, too?

Now, there is a smile in two, but what about the class that grew around you as you worked in this work for many days or weeks until you arrived with this class at today and in your own way? Are you going to have a baby soon? Are you able to practice hosting a picnic, too? What do you think of two women and one man who are able to do nothing all day, but seem to have it made? Are you afraid that anyone who is not working in the traditional way is not going to be able to establish a work that you can use? Are you ever aware that others do work and care and deliver what they do, but do not work as fools do—only for the money to buy things they will not be able to use.

You will find if money is overdone and it is now in some countries, some others are unable to get as much as the top levels have done. You have to understand that if you take from all over the land and never ever care about any man or woman again, you have lost it and will never regain it, but then that might be your plan.

You will find as we rise and fall and the lines go into time, we are able to continue to write long about tonight. We want all of you to know in this book there are letters and lessons others prepare and share with you, but you also have to write. You might not like to write, but we require that you write when you read this part and you will delight in what you write or you are not sharing you with You at this time in your life.

We will include at the end of this session a few letters these people who are working for you did away from the class today, but you must also write and include this work here and now for you.

Note From The Scribe:

(In the last session you were given an assignment to do. In the space below, write in your revision of that work as you remember it. You may have already grown beyond the work you did then. Check and see at the end.)

As the Scribe writes away and says nothing about it all day, are you as easy as she about not talking all the time about what you say in writing some days? Are you able to write and listen and do what you like? You can, but writing helps you to pray and mind your own business everyday.

You will harm no one unless you write of ugly or mean spirited ways others have today. Why not imagine that "they" whomever they may be is not going to be able to see you anymore? Why do you go after people whom you do not adore?

You have to see the contrition of human beings when the agony of this life is over? No, but you might like to be in the next light and see many crossing over into a brand new life. We can. You will learn and then try, but not until the end will you know if this exercise turned out right.

This is an exercise in delight!

You will expand the lungs and breathe into your upper and lower lobes as deeply as you can at this time in your life. We will help you to expand and view the joints, too, but release all pain within you.

Your back is the way it is because you either are pleased with what you do or you try to hide from you. If you sit and stand erect at times and then slouch, you might be able to do that now and not hurt you, but it takes a strong body and back to be able to slouch much now.

You will breathe and erectly sit in a chair with both feet properly spaced about 2 inches away from the front of the knee and you will let the feet be. Do not think of the feet now. Your mind revolted already. We know you and we smile.

We want you to remember that if we command you ever, you do not do anything at all or you do it because of fear of us all. We want nothing like that again.

This is an exercise in being you.
Look at you.
See what you love to do.

Will you want to write, too? Are you so excited that you could ride a horse and never be upset if it upset you? We want you to ride and fall and see if it is at all as upsetting to you as not being able to talk at all.

Can you sense this is a book being talked about as it is performed for you and worked upon by a group unknown to you? Are you the group or a personality that just picked up this book and glanced into this page and does not know what to do? You will follow this page and grow or you will deny that you do know what to do to grow.

Now, let's all get back in tune. We were interrupted too soon.

The next lesson is not about you, but it is always about you. You have to understand that you are now in ecstasy or you do not plan.

We said this was an exercise in fun. If you are commanded to do that again, will you do what you did? We want you to exercise your own mind in time and make it run again. Run with the wind!

Can you see your mind free? Are you able to let your hair and mind flow in this time? Why would you agree if you had not hair or you could not see? You can remember them if they are long gone and you are still on the Earth to be. Remember, you are a product of genes and you wear your own mind most of the time, so recondition the mind to accept what you have inside or change who you are to be the same as you are inside and outside all the time.

Why? Stress is in the work you do that is not you. You have to see that if you work and do work you do not like, you build you and you work for you, but you also are making a gap within you that stretches you or it rips you. Which do you do to earn the money you need for you?

You do not work? Why do you ever say such a lie today? All work regardless of the wage that is paid, but some are outraged at how much they work for no money or prestige today. Why? You are guilty of too much pride we could say, but it is the society and what you prize today that makes you feel guilty that you are working for you. We admire you if you do.

What if you could find a huge volume of money and it was of no use to whomever, and they gave it to you? What would you do? Are you critical of you enough to be able to manage such a sum and not abuse you? Are you so silly that you would spill it out over the Earth in a burst and assume it would be refilled for you?

Why do some live and laugh and begin again and others crumple at the first regret of life?

When you see life is not as bad as it is or is better than you can be, you are full of energy? No, but you are sure to know more and more about the world than you do now. Why? You have to prize a person in order to want to marry, but if you then decide you no longer have such a great prize, do you divorce them in a hurry? Not if you have a reason that is not good.

You have to see you are fair and equal to everyone on Earth, but you are not the only one of you who is working this life for you. You have several levels or planes within you that grow and assume others and let go within you, so be sure you have time on your side before you decide to just let someone go.

You must know one or two people in every group around you let go of someone and all know of true grief from having lost to the Earth a person they loved, but do you act like you are the only one on that path? Are you sure you would like to be reminded that others also have divorce, death and illness in the back?

You let them know? Why not push them away? You do when you act like you are the only one who has ever had a time with no fun. You are not alone, but this is a class in having the time to be on line within you all the time and have fun. You will know when you are out of sync by the line of grimness that makes you look fatigued.

You have to be able to laugh. You have to be able to relax the tension from the work you do that is not you. You have to do that faster than you now do.

Why are we so insistent that you laugh? The work of this situation is such a lot of work for you that if you are too seriously involved within you, you will collapse in about the third class and not be back, so let us all pray today that you will find enough fun and be able to play.

You will be back if you have a lot of fun and a strong back, but if not, try anyway to assume we can help you.

Your own lesson is to have a ball today, but we are not spinning jokes your way. Why? Life is not that way. You have to see within you the way to have a good time always. If you sit and cry and moan and complain, all others soon find the door home to another. You will find there is a long line of people who pine to be alone all the time, but who are they? The unhappily wed, and the single parent dreads that one day they will also be unable to wed because of the child they bred. Why? They believe the married are all pleased and these things we say are all in your head—but not in your way.

Today remove all thoughts about another who once loved you. You will then be able to center your own approval on one who is in love with you or is able to love you or will be in your life soon.

How can we predict you will meet a new friend soon? You do all the time now. You are who is dedicated to being you and refusing to admit others to be a friend to you.

You are who smiles at no one in order to be able to not take on anymore work for you again. You know what to do, but you do not want anyone again if you do not smile at them.

Your mind will say to you, "Why not marry," provided you are single today, and you say back, "I am married today." Is that the way to be today? It appears most people do not respect marriage as a rite of being a partner and working beside another today for life and not so concerned about the pay they might have made if they had not merged that way.

You will find the Church is not opposed to divorce as much as it was before, but that is because of you today. You decide what the Church will ask of you and why you will do what you do, but no one else can make you do anything you will not want to do. You must take responsibility for building you.

You are who is taking the body and pulling it apart or building it up day by day. You are who is taking you apart mentally every day and in all ways, but if you never push you to study or do things mentally for others, you will fall into disarray only if you have no discipline in you and that generally comes from a lack of communication today.

You will find many mothers are totally blind to their own enemy, and they think that another mother is unkind who prevents their own child from harming their own life one day by disciplining them. You have to socialize any child into the life of today. All come the same way and only those who are brought up in the right way can be in the society you would like one day. You must take responsibility that you are who is raising up the world today.

You will find if your mind is ill and you are unable to fill your body with the proper amount of food on any day, you cannot spiritually soar or you feel you are not as well as you were the other day, but it is false. You are still ill if you are well and well if you are ill? No and yes, but of course, you have to decide what to do in any case and if you feel ill, why do you say otherwise and make stress within your own lives?

You must do more on a constant basis if you want the aging body to not decay ahead of its day. If you want to ignore and treat the body only when sore, you can decide to just end a few days earlier than your own body was built for today.

You have a hopeful or hopeless look on your face most everyday, so look at you and find out why you are as you are today. Look in your mirror and see what the time is and why you should not waste a day.

Your mind is now a glass of water and you are to drink of it whenever you need it, but you must get to the point where a glass is not enough on some days. You will be thirsty to know more about us and others and you will drink more that day. Some days you will not drink enough to keep the mind busy and out of trouble all day. You will pay. If you are sorrowful and sad and lonely and disappointed in others today, look at your mind and see that you have not used your time.

You will find those who are busiest all day have the best time at night when asleep and so they are able to play longer than you today if you are not working to complete the way you are to be today.

The fingers of the Scribe are not alive to you, but to the few who do see what she is doing for you, you will understand she never sags and frowns at you in any way. She is not as young as you? You are all about the same age or a few of you might be as old as the Scribe today. You are all alive in the same way, so when death comes to you and it will one day, you pass the same way and you move along the same day, but it may not look like it today. You will find out that the man who is upset with the past is not in today enough to be able to play, but if discouraged by others from lingering always in the old days, he will also begin to brighten within and have a great day.

You might not like to brighten the life of another, but it helps your day. You will find that older and older generations are passing away long before you have had your day, so listen and find out what they did to play. You could also ask them to pray, but most of you are not listening to your elders and laughing with them today. We are.

We are also listening to the children when they are afraid of you today. You haunt the past with your own limitations which you complain a parent brought to you and never helped you to do what you came to do, but is that the truth or just your own way? You are either a happy person within today or you are not. Decide which way.

We have played today, but all who are working in the same way are working so hard that we will teach you to relax when you do this work for You.

Sit now and pray about the day you had and why you had so much fun in it. Look inside it. Look at your grin. Are you able to smile? Are you going to win? Why not look at you and win and go within and smile about you again and again?

This is the end of our time today, but when you all get done working on this session within, you will find there are three women today who will not be able to say we were not listening to them. Are you one of them or a man who feels left out because we mentioned women to them? Why stress the sex of one or another so much as you do today? You are dismissed.

If your mind is unfit and you have no time to do anything about it, what good is life for you? You will find there is nothing in the work which is not you, so do whatever you do and enjoy the profits from it. Don't work for others and never share the profits with anyone? You are unfit then to work within on you. You work in the same way today inside as you work outside in the world around you.

Some of you give so much time to others that you wonder if it pays you. It will help you more than if you sell that same time today. Why? You are not thinking about the greed aspects if you work for you and the help it provides others to do their work, too. If you get inside the work of you and find greed is there and aspiring to tell you what to do, what do you do? You work to free you of all money in the mind first and then you begin to see how God provides you with what you need always. That simple truth will then end the dependency upon others to tell you if you are a success or what you will need to succeed.

If you listen to a warmonger or a bargain hunter talk about their success, is it not very similar? Are you masking the anger within you in order to shop and buy what others are not able to have or would never want anyway today? Are you upset if you buy the work you need to do today? You may not realize that if you are always reading books about success that you deny you are a success today. Why?

If your most original idea to date was to advise you that you have no way of knowing you today, you are a success and will have to advise others more about the way you arrived at today. If, however, you never think of ways to be wise or go inside or do your own work in your own way, you will not have time to listen to the work of three women who are going to talk about the way to be whatever today.

The first letter is about what you would do and why you would not want anyone else to try to be you. The second letter is not as open, but it implies that you, too, can be like this woman inside. You cannot, but it teaches you a truth—be you. The third letter is not about you or anyone you ever knew, but which letter did you read first?

Your mind will confuse you into believing these three letters are all by one hand over time, but they are not. You are who is writing in this book all the time. We will now give you the letters to read at your leisure or you may decide to study them one at a time.

Group response:

(There are many different personalities inside the one called Sharon, but the real me is free. The real me is free of all fears and anxieties and concerns of this material world. I have been many different personalities in this lifetime and it seems like all of those people I have been are now non-existent. I can remember how I acted out my fears in the behavior I had toward others, but it seems to be like a remembrance of a dream. Those times and events are over for me and for the personality I was at that time.

The real me is free. Free like a dancer swaying to the music, dancing because of the joy and love she feels when she is dancing. Unencumbered by worry or pain or doubt, but safe and happy just to dance for the joy of dancing.

These personalities we all have are fronts, like movie sets, they hide the real essence of who we are—pure love and light all connected together. These personalities seem to separate us to prove that we are individuals whose actions and thoughts only impart the one. But it is all an illusion when I see a personality trait in someone I dislike. I know as a human being, I am also capable of showing that side of me and it frightens me to see that trait, perhaps an unloving trait as I see it, reflected back at me. But I also know that we are all much more than we see in the mirror—these bodies, these separate personalities. These individual lives are all window dressings that cover who we really are, and now I know that I want to live knowing and showing that real me to all I meet, and in remembering who I really am I am free.

Each time I see something in me, like actions that bother me or cause me to be less than peaceful, it is a reminder to me to remember who I really am, and who I really am 'is free.' We are all free and we are the dancers who just love to dance—just because we do. We are all together remembering our love for the dance and for each other as one.

A Poem by Me

**I look in the mirror and what do I see?
A reflection of a woman looking back at me.
I've seen this woman for many years
Now smiling or crying and wondering how
She found herself in this place and
What purpose does it all serve?
There must be more than this cotton-candy
Life full of pain and fear and anger and strife.
She was so empty and directionless for all to see
She saw many troubles and felt life unfair and
Prayed for the day she would not have a care.
She asked for a miracle and beseeched The God of All—
Give me a sign, answer my call!
What would you have me do here? What's left for me to do?
Why do some seem so clear about all, while others are so blue?
Why do some have so much and others not at all?
Why do some lives seem so easy and others always seem to fall?
Her questions were sent from deep in her heart,
And she cried out for answers about what was her part.
Her mistakes they were many as she learned and she grew
To listen inside for the answers she already knew, and
She forgot many fears and doubts that would appear
To keep her off course for perhaps just another year.
But she knew in her soul that she wasn't alone and the
Love that was deep was her only true home.
And there she would find all that she sought.
From every source outside and down the roads when she felt lost,
The knowledge she had to answer her pain, was always inside her
Forever to reign,
And the woman looks back at me from the glass with quieter eyes
Since more time has passed, and as I search the reflection I see
far Beyond here.**

The reflection fades and disappears and all that is left is all that We are—
The brilliant, colorful light of a star.)

Whatever you do and whomever you see are two ways to be, but the first letter is not the one you will remember if you have worked beyond that time inside you and are now working to do something more with what you have in store for you. You will now read the second letter and find out what you need to do to be you, but will it be you if you copy what she is saying in her letter and more?

Group response:

(There have been, both in the history of the world and my own personal history many teachers who have tried to teach me how I should live my life. There are numerous qualities and values that could be listed here and would somewhat attempt to describe who I am and who I want to be, but any list would be incomplete and inaccurate since I live in the real world and I am constantly changing as a response to my environment. I am never going to be finished changing me because I can always be better, but one area of my life I wish to enhance right now is to have more fun, to laugh more and not to take myself so seriously.)

<u>The ABC's of Being Lynn</u>

A.	ADAPTABLE	-	Be open to change and be able to 'go with the flow.'
B.	BALANCE	-	Balance your spiritual self with your worldly self, keeping body, mind and spirit in harmony.
C.	COURAGEOUS	-	Courageous enough to speak up for injustices and to speak your heart and mind

D.	DEPENDABLE	-	Be a person who can be counted upon. If you say you are going to do something, then do it.
E.	ENERGETIC	-	Have the spark of life. Be able to energize yourself and others around you.
F.	FAITH-FILLED	-	Have God as the center of your life.
G.	GOD-LIKE	-	Try to recognize the god in others as well as yourself.
H.	HAPPY	-	Smile and be content with your life. Remember it is you who chose it for you.
I.	IDEALS	-	Live within a strict moral code and always strive for excellence.
J.	JOYFUL	-	Make a joyful noise unto the Lord—Sing!
K.	KNOWLEDGE	-	Be in constant pursuit of knowledge, for teachers are everywhere.
L.	LOVE	-	Love unconditionally. God first and all others will follow.
M.	MERCIFUL	-	Have a kind and compassionate way with others.
N.	NURTURE	-	Nurture strength of Spirit in yourself and others.
O.	OPEN-MINDED	-	Something can be learned from everyone.
P.	PRAYERFUL	-	Spend a portion of each day in prayer and/or meditation.
Q.	QUIET	-	Be quiet and still. You will hear so much more.
R.	RESPECTFUL	-	Be respectful to all of God's creation. Treat others with respect, care for the Earth and respect its balance.

S.	SENSES	-	Develop the third eye; see self as I am. Speak—Up to myself and others who are unable. Hear—The silent cries for help from those who are emotionally wounded. Taste—The goodness life has to offer. Touch—Others' hearts and lives by being a positive influence in their lives.
T.	TRUTH	-	Seek and speak your truth quietly and clearly.
U.	UNLOCK	-	Free your heart so that you may always seek your highest self.
V.	VIVACIOUS	-	Have a great appetite for life.
W.	WONDEROUS	-	Be in a state of awe.
X.	EXAMPLE	-	Your life should be an example for others to follow.
Y.	YOUTHFUL	-	No matter what the age, find time to play.
Z.	ZEALOUS	-	Pursue and practice the lessons we receive from our teachers.

(When it is all said and done and I finally pass on to the next plane, I want to hear whoever greets me there to say, "Well done.")

What you will do now is sit and study the third letter and smile. You will not be able to understand anyone at all, so read as if you are the letter and the writer is trying to tell you how to be you and do what you want to do for you.

Group response:

A New View of Kathy

(I once sailed the stormy sea of life—tossed back and forth in an ocean of Earthly lessons, never knowing what to expect as life's ups and downs took me by surprise. The peaks and valleys I rode like a roller coaster, left me wondering if peace would ever find me.

This other me never knew all the experiences I was participating in were molding and shaping my very existence. All these obstacles I was overcoming and learning from were only stepping stones and building blocks to birth the new me.

Like a fleeting glimpse in a mirror, the past is a vague memory and the person I was is gone, but certainly remembers the sting of the lessons learned.

The new me is stronger and has a burning desire to do all I came to Earth to accomplish before I go home.)

Now that you have read about what others do, you will be able to list here what to do for you. Do the list in your head first, but be sure to jot down a word or two to remind you. You will not remember otherwise if you had this idea now or it just grew out of doing the other two.

1. ____

2. ____

3. ____

You usually need more time to start a project, but if you do not, let the line stand there to remind you that you did have time to develop you first.

Whatever you write or say you will do is etched inside the brain in a way that makes it a mess if you never follow you to the end or do the work you intend. Please remove all false starts now and command the mind to not bother you at this time with problems you cannot do for you. YOU will find that You and you are doing what you came to do, but when?

CHAPTER 13

The Will Is Not Without Work

If your will power is so little and so weak you cannot be you and you are always meek, will you be able to descend or ascend within when your life is over this time for you? You will.

You decide and follow you through to provide you with the will to do whatever it is you intend to do. If you never decide to do anything at all, you will not be able to be you or do anything now. What work would God give you to do if you had no way to follow through now? Work that would force you to decide what to do!

If you sit and do little, you develop nothing within you unless you work within to begin a new life for you.

If you sit and do nothing inside you, do you work for you? No, but you might in time become so inclined. Why? The boredom or tedium or lack of excitement will in time force you to do something. That is why you will find many do nothing until after the prime of their own lifetime.

What if your life is now prime and you are not doing a thing to help you? Would you know who you are and where you are most inclined to spend all your time? You know exactly who you are at all times, but you might not do anything to help you. Why? Your mind is so preoccupied in others' lives that you are not living within you.

When you decide to divide your life up among many others who are not at all like you, you might divide up all your time, too, but it would not be as bad for you as to spend all your time with those who think exactly like you. Why? You would never develop the level of tolerance you need to expand and develop you.

You are told to work and respond to others with respect, but many of you never do anything at all that would help you. Why? You do not believe you came here to Earth to do anything at all—and then you die. Why would you want to arrive at a planet on time and then not work on time to find out why you wanted to do this work for You? Think about it at this time.

If your mind cannot stand sitting and doing nothing at all, your mind commands you to do your own work. You command nothing if your mind is always in charge of you. Which of these statements is true? Which one talks to you? When you are told to think, do you?

What if you are old and gray and no one is there to show you how to pray, would you know the way anyway? No. You have had to be young for a long time to grow old and if you still do not know the way, your mind has held you captive all that time and the will is not strong enough to let you go your own way. You have to develop enough within your will to be able to sit still, meditate within you, and then be able to go without a lot of crying within you.

Your mind might not like the idea of you not being able to go and not being able to outdo those around you, but the soul will always come to the rescue if you even ask at the last moment for direction and help to go. We are not in that work. We are here on Earth to help you prove to those who are not working at all, that it is better to work now and have a great life and enjoy this time and then go as a group and end the work you all came to do—time.

Whatever you do, do it for you. If you do anything at all that is not for you, it will only confuse the few who are you. You are not a single unit? You knew that by the time you were two. By three you had learned to integrate into a few more of the old works you came to do, but by four you were trying to learn more about the world and why it was not working as you were told.

If your child of six is not able to count, you worry that perhaps the child has missed something in life or is neglected by others; but why not worry if the child has no conscience?

You have to notice that today you have a large climatic change moving within the countries in which you choose, but most are now accustomed to it. Are you able to understand that the rivers are changing their paths? Are you willing to let the floods disappear and take houses back? No. You will and you work and you state over and over that you will prevail and live in the path of the rising water, but you will not state that the Church is going to get you back on the path. Why?

You have a will and your mind is full of values that you accept from others, but you are not able to understand a country that is imbued with a lot of power must act with the power in its own best interest or the world cannot last. The United States has been on a crash course for months of the Earth's time and not admonished its citizens enough to take crime and defeat it on its own terms.

You might decide now that we notice you and others, but always speak firmly, and that would make some people laugh. Why? They are not in tune with you or with anyone who is on time.

Now these two paragraphs seem to be in direct contradiction to what we normally do, but do you see the first paragraph was not for you? Did you see anything about the second that was?

If your mind is now unable to unwind and take time to enjoy all you can be, when do you think you will find time?

That line is more like the work we normally do with you and others? You are now following each line and not listening to the time working into the work of others at this work if you think there is a difference in the lines.

You will now see several different kinds of people will help you to become the best personality you can achieve, but you need to have them around now. You cannot just do nothing and feel okay. If you feel your mind is leaving the ground, do you have to ask why and decide immediately not to let it go that way? You have no will if you cannot just be you and float.

The will is a combination of skill in manipulating time and desire within one hour or two to do whatever you came to do. If you cannot continue to follow the work, you will stop and remove all the work you do and not be happy with anyone else who continues to do the work. The skill you have developed within you is will, but you will not be able to see within you anyone who is not going to like you. Be still within you. Be able to build the will into the strongest part of the physical being you may be within you. What? Read that part over and over again until you know what will is and why it is part of this work.

Your work on skill building and will is not the same as it would be if you were meditating every day, but if you will meditate and work all day, your will is so strong that you will hold together long.

When a long sentence comes along and talks to you, do you feel it will not be able to help you in any way? What do you say? You always make up another version of whatever you think you hear, so make up a sentence today. Use the work of the last paragraph to restate your own day.

The way to pray is not to do anything at all? You are who is in need or you would not call. If you have not tried at all, why would you call? You have to see that no one will believe you need anything at all if you never tried to be or do anything at all. You will fall. You will not be able to stand up tall, but you might be able to sit all day.

Whatever you decide to do today, sit and work inside and work all the way through to the end of this day for you. You will not be able to decide anything at all if you never find time now to do this work today. Will is why you would decide and then not do what you came to do.

You will find most people are not going to say no. They will talk and talk and will not show what it is they do not want to do or do not know. Why? They feel powerless inside and do not want anyone to know.

If your will is strong, you might pull out a joint or so and not be able to walk as far as you would like, but you will strive to leap up and move forward faster than ever now. Why? You are determined to move on with this life and all who are on the Earth are beginning to rise. What?

Yes, you are here to help the world disappear, but you have to know why. You cannot disguise the why and when of your own life. You know.

When you go forward and see what another is trying to do with a life or two, do you envy them and try to get them to work on your life? You are lazy if you ask anyone to do what you will not do. You are crazy if you let someone undo what you did for you and have always done for you and will now be able to do, but the craziness may end.

You will find if your mind calls out for you to find a friend or two, you can go within and find all the things you need to know about you—but would it be easy to do? No. You have to work to develop the will and the muscle and skill to excel within you.

Your moment on Earth is over when you decide to never work or be you? Who knows? YOU.

If your mind is full of designated drivers and others who take over for you when you have no control, is will the problem or is it the lack of working within you and doing what You sent you to do?

Skill is not the ability to outdo others, but to do whatever you have to do for you and win the work over to the next world when this one is over. You cannot see anyone now unless you are able to find one or two who are like you, but that is easy if you just go inside and look at you. We look down and over and around, but only you can go inside you and know what to do.

Grow out of the past and enter the future and make today last until you know the way. You cannot erase today until the next day is clearly defined and able to stay that way and not collapse if today is taken away. Today may last for a day, a few hours, a year or a life, but it will pass. Why not let your own life last until you know the path to the next place? You will. If you do not, let the mind remind you over and over of the way to develop will power, but it will not help you until you know you have to do the work, too.

Working on you is not the way to do anything at all for you, but if you do work on you, you develop a sense of who you are and what you can do. Will is what you develop when you work on you. The day is over.

Did you feel brand new?
What are you doing today?
Are you ready for the next day, too?
Are you feeling a bit depressed, lonely, or blue?

When you leap and jump and make sure of nothing you do being able to follow you, you do not help you. Before you jump or leap into the next day, make sure you know what way you will land and when you can best do it for you, but if you cannot explore it enough today, go into the mind more and let it accept that the soul will know the way and let you ascend today.

If your mind is refusing to accept that the soul is there to stay, make sure you know why you came to Earth and why you will not stay. That is the best way to do your work and help you and not delay the soul in any way. Why not ease up on the way you will help you today and win all the things you wish to do, too? We will then be able to help you, but first you must decide what you want to do. See? We always remove the excuses you will bring to this work before you can worry so. You will want to do three things before you begin to work on strengthening your power of will.

1. You will not say you cannot be or do anything today.
2. You will not say you are afraid of anyone or anything today.
3. When another speaks badly of anyone, you will speak up and say what you believe is the truth about that being today.

What you do and how you move you are skills you have learned, and whatever you do, you have to remember you are here to do all these things to help you get to the next avenue. Your own work is going to follow you, so be sure it is now done by you. If not, the other person will be able to do more and more and you will fall through and not be able to do much for you.

Time and time again you have asked a friend to do something for you—what was it you were afraid or too lazy to do?

If you are lazy or afraid, you do little for you. If you are a coward or know not a trade, you have very little you can say about you to others who work very hard, but you might decide to lie and say you do work hard. Why? The conscience is part of the will and it makes you aspire to be more comfortable still.

If you cannot sit still and be you when another is talking about what they do, you are not working inside to develop you. If your will is still not developed enough to sit and watch others do what you know is not wise to do, your own will is not developed enough to let you ascend at the end of this time on Earth being you. You will have to return and work within you until you can let others do unwise things without you.

You will find many people try to tell others what to do in order to inspire themselves never to do that at all, but do you?

What if you were afraid of lightening and it struck you? Would it mean you were afraid of it and attracted it to you? What do you think?

Things are there for you to wonder about and remove from your path, but people are there for you to investigate and respect and learn the way so you do not have to do it all that way yourself by the time you cross over to the next gate; but if you have so many people who block your view, you might never get to know you.

Normal people and frugal beings are not that much inside you if you work and work and spend all that you accrue on treating others to things you do not need for you. Why would you spend all your money on a child when loving the child is easier and better to do?

Think of all the reasons some of you talk all day on the phone to people who cannot see you.

When you are able to sit and enjoy food at the store, why would you spend more than you need to buy stuff that will never feed you?

When you buy stuff that is not of good value, are you buying it for you or trying to spur on the economy more?

When you try to develop another's life, do you think that it will benefit you?

Are you spending you doing things that will never benefit you? You are if you work for another and expect them to then turn around and do it for you. You must learn this is not the time to martyrdom pursue or do anything that would ever hold back you. You have no time to do anything that is not good for you. The time has come to be able to run. You must assume you have time to do all the things you have obligated you to do, but otherwise, you have no time to waste on developing the lives of others who are able to do that, too.

You will find if your own mind is too overbearing and you have no will, you will run around and try to criticize whatever others do. That is absolutely true, but you can spend hours debating that issue, too. If you do, you waste precious life moments doing nothing at all for you.

To legally entangle you in order to gain a dollar for the future is the worst kind of need you can develop within you. Look at the fraud and see the fraud was done by one who never lived until it was all the way through to the end and the money was shorter than he or she thought. If you were harmed, God will revenge you and take care to amend what you had done to you; but if you play God and try to avenge you upon another who is now trying to amend what was done, you will find you lose you at the end.

What if all these character building exercises never work? Are you full of energy or power? You will not be able to pursue this work. You will never be told what to do or where to go when you do ask for help, too, but you will know the next time to do your work for you.

When you accomplish a major life work, are you flat? Are you tired of it? Are you retired from it? Look inside and see if you can find something better to do and how you would like to do it for you, but be sure you do not sit still and do nothing inside you. If you sit still and never build the will, you will collapse and spill all you ever built.

Whatever you are and whatever you will are about the same if you are powerful all your days, but if you end poor and disheartened in any way, you let your own power dwindle into whatever you had another do for you. You shall now look to see if you are doing that now.

What if you have to teach someone a class and it requires you to let them take over what you do, would you do it to prove to them you could be the better by letting them take away your power or would you be teaching them to let go of what is not power? Think on that.

Look inside and meditate now.

When you are able to think of deep and difficult work, think of the things you might like to do. If you cannot find anything that will open you wide, you will shrink as you grow older in the world, too. You must work to open the largest avenue of you? Why not? You could open you to the next work by just adding a few burdens to you once you have all your work done and are able to run, but not until then. If you try to take on a burden or two before you are ready to leave for the next tide, your ship will run out and not be able to save you.

What you save and produce and put away for you is yours only if you check it and request that it be used by those who are trusted by you. If you never sense that fools run most of the loans in this world, you would be angry enough to never invest in a bank this time, but if you never have given a thing to anyone, you might be better off to let the bank give it for you.

What a long way to come and save the day for you! You might not like this lesson on you, but it is one that comes and goes and does not stay unless you know the way to build you today. Power is the will and will has to have power if it is to save you.

Today you will pray!
Did you?
We will now go inside the widest avenue you grew within you.
Where are you?

Are you able to build within the walls of this street, a house that is new and big enough for you to bloom and do whatever you came to Earth to do?

What are you going to do if another comes inside you? Look up and praise God that God is able to come in that way. No one else is permitted to open you. If you open you to anyone who is not God and of God and doing work for you that helps you to prepare for the day when you will end working this way, your will, will overpower no one at all but you.

You must not open to anyone because they do not like you. Most of you do that today. Why? Your power over you is too small for the mind you grew. You want to believe that you can talk about others, but will they love you? What do you think will happen to you when you talk all day about them to others and let others talk about them to you?

We notice a few of you blanch at the idea of anyone not liking you. Why? Do you really love everyone you meet today? Are you walking down an average street and not able to see anyone there who is not going to be unlike you so much that you worry they might steal or take away something you have made for you to keep? You would be a saint and that is possible today, but not like most who walk the streets with their money between their heart and their head and feeling incomplete.

You will now develop a new way of looking after you today. We want you to do nothing at all for those who are not able to do anything for you. Can you use your power to do nothing still? You will, but wisdom shows you the way.

When you are able to sit and work inside all day, you will, but if the will to work is still in decay, you will not stay at the work longer than a moment a day. Why? You do not have the moral stamina to resist decay.

Decay is there for you to notice so you will grow and move into the work you came to do. When you see another refuse to grow or move up inside and do the work they came to do, do you feel they will not want you to help them, too? Walk now and see if a new idea comes to you.

If your mind is not walking at this time, why?

If you cannot walk and talk and work within you all the time and not have to physically admire it by doing it, too, you will find a way to meditate to a different level than you do today, but if you already know how to live and climb and give inside all the time, you must examine why you pine over anyone at this time in your mind.

You pine and ache for women or men if you are not one who is able to see inside that you are the only one who will be there for you at the end of time. You are who is going to have to know what to do to ascend and be able to plan that end for you, but do you know why you postpone learning after you once leave your natal home?

You believe you are an adult and can be all you can be, but then you deceive you into doing nothing at all. Why do you say you are an adult and brave and kind and able to help others? You want to believe that someone else has less than you do and is unable to feel like you do, but we know you are just rising in your pride when you set there and do nothing on you and say over and over that you want to help another do more and more this time.

You are who needs to do that work for you. You are who needs help and you must be able to do more than you do before you can surrender into the next avenue of time that is going to be there for you. You will have a few streets to cross and then an avenue or two if you are not near to the goal you came to achieve and be in this time and place, but it is you who is doing this work and no one else is going to do it for you.

Your mind likes to assume that you have more than another and can help them recover, but that is a fool's idea of being up and above others who might just be above them as much as they are now able to be today.

You will find that many humble women and men do not say they pray every day and one of the proud can even seem to be so humble today that they will say to the others who always pray, "I am a wonderful meditator or whatever and it is because I pray and work all day." Such a prideful way will automatically erase all that goes that day.

You will find if you are too into your own mind all the time, the mind will erase that the Spirit is in this place. Why? You are to learn how to manage your mind and find the time to develop will power at the same time. If you cannot, you will find another is able to do much more than you ever will. We want to remind you if you are very pleased with you and what you do in a spiritual way today, you will lose.

You will find that some find the timeline and are on time for a long, long time and then still lose their way. Why? They begin to not pray and meditate and do whatever it was that took them to the top or wherever they were going that day. You must not stop. You have to move and get your own life together everyday. If you do not, you lose and you will not stop.

You are here for a moment or two, but you might feel you are trapped in a zoo and unable to do anything you would want anyone to be able to do. Why would you do that to you?

If you cannot know why you trap and upset you so, you do not know you. Do not attempt to help anyone else again when you have nothing you can lend them. You will both drown. If you are upset that another asks you to help them to grow into a better spiritual being than they are able to be today, would you be wise to tell them lies about what you do and why? No. You must say you do not pray enough to be able to talk to them about what to do and how to do it today, but when you do know, you will be allowed to show them the way. How? You will live a prosperous, happy and united way for you today and all will see you are a very spirited individual who is showing the way. You must not say you know or you will be told where to go.

You have to see humility is not the same as being humble today, but that is the right way and the only way to seek God everyday.

You will find a credentialed minister of the Holy Spirit is one who prays every day. You are a minister of you and what you stand for, too, if you are always trying to be you, so never assume because a man or woman is able to survive school and get into a better role than you that they know more than you do. You may not be helping them at all if you let them put you down and stand upon your ground, too.

You will stand up for You. If you do not, who is going to know you? You do not!

We want to say that some today seem to piously prompt others to say things that they are not happy to repeat on another day, but are you so fine and wonderful inside that you would say such a thing on any day? You must watch what you say.

You will find that the will to talk and be talked about is not the same for everyone today, but you will be talked about as much as you like if you do not live as others who live with you today. You are not inclined to want another to do anything better than you over time, so get into your own work and do it forever and not notice that others do not need any help from you at any time.

Your skill and your will are together when you succeed and believe that you will do whatever. You can add skill and will together and succeed and still not believe that you put them there and worked within to be you. Whatever you decide about you will arrive in time, so decide to be wise. If you are a fool, you have not used what God gave to you. If you are a fool and have no one around you who is like you, you will arrive fully developed by the time you die, but it will be because of those around you excelling beyond you and pulling you through this time so you will be able to go with them in time. You must not be one of that kind at this time. We need you to do work that helps you to grow and develop and aid your fellow man and woman in time. When you teach or preach and do not practice it at any time, all who hear you will in time know you are revealing the liar within you, but you might not notice it now.

When you talk to you and walk within you, are you doing it in time?
What did you do when we asked you to walk within you?
Are you still walking and talking and working within time and doing what you said you would do?
What time do you feel?
Are you all aware that the time you feel is in air?
If you are real and the air is in there, where are you and why is the air not seen at all by you?
Did you ever wonder where God exists within you?

You are who is trying to hide God from you, so admit that you are upset and God is. You then are able to know within that God is there and taking care to help you win again, but if you are so pleased with you, you will not realize when God leaves you.

You do not know that God can go? You are not wise then, but some skies are so rosy and blue always that the owners of them never believe God is in them and assume they are in control all their own lives, but you will see that is not the case eventually. Why not know now?

You will find Ray has had a way of being himself and has had to play at planning a picnic for today, but he is not sure he really did plan for that event today. Are you able to now play with Ray?

You will find that if Ray is on time and you are able to bend or recline, you will see Ray and be able to play with him over time. He is a musician and he is a man of great interest to most men and women, but he is not at all as he was in olden times.

Let us all admit that we knew it. We did, but you are all human and you are all permitted to look into it.

When you look into a man or woman and see them within, are you permitting them to be free of you then? No, but you will see that if your mind is free and easy and not too hard on them, they will tell you much about them. But, if you are hard hearted and have no time or reason to be with them, they will probably not want to talk to you time and again. We want you to listen as we work within you to see what you think Ray is going to say today.

If you can see what kind of picnic that Ray was asked yesterday to do for you today, you will find he was so busy all day that his mind had nothing to do with it. You will then be able to assume that he did it spiritually then? No, but it could be that he did. We know as soon as we alerted him that you would be listening to him, his mind awoke and he wanted to smoke and he was sure the fumes of his own throat would not hurt him. We want you to know there is no smoke that can harm him from within, but if you want to feel like a joke with him, smoke and see what it does to him. You will not do it, but you will feel that it is something he is conquering within.

Up until now, his tongue was easy to open time and time again, but now you are all listening to him and so it becomes a bit more difficult for him. You tune him in? You are all in tune with him if you are able to do this work for you within. What?

You are all in tune if you have truly been working to do this work within this group and are now tuned in.

The space provided is because one or two who are about to learn what to do need more time than another will need to use. But, let us go now to Ray and the parade he has in his mind to do. Ray, we want to ask you what day the picnic will be?

There is a pause because Ray is picking up so much static from thee. Please stay in your own day. Ray will come to say what he is thinking in this day of his today, but it will be in your day someday. Ray, what day will you be able to meet and speak to another about the picnic and when will it will be?

Group response:

(The 28th of May.)

You have no need to be upset, but you are still upset over things that are not of any importance to thee. You are involved emotionally and physically and even mentally in work that is not supporting you and what you will do, but we will ask you to think no more and let the day appear and sway you into that world of play. You will then be able to say, "I see me and others at play, but it is not today or is it today or near or far away." You only have to let the Spirit know you are able to go within today. The Spirit will play.

Now our old friend Ray has put away all his cares for today. It took him a while to settle within and you can all smile, but it is that way with you today if you are unable to see him at play.

Now that you are open again, let us all ask you when you will be able to do this picnic, too? Ray is going to be ready for it by the end of May. When do you plan to play with him all day?

Now Ray, what day of the week is the picnic to be?

You continue to confuse you by using the mind, too. You have to let it go and just be. If the calendar is confused and it does not agree with you, it will one day, so just say what day you want to play.

Group response:

(Sunday.)

That is the day you must set aside every week for your own beliefs. If you are in any kind of pain today, you need to be able to see that a way is coming again for you to determine when the weakness will end. You are to play every day, but you must do nothing on Sunday again if you are to ascend into the highest end.

Now that we show you all how, can you do that? Can you decide what day you must set aside for you to work on you and then provide you with that time to be you? No? You are then not going to be able to arrive on the other side with your friends.

You all have to have a time to be with others who are not like you and who are going to help you learn to assert you, but some of you will find time is about to end. You will be able to end such assignments by the time you die, but why not learn to seek out friends and mend the ways you work with them? You can then adjust you to the work of the world and them, but you also learn to respect all you do, too.

You are who is upset and blue if you do not talk up and say what you want them to know about you. No one is going to know you unless you tell them about you. They may guess and they may gossip on some days, but they will not know you until you say who you are and why you still are there that way. You cannot end that day with them until you find out why you are there with them. It is God's way to understand you and them and place you together and make you play with them all day until you can be moved to another way of being you.

You will be told to work until you are old only if you are unable to learn to play and be happy all day regardless of the pay or the way others are today. You have to do whatever it is you must do to stay away from the crowd that is not going to help you, but if you are unable to see that anyone is as able to be in a group of three and pray with thee, you are either too proud or not living in the proper place today.

You will leave any place that is not good to be if you want to save your family, but if you are an adult, you could live within prison walls and not be upset by anyone who is difficult to be with at times or always. You create you and you decide who will upset you. Decide to let you abide in peace and harmony and not be upset by anyone other than God if you are on the wrong side.

You will feel pleased and in harmony beyond your own line of communication at times, but that is because you are human, too.

To be pleased and to be flattered a lot is not the source of your own relief, but it can feel good if you never get too much of it for your own good. We will help you to help others without spoiling them and their lives inside, but you all have to stop lying to others about what you do and what you respect in their lives.

You will find this machine is hotter than you are inside, but you might feel that you reveal too much about you when you get hotter than you feel. You are not going to upset you if you explode into the right avenue. But, if you explode at everyone about all you know and why you are so right about it at that time, you will ignore them, and you will be upset when they go. You have no right to ever bombard others with spite, but if you are right and you feel they are overcoming you in some way that will hurt you or another that day, speak up and say what you feel is right. It cannot hurt you and it will go further than to just say you knew what you wanted to do, but you rose above them to be better than them. You will have no more work to do if you use a temper to rise above others. You are not going to fool anyone long if you say you are calm and you are not.

You will not talk about another after you refused to help them do any planning within for them or you. You are who is plotting then. You could say, "I am so wonderful because I am never upset with anyone," but who are you talking to?

When it comes to human nature and whatever it is you talk about now, you have to find someone who is about your own age to go further and further? No, but it takes time to see that if you are wise you will seek out elders all your lives in order to know what is going to happen to you over the next ten years or so. You could ask a person of the same age, but what would they know? You have to show you know who you are and why you have to go, but you will know about it because all of you are here inside working to go.

We are not slow, but we will ask you to let another know who you are and what you will do before you go. Do not be bothered ever by anyone who is not in the same work as you are, but be able to understand that whatever you are doing now is going to be done over if you cannot find the silver thread that binds you all now.

You have found that one kind of annoying person will seem to be worse over time, but you will annoy many over time. You will, so be aware you must look over the way others annoy you today if you are to be able to say you never upset another that way. You are also able to see many are unable to be as they must be. Save the day? You are here to live and be you, but we must say that now you will be like Ray unless you leave him and go within you for the rest of today.

You can join anyone at anytime and be with them, but do not do it unless it is fun. You will pick up static from everyone if you cannot protect you. We want you to be able to see that others are not stronger than we or you or anyone who is of God today, but there is a fear that someone could be near and steal from you and take away your day. We will not reveal who is saying such words to you today, but it is perfectly okay if you say the word 'you' today and see that you fear you and others, too.

When you feel good and sincerely want to do good, you are going to do it and not say a word about it. You will be you or you will change you from your usual way.

If you change you in any way, you are that personality until you change in another way. The day is now concluding in the group which is teaching you to channel within you, but if you cannot find anyone of them on line, just tune in and we will help you work.

You will find a group of nine is very powerful and automatically is able to turn you up and on line, but eight or seven do fine. We never worry about you, but you could find that if you were to overdo working on another over time, you will not be able to do your own work on time. We will not give you any excuse because you were working with Ruth, but if you need to do anything for you and you have to do something for you, please see Ruth and feel within you that you can write inside and work all night to be as you are. That does not require pride, but to want to write for others all day and all night and know whatever they are doing that day is to seek power over others and you will most certainly lose your own way.

You will not gossip ever. Why? You adopt unto you whatever you talk about to others and if you are unwise and talk about others' lives, you will find that yours will not run smooth. You will find your conversations on time will end. You will not do that again. We want you to realize that it is no sin to be you within, but to tell lies to you all the time is to lose you over time.

When today is over and you know the best way to live today, it is over and cannot be of help to others, so do not criticize them for not living like you then. We will help you to do whatever you want to do within you, but never ever again pray for another or someone whom you do not know and ask us to talk to them or to take over for you and work on them. We are not here to imprison you again.

You will ascend to the next level of your own ascent when you tune in and listen to You, but whatever you must do, do it for you. If you slip, do not admit that you were the one? Why not admit it so others will not slip in it, too?

You are going to know what to do when you are through? Will you do it? You are who is sticking you into a corner or you are who is soaring within you. Please sit and see who you are and why you perform for others more than you do at home for you.

This is a time of time and you will admit that you have no limit set within you until God comes and tells you, "This is the limit."

We are not tired, but if you are, you can change into you again and just sit. We will know your limit, but you are here to be you and then grow up into a bigger moment or so and then be moved into a bigger view of you. Let's go. Let's really know who we are and why we limit this life to doing only what we think we will like. You have to do the work for you and life is such a grand adventure for you, so live in it and be in it and think of you.

When you go from this work, you will know what you did in it, but some already are there and able to see you and show you the way you are going into the next way, so why not ask for help on any day when you are slow or upset and cannot go your own way? You will be able to know today what to do, so pray and ask God for help and then go slower than you would normally go into your own day. Perhaps a new day will open to you that way.

The day is over for all who have worked with the Scribe and done all they came to do, but some of you will remove so much of this work and never do a thing for you that you will continue to work forever and still not be able to cross over at the end of you. Why not adjust you?

When you adjust you and do what you came to do, are you complete or just a positive being who is here to succeed? Both. You will find that your mind is complete and your work is succeeding when you do what you want to do and it works, because it is good for everyone who is working beside you—and you know. You know? Yes, You know if you are doing great or not. Which way are you going today? Show your mind you are able to judge you most of the time, but only when the will is pushed into a panic does it want to stand still. Let your mind go. Get inside the will and build.

The way to build willpower and power to do whatever you want to do is to sit and stand and work in a grand manner that promotes the work and not the way you feel about you. The power to be a great man or woman and then not carrying through will generally produce the biggest fool, but the inability to move or do anything without many obstacles being made less by you is what makes you powerful enough to survive and live the best of all lives. Which life is offered to you?

You will find that whatever kind of life you have, the best is inside. Go in and see who is there. If you find no one is available now, come back again and sit. You may be rushing You a bit if you have not been around in that part of your work for a long time, but the will, will sit and the power will generate within you when you do the work you came to do and are committed to it.

When you move, electricity is generated, too. Use your wit and stamina to commit to work that makes you do more and move more, too. If you can find another who is as committed as you, you both move more, but each must remember not to split into a common contraction by doing less and less and not fulfilling the lesson you came to do. We will now commit to doing nothing for you so you will work and develop within you more, but if you try hard and cannot find the work, we will rush back and forth until you can do it for you.

We have a few things you must do for you, so commit to doing them by the time you return to this program again.

We want you to do nothing at all.

Yes, we want you to sit for an hour or two and do nothing! That is the hardest thing for you to do if you never commit to being you. If you already do, you deserve this time alone within you. You will come back to this class when you have done it.

CHAPTER 14

The Worth Of You Is To Be You

When you are not able to do anything at all with your own life, you leave, but it may not be until the end has come to the body that you learn what to do to live for you. That is why there is grief and sorrow.

Many of you never think of God at all!! You seize every issue and every view as something that you do. You never believe anyone at all is like you? You think all are and you normally view them as you see you. If you are not aware of that now, you will learn it all.

Why do you want to be another or be anyway that is not you now? You have to understand that it is always in your power to change and become what you truly believe you are. You can now see that what you are and what you do are ways to see you as a human being and as a spiritual self that has no reason to be a human being except to find out more about humanity.

You may see within you a way to play and do whatever you like all day, but do you follow that through? No. You all work as if you were out on a date or you work as if you had all day to do an hour's work and then you complain that the day is too full. What are we going to do to help you? We know, but do you?

If your life is full of things you cannot understand about you, what will mean anything to you? You might decide your mind is full of ideas that will never be used, but are you using them for you or just accumulating what you think others may expect from you? You will stop expecting!

What? You think that expecting much creates a self-fulfilled life? That is not good advice, but if someone taught you to sit and watch and let others decide what you should do with your life, stop it. You must sit and look inside and decide why you came to this life and then pursue a plan that will take you to that life now. You cannot afford to wait.

If you love to listen to dire predictions about planets colliding and you expiring at the end of the world, you miss the point. You are a planet on a planet of many suns and stars that will collide before you leave life. If you learn to admit that you are able to do more and more for you inside the spirit before you remove you from this planet, your mind will be made ready for the next state of awareness, but better yet, why not be you and go inside the line that is You and ascend at the end.

What goes into the mind when you hear others talk about ascending all the time? Are you able to understand what it means and why we are always trying to get you to pretend to fly so one day you may go inside and fly to the other side? Are you able to practice now to leave this life with no false impressions left of this time? What do you intend to do with this life?

All questions expect you to stop and look, but most of you just fly over one line at a time and not think at all about the way you are inside. Why bother to read and study at all? If you could find a way to just be you today, would you do that and never again need anyone?

What is the end? Are you the friend you think of in your dreams and then pretend to find your friend over and over again? Why are you not easy within you now? Why would you think someone could open your mind or shut up the view they have of you? What do you do for the money you spend?

When we end on a mundane note, you all seem to note that work, but do not seem to weigh the other questions as highly. Why?

If your own admission of failure is that you cannot buy a big car or live in a mansion that others envy, you have placed you in a terrible view for money. You are not spiritual enough to even want to end this life and float up. Why be so rough on you? You will find the younger you are in your mind the more money preoccupies your day, but some older ones still want to be surrounded by money rather than those of their own age. Why?

If you are starting a new country and need people to do the work, what kind of patriarch would you want? You would? Why not a state in which women and men share the work? You have always seen the work of the man as superior to women in this time, but now the time is almost at an end and women are becoming more and more like men. What is happening at this time to men at the end of their time?

You will find that many men fight now for the time when they can still be of age and find some woman who is going to keep them or take care of them, but why would any woman alive want to do that for them? Money? You must think woman are prostitutes from birth if you think that or you would describe such a man as a jerk. We would say that such a man was unable to understand that life is at an end. You will find all men at the end of their lives are cared for by women and not men, but that is not always the way today. Nurses come in many shades and sex is not a critical factor today, but it is not the way you want your life to be today to sit with these enlightened ones in your old age.

When you decide that the old ways no longer meet your expectations today, you drop them and then forget to observe any new ways. You have to replace things or they will not be able to help you again. If you stop going to church because they are not at all talking about your own life or what you are inside, you stop the process of change and do not want to do anything religious all your days. Is that right?

What if you had never heard of Christ, Buddha, or the Islamic life, would you still be you and have such a one-sided view of their life?

You might believe you understand the creed of other human beings, but not if you have none in your own life. You cannot understand anyone if you do not have a measure to mark against them.

Your mind is full of ideas that some ascribe to all the time, but do you? Are you full of ideas you alone believe in? That is hardly true if you cannot be you and not have the world around you. You will find only two or three people at any time live totally inside. The world cannot provide a place for anyone who is working in this time to just sit and do nothing at all, but some try to say they are and have found a way to be paid all day for doing nothing at all. What kind of person would take pay for doing nothing all day? You, if you do not work as you are telling others you do.

When today is through and your work is explained to you, what do you think will happen to you? Think of the time to come and why they are not going to be able to fully be inside you and help you and go without you. You are a member of a clan or group that gathers around you. You need to ascend at the end, so why not pretend that each group you meet is such a group and will help you go fast at the end to the next avenue within you?

Where is the end? When is it reached? You decide always what is the last way to do something and why you will not retreat and do it over again. But whatever you do, think of you. Think of why you let you do nothing or do too much for others rather than look inside you and do what you came to complete.

Your mind is sweet only if you say nice things within to you all day. You will not like you much if you do not live a good way for you today, but if you have been forced by another to assume a new way that does not feel like you all day, you will rebel and not work for them at all. You will not be upset if they talk about you? You may, but do not let the tone of the mouth of a bitter person upset your day. You are here and now told not to listen to fools. What? You heard what you thought.

You are not to sit and stand and pretend to know others who are wiser than you are. You will just accept that you prefer to sit and listen to someone boast rather than do your own spiritual work. We abhor those who stand up and pray and ask God to release another, from what? Who knows you if you alone are doing your work?

You will not do anything that sounds like a boast if you are still doing work. Why? You will not be sure God is not listening then and will teach you a lesson again. We would not boast at any rate, but that is the way of men and women.

You might believe there is a rate of production that is good to do and money enough to fill you, but that is in your own mind. You decide what is enough at any time. If you feel good and have spent only a dollar on you, are you the fool or the one who is still upset after spending all the wage and not having enough to pay for the food and lodging for that day?

Are you a fool today? Look at you and then pray for you. Why would you pray to find out if you are a fool today? Fools never pray.

You will find many are confused about what work to do, but if they just look inside, the work comes into their lives. Why? God provides whatever you need to do to take care of you.

When you are able to see people look at you across the table and smile at you and talk about subjects that interest you, are you able to feel happy about you? If not, you are in deep depression and must stop!

You will depress you into submission of a situation that grieves you or you will talk it out and not feel so blue deep within you. Why talk? It takes time for you to see you are not at all as bad off as you seem to be. If you hear your mouth talking over all you have done or not done to deserve such a poor relationship with you and your mind, you will begin to not listen to you and revolt and get on with your life. It works. You will also try to sit longer and dry your own eyes. People do not like people who cry on them all the time.

You will find most people overlook others when they are negatively involved in their own lives to the extent that they cannot fend for themselves. You begin to expect another to reveal what your life is to be or you expect others to feed you for life or take care of you without being told what you need. You will depress them if you do that too much, so you will then have to feel such emotions yourself in order to teach you not to abuse others.

If you are abused and do not stand up for you, you will not love you much, but you will also learn to hate the other. Why not save this relationship? Why not say why you refuse to be abused or neglected now? What is in your mind that confuses you into believing that you are not you? You are not able to see that God is your own work and what you do is work within you to ignite the spark of God within you and do the work you came to do. If you shirk such a simple view of you, then dream and believe in a more intricate plan, but this view works.

What you have to do is develop a total view of life if you do not follow any particular religious view of you. What? You are religious inside you. All are told to come to Earth and work? No, but the missionaries and their like, like to come back to work on Earth. You may find that is why you always look for people to save.

You cannot save you today, but some of you work all day to save others from themselves and what they may say. What do you think that line of work will do? You are who is going to save you, so can you also save others, too? You will know when the last day on Earth is near and you are able to go into the next path, but until then, you will only know what you can find within you.

While a man or woman may not like you and do not want you to be around them, they may still show you compassion and help you to know who you are and how to go about your life. If such a man or woman helped you earlier in life, you will not love them as much as you will learn to have compassion upon others the rest of your life. We know, but you may not agree that this is the way you will grow. You will find men and women who have families before they can pass into the maturity of this life are prone to not know what to do. Can you succeed if you came from such a seed? You are not to judge those who knew only what they were told was right when you are now able to go inside and correct your own life.

What we are doing now is cleaning you up so you can excel at what you are doing and seeing within you. If your view of you is clouded with despair and things that you do not know, you will scare you into never going there. We want you to love you and take good care of the spirit there. If you cannot, who will?

If God does not go inside the mind and clean for you, who does? You in this life. You create what goes inside the mind all this life. You could decide to let nothing enter and be a dunce. You could decide early to announce to the world that you will do much and reach the stars, or not. It is not that the mind is so much of a machine as it computes your chances against what you dream. If you dream much, you enlarge the mind's idea of what you want and it then lets you go beyond what others would normally expect you to do to excel.

Computers are not that very different from each one, but some are used by experts and some by those who want nothing much. Which one will succeed? Neither will the computer succeed or fail unless there is a disease to the software and that is like the life of humans and such. See? You can go inside thee; eliminate whatever is not working and install a new program whenever you please.

If you can use a computer and excel beyond what others normally do with it, are you able to now fit inside you? If you cannot, you are not working enough inside the work you are to do. You are ignoring you. You are trying to limit you from inside and it will not work. You have to let you soar if your wings are not clipped by those who would want to make a slave or a fool of you, but only you can submit to it.

What we have now is a day in which you will either decide to grow and admit you like it, or another day of agony being you. Which is it?

The day of the week you fear most is the day in which you are unable to appear as you are and have what you need to be as wonderful as you can be, but what time is it? Time? Yes, are you on time?

When the day of the week does not match your energy or your idea of what day it should be, you are out of sync and your work will not collectively be as good as it would be if you were in the same day as you thought it should be.

Ever say to a friend, "I thought it was Saturday and I see it is Friday"? You are behind you again. If you think it is a day further away, you are too far into the future for you to work as well as you would normally work within you. You can see that many of you are out of sync and know nothing at all about how to make the timing within thee work.

You might say that one fellow has a bad day, but when all of you are out of the limelight and have no life, what do all of you say?

You might say if you had a great day and everyone smiled as if they were happy that day that all of you were pleased to be alive, but are you able to know if that is right?

You can line up your own line of time with anyone now. You can and will begin to find time is real and not just in the clock that sits on the shelf and counts out the minutes that take you into the next hour or so. You will find your limit is time. You always talk about having enough time to do only so much, but all of you do whatever you really want to do. You always have time to be you.

If you ever doubt any lesson we use for you, you can choose that lesson and go into it and learn from it and expose you to the lesson of it, but time is another kind of lesson this time.

We want all of you to sit inside you and listen to what these people all said to the Scribe about the things they did in their head when they did nothing at all for an hour or so and had no place to go. We want one person to volunteer to talk slow and let the Scribe write up whatever it was that she did on this side to make time to go out of this life for an hour or so. Can we have a volunteer please? Kathy?

Group response:

(I went out on the porch—it was cool and I was very much aware of the birds, insects and street sounds. I looked at the clouds and just sat in my rocking chair and rested and became aware of the things that one never pays attention to in the normal schedule of a fast paced life.

The church bells chimed on the hour and half hour and that's how I knew I had completed the time on the porch.)

Now, Katherine, what time did you think you were out there and when did you go there?

(It was 8:30 a.m. to 9:30 a.m. and again from 4:30 p.m. to 5:30 p.m.)

What kind of emotion was within you and how did you think the day was when it was over?

(I cleared any thoughts of what I personally needed to accomplish that day and I proceeded to relax. It made me feel good to complete the assignment and made me realize how important it is to give myself this kind of time alone. It was harder than meditating.)

That day we were in the world and you were there and we saw you and watched what you did to move within your own head, but did it matter to you that we watched you?

(No, but I knew you were there.)

We are a group. We move within the group of people who are always trying to do more and more and more with the work that we scribed to use in the world, but we are also alive. We feel that the emotion was real, but you were not as you are today. Why?

(I guess the concerns of everyday life affect me more than they should—especially with my business.)

We are not concerned about you, but we are concerned that you are not the same as you were when you sat and had a total way of being you. You were not upset, but you thought of us and we were sure you knew that the lesson was good for you, but you do not like it enough to carry through and do it for you. We want you to think of you and take two minutes every hour or so to be you. Do nothing. Sit or stand and just be you inside and not care about what others might want you to do.

You will now get your own salon and a lot more like you will be able to see that having you as the perfect mother is not the way you intended to earn your pay, but it is the way you do earn your way. You are a perfect mother today.

You often confuse being in love with you with being conceited, too, but that is not the way we see you today. You are not to pay anyone ever to tell you what to do about your own way of being today. We will see you get all you need, but you will not be able to say you had to learn anything over that another erroneously tried to teach you from the other way of life outside. What we want Katherine, is that you begin to use only the things you want to use and not see money within. If you like a special type of brush or shampoo and it is not going to be pricey enough to some clients for them to boast that they use, then say you use it today because it works in a very special way. Do not ever again do anything because you think it might pay. Use you as the guardian of the way the salon works everyday.

You will find many others were working still in that salon for you in a way, but now the others are gone. Only you and the one who is going to be the next you is working there for you. See you in all that you do. We do.

Now there is a woman and a new man that are also going to say they took time to do nothing and it was a great way for that one day. We want all of you who read or work or listen to our work, to stop and look inside you today and figure out a way to do nothing all day.

Yes, you can be you, but only if there is time within you to do nothing but love and be loved by you.

We will now continue and ask who will now share with you what they did to earn a few points, too. Jack?

Group response:

(I went to work early on Thursday after not getting much sleep the night before. The assignment was on my mind and I planned on doing it as soon as I returned home. When I got home, I was sleepy and decided to take a nap before I did the assignment so I would not fall asleep while doing my homework. I awoke from the nap with an alarm and wondered if I should use an alarm to time my hour of doing nothing. I didn't know what to do, so I looked at the clock, which showed 3:09 p.m. and I sat in a chair and cleared my mind. As I sat doing nothing, I nodded a few times and went into nowhere. It wasn't that easy, but it was. I blanked everything out.

The phone rang and I opened my eyes and I saw that it was 4:10 p.m. I was amazed. I knew it was you waking me. The call was very important to me. I said, "Thank you.")

We are not going to say that we were there all along, but any time you need to be sure you are up and awake, just call in an alarm and the phone will ring or the dog will bark and we will sing. You can find us in the dark. We are not like the Guides who tend to find you in the mainline of your spine, but we are not in the spiritual realm at all at any time. We are in the work you are. Yes, the ideas you build into you are there in an energy form. You then decide what to do and it becomes another view of you, but it is there and you have to take care not to use too much energy or it will never ever happen to you there.

We are aware this is new to you, but some of you automatically knew. How?

Can anyone say they always thought that we were in spirit in some way? You all did. You all thought we floated about and we were in your way at times or we flew away, but it isn't that way. We know when you work because you are the way you are today from the work you do everyday. If you do not work, you do not decay? You do in a way. Muscle will deteriorate and blood will be excreted throughout the day, but you will be energy completely always. You are not of flesh and blood or spirit when you are doing that work.

You are in spirit now. You have to smile to think that God is inside this work and caused you to do work for you? No, but you work and you develop and teach you to do the things you must do in order to rise into the next most important view of you. The spirit is arriving and will take you to the top for the next view of you.

We have one more who was able to do the work of nothing at all planned within you and was able to spiritually evolve into another point of view. We want one woman of the two to speak and talk for you. Sharon is going to do this chore.

Group response:

(It was 9:00 p.m. and I was concerned I would fall asleep. I lit a candle in the dark, and because there was moonlight coming in through the window it was not pitch black in the room as I watched the flickering candlelight. I thought about how amazing it was to watch the flame doing whatever it wanted to do. I should do this more often I said to myself as I sat and listened to the sounds of insects, dogs barking and other night sounds. How noisy it was outside at this time, but then I watched the candle and saw that it was just being—doing nothing, it was most comforting.

I thought I fell asleep for a few minutes, but I didn't, I came back. I didn't feel like I was back 100%; somewhere between meditating and sleeping—if there is such a place. I remember hearing, "Stop and let life catch you." I thought it was from one of the tapes I had heard before.)

What you did was relax and listen to the world. It was nice to be alone in the dark and have a light, but you were you and you had to hear what you alone were there to do. The light flickered and taught you to dance within you. Your mind was completed and you had no need to think about work or doing anything you did not mean to do. You sat there. You felt you within and grew. You will do that more and more until it becomes a ritual for you to do whenever you feel overwhelmed by what you do. You will see that the ritual is not that deep or involved that many cannot join you and bring you into the view of them, too, but watch for them and make sure you do not join them.

You will find your own life is to be your own life and if you join the spiritual realm and make them always aware of you and let them use your air for them, they will often take over and do too much of their work and not let you do enough for you, so beware of them, too.

We want you to know there is nothing weird in the air around you, but if you dare to see anyone at all who is not with you is there, you will find that time is not a problem ever for you.

You will find that time and people and matter and whatever you do are just there. You will find if New York is on your mind, the people there do not mind. You will find if you were to dream of a scheme to make you go there, you would go in your mind first and see if you really wanted to be there. We want you to learn to plan more and more for you to go into the work you adore and let the rest of your day go more.

What you do is not what others may do, but you learn from others when you go inside you and abandon the world to do work others cannot do.

You and your crew, Sharon, will be able to do more with this work than others have done before, but you will know why you cannot go anywhere other than up once you do work for you and see that others are always there to help you be and conceive the belief you must have of you. Competency is not hard to achieve, but lonely and confused women may not see you as anyone who has a problem. You will know. You will be able to show them, but they will go from you with the assurance that you are now you and not able to understand why they cannot do their work in time, as they are able to.

You will work and you will not shirk your own work, but you will know more. We will show and tell others that you are here to do well for you and go forward to the world and teach others that God is well and able to heal them with a finger or a touch of the hand that is real to you. You will know why you have to show and tell so many who are going to want to do nothing well.

When this day is over, you will join the others in a farewell to the work. We are not here to tell anyone what to do or where to dwell or what work they can do well. We are here to help all to ascend again and again until the end is near and God takes up the sphere of wonderment you are. We will be near, but you will all be able to work as a group forever if you are able to be here.

We will all of us and the Saints within you be able to do more and more for the world, but you all are going to be told nothing whatsoever about the way to publish this book today. We are going to end in a flourish never, but to surface from day to day and work in this way.

We will not say this book is the only way to teach you to pray and work all day to ascend one day, but it may be the only way you will ever hear from us after today.

When this book is open to a page and that page is clearly not at all what you intended to read or do that day, do it anyway. We are in the work. You will open the work to any page and see that this work is you in some way.

Be aware this is the way you are today, but in the pages of a book are many others who look and look for those who are willing to read or work that day. You are all here to do your work, but we are always there within the work.

You will tell no one of your own work unless you are able to teach what you have learned to do. No one can be sure they are not talking to one who is far and away above them that day, so be sure you do know what you say.

You will encounter angels along the way. Work for you and be sure you know what attitude you are and work for. If you are not holy today, you will find that holy men and women are on the rise at this time in your life. You will find them everyday or so and they will show you the way.

Today we want to thank Ray and the men for being willing to share with women the work they are. We are also aware some are not there who normally would be because of committees that are in their lives before we arrived, but you are here to know that life is never a dull course and never to survive any other life, so enjoy all you are.

We want to thank the Scribe for being alive. She is very good and very decent and very much misunderstood in this life by those who are not aware of the work she has inside, but that is good. You would not need a scribe if no prophet were alive. You are able to see that the work you achieve is the work you have inside. So, if you believe the Scribe has written all these lines, ask the crowd. You can be sure not one of them is going to believe that you cannot conceive of the Scribe writing out letters as you hear her read.

You will find no one else cares about you as much as we do. Why? We are in the work you do and if you succeed and breed into the world a bit more oxygen and love and water and such, we can do more and more. We want you as our students to prove to the world that life is pleasant without any strife if you do what you are called to do. We do.

When you feel that you are pressed to be unlike you, think of the Scribe. You will laugh inside. You will also see this is a group of committed beings who are trying to help all on Earth to excel and arrive on the other side without a problem or a thought about the Earth that is now going to go into another way of living today.

When we work and play and you pray to be one of us one day, we think maybe you know that we are happy at what we do among all of you. Do you know that or are you just assuming we work for pay?

If a teacher is told to work and do such things that a teacher need not be, would it help to be paid a lot? We do not know. We work for love. If you work to do what you want to do, you will never be able to sue anyone for not paying you. You will be inclined to want to praise them all the time, too, but don't. We want you to contract your mind now and sit inside and see who is there with you.

What did you see? Are you able to now see what we are and where we are and how many we are? What kind of memory do you want? You can choose and develop one of those in which everything is detailed and remembered and it takes you so long to talk about anything that others grow tired, or you can develop a selective memory that just reports on the major events in your life and you lose most of it in months. What works best?

When you decide what to do, why not try it for a month or two and see if it makes life better for you? When we ask so many questions as we have in this lesson with you, are you able to memorize all the lines?

You will find that many of you memorize the lines of a book in order to quote and never do what the author or teacher was trying to help you do. Why not do the work and forget what they said to you?

If you read about a boat and the stars and a crew, are you a crewmember or are you the captain looking about you? Look for you. See whom you choose to be in any old movie, and you will learn a lot about who you are. You will seem to always select the hero or heroine if you have mapped out a lot. If not, you might see yourself as a servant or a lady in waiting. You will find you will not be upset as much if you are not waiting as much and are able to command others about, but one requires many hours of work and the other does not.

You will find whatever you want to do with this life is going to help you regardless of what you have inside you now. You change by doing something new and you provide a better life for you by becoming proficient enough to do it for a livelihood or you feel better inside because you can use your pride to make you a living from your work. You will not waste hours on playing games that never pay you. That is what your mother forgot to mention to you if you still sit and do nothing at all and seem to be playing for fun when you never talk to anyone around you.

Bridge the gap between you and old friends by playing with them. If you have time to talk and walk and do things with them, you will find they are going to be there until you die, but if you never say what you think today, how can they know when you are going to go?

Work today to see which way you will want to be tomorrow. You can decide today to open another way so that this one will not stop you if someone else blocks you, but it requires persistence to win a better life when this one is consistently blocked by you. Yes, you are the only one who can constantly stop you.

If you have a reason to do things you want to do and it makes you upset being you as you are today, what is it you want someone else to do? You might decide then to do it yourself. Work inside now. Look for a friend who often stops and helps you and then goes inside and makes their own day. Look at that friend and try to do what they do with you. You will then mend that part of you and be able to make a new friend.

If you are totally dependent upon a friend or an enemy that is not able to hurt you, which one will build you again and again? The enemy. You cannot be hurt by anyone who is now a lesson you learned and many enemies are so bold that they help you before you even know what they are trying to yell at you. Listen to those who are your friends and find the enemies among them. Look at your enemies again and decide which of them was the best friend you ever made in school or wherever and why they now are to take some credit for helping you change you into a better personality today.

Look at what someone says about you. Do you like praise? Are you surprised if someone flatters you and says you do things you know you can do? Why? You must not be maneuvered ever again by someone who is only trying to move you to do something for them. Make that a motto and use that always to determine if they are a friend.

If you work and work and stop that work, will you confuse you and make you upset you have to end that work? Not if you are wise and disguise that work as work you do for you all this life. Once you have found a job you like, look no more unless the wages are not high enough to keep you in the usual way. If you hate your job, get out.

What do you want from you? Are you sure your complaints about others are not about you and what you do not want to do to help you?

Think now of yourself. What thought came to you?

What are you going to do if no thought ever comes again to you? What? Yes, when this life is over the mind shuts down and goes from you. You will not ever again see that spot on the work you do, but it will be locked in time for you. If you revisit this view of you, the mind will renew its work for you, but otherwise the mind has no life and will not follow you.

The soul, however, is you and will always be you and has to submit to many things you do to it. If you are unable to fit inside this lifeline, you might even harm the soul a bit. Why? You forget to nourish it.

Poetry and art are the favorites of Earth beings to nourish the soul, but you might not see it. What? You might not notice that nature is God's artwork and men are always trying to disprove it or improve their eye, but God creates it over and over so you can enjoy all of it within you. Yes, the eye is a mirror of what you look at when you are outside and you carry it within you.

Create beauty in the inner city.

We would advise all of you to create a beautiful park and plant as many trees as you may believe will survive in that part of the Earth that is now dark. Go there and put aside the past and believe now is the time to impart wisdom to those living in the dark You see? You have a purpose now if you have time and energy and no part to play in the work of the Earth today.

Now if that work does not make you want to play and work with others today, look at what work you do instead and how little or how much it helps you. If it does little more than pay you, why do you not volunteer to work on the art that God will supply you?

When you have time, and you do, what do you want others to say to you?

If you speak foully over the most part of your day, what kind of message do you think others will use about you? Four-letter words are used to confuse the soul into not believing in you? No. The soul is perfect for you and will perfect you if left to show you the way. Swearing and comparing others to you is not the way to perfect you, but it will betray you as a person others will prefer to avoid most days. You are who is preparing you, so do the work you would want another to do for you.

If your day is over and you are about to pass away, read this book in the old way and then go back and remove your owlish ways and let the work, work for you. What?

You are all going to go away at some point in this day, so work and work on this work until you know the way home and how to go. What?

You will find we are preparing you for the end of time. It is not the end of the world or the end of space or the universe colliding all over the place. It is you dying and not being able to return to Earth because you have tried to eradicate that planet for doing what you asked it to do—provide for you.

We want you to notice that you have all found truth from this work and Ruth is not the only one who is writing for you, but are you now writing when we ask you to write within you?

Look now and write a paragraph about you. We left no lines so you will have to write within you.

Now that you have a lot to laugh about or you may be upset all day, think of what you said about you.

Are you proud of you and willing to share what you do? Why not share you? You can talk about you, but beware of talking too much about what another is like or you will be blaspheming God of All with what they came to do. Yes, you know not what others are here to do. You only know you, so get down to business now and work within you.

Write up a letter now to a family member who is far away from you. Do not say you know no one at all far away when you always have elders who have passed beyond this time with you. Write in your mind and save time.

What kind of letter did you write?

What kind of life did you want them to know you have at this time? Look inside now and see if what you wrote has any meaning now. Are you able to smile or are you frowning now? Look at you.

Once again, did you look or just leap ahead? You will not pass over anyone else by not following up on what the rest of the class is doing and removing now from them. You alone work as you are and are able to remove anyone or any idea that is deceiving you into not believing in you.

When this class is over, leap up and down, but now sit and stare inside you and hum a song you learned when you were young.

What song did you hum?

When you cannot hum, you cannot calmly work within you. Look at you and see what is upsetting you enough that you cannot go inside and be you all this life.

Welcome to you! Sense the fall of man is what you are prepared to do. You are not going to spring up and stay in the work of this day forever, so get it done now and see that tomorrow is going to fall exactly where you would want to be when that day comes to be. You are dismissed until we meet again.

We stopped for a moment in order to thank this crew, too. We have seven teachers gathered around you. You are here in this room with a tutor for each one of you, but the ones who are not here with you will bloom, too. You will find today is a fine day to be you. God is the wind and we blew you into the world with a huge burst of air and it was that kind of day when the Scribe tried to enter the airways, but we laugh as she would with you about the wind blowing you into the work you do.

We know you all feel a bit tired and sick of the work you do on Earth if others do not appreciate you, but why do you do it then to you? You must see some benefit for you or it would not logically calculate into money for you.

We want to thank you for this time in your life when you can read and write and work in this book and change your own life, but some of the readers and writers will work now in a different life. We know, but do you?

CHAPTER 15

This Is The End Of The Work, But All Of You Will Work

The end of any work is not the same as the beginning? Why not? You only begin to assimilate and incorporate the work once you have gotten into you all the work that the teacher or teachers have combined to help you learn and do. You will find that now you are done with one phase of the work and the harder part is about to start—you must live it, or you will not have worked within you at all this time to learn what is in it.

You will find the team of people who gathered on the Earth now are all on line at this time, but some of them will still not realize that time is what holds all of them in the same line. If you meet as a group at irregular hours, you do not compete with anyone at anytime, but this group met on a regular basis and all had to make arrangements to be there and be there on time—as you would call it.

You will find whatever you do with the material in this book for you, it will still work into the major avenue of time and teach you what is true about you—or it may even tell you ways to understand others around you today, but it is you. You are who is going to do this work. If you do not, you are not able to do anything inside you. Why? You never follow through and do what you want to do.

If you start a job and fully decide you will do this work for you, do you hurt anyone else by not being fully committed enough to do the work for you? You do, but you might think that you did not. Why? You are not willing to mind the mind. The mind is a tool that uses time to decide what to do and helps you prioritize this life, but if you do not use time as a tool, it will rule over all this life. It will take you all over the world in a few hours or maybe within a month or two, but you decide whether or not you will fly.

When you decide, what do you do? When you decide, you start to declare to you that one thing is more important than the rest that you are looking for, or working on, or doing now. You prioritize them and decide which one is going to be done before the rest of them. You do that all the time.

If your life is boring and has nothing that interests you, you do that to you and no one else can change that about you, but you can. You can decide to select more risky adventures that you would not normally choose or you can do exactly whatever bores you. You have to trust the risk is not going to be too much? You decide always how much risk you can take and then hesitate until the risk gets too great. If you decide and move, you get the first burst of energy within you and usually you can jump higher or wider than later in your life or if you delay your decision for another day.

If you decide wisely to think about what you must buy today, you may decide that buying a large purchase will always require a day's delay, but otherwise, most decisions are better to be done right away and not delay since you will not do whatever you cannot imagine you can do right away.

What you do now and then for fun is not the usual way, but if you do it always the same and everyday you never change any of the ways you have fun, it will be boring to you by the end of a few times you put it together on the same timeline. Space and time make things less boring or more by the way you space time together or stay apart over a couple of weeks or months. You are who sets you up to be bored by using others too much today, but if you do feel you cannot face the same group everyday, you will say you hate the work or whatever instead of realizing you are bored with the same work done everyday in the same old way with the same old group gathered around you. You could leave, but why not decide to change you some way everyday or so? You can change you enough so the group is never exactly the same on any given day. You are the one who changes everyone, or you are changed by ones who are not able to stand staying the same old way.

When you change you or do something brand new, you might decide you are a better or worse person than you normally are, but it is not the case. You are still the same regardless of what you might try to erase by a harmless display of whatever today. However, if you continue to do it over and over, you will become the new being and have more time to have fun or less—depending upon the way you sit and work and confess your mind to those who are around you today.

You tell others what you do today, but they may not feel the same with you or about you. Why? You will alter your own aura if you cry, if you laugh, if you are not stirred up in anyway, or if you do not like what you stand for.

When you decide to read or write and advertise to friends that you like one of them, do you feel they look up to you more than they did? Which work does more for you? You could say that boasting today seems to earn more pay, but writing and reading instructions will pay more than ever before because so few are really educated today.

You will want to do more and more for you once you find out that you bore you? You might decide to not bother at all this time. You might decide to sit and let the tide take you from one side to the other again. You might decide to just rest on your laurels again. Why? You do not believe you have to work to reach the other side of this life and begin to ascend.

What kind of ascension process do you want? Yes, you can choose what time and what kind of process you would like, but it could be increased or reduced or eliminated when the time comes for you to cross over to the next life or two.

What and how are ways of making excuses for you. If you always use such words whenever someone talks to you, you are not questioning them for you to know what to do, but stalling in order not to do what they are asking you to do. You always grasp immediately what you want to do, but may ask for more facts. You stall when you hear something you do not want to do, so some of the folks who started this work are not here with you. They lost the way and will not be back and in line someday with you.

When you seek another to cross the world with you and you do, do you feel they saw the world the same as you did? We would not dispute you if you said you could never stand to sit and walk and talk and eat and sleep with the same two people all your life and not at times be upset or disgusted with the other one, but we would offer that you would have had time to really alter that one. Only if you spend a lot of time with anyone at all can you tell them what you believe and how you succeed. All others are merely advertising that they are doing whatever again.

You will work now to decide what kind of life you will realize and do the rest of the time you are on Earth. What?

Yes, you decide now, and tomorrow will bring that work for you to do or those people back inside the line that is you and redo what you once thought you could do, or you will continue to sit and do nothing inside on you.

If you decide to sit, you will change a bit, but not enough to stop you from not feeling good when others begin to leave you. If you are not working or prospering enough for you, you resent anyone else who is. Work on your own work and you will prosper, but not more than the effort that you put into it. You must feel you deserve it or you will waste your work and get very little done with it.

When you are given money or material goods, you do not seem to use them as if they were gifts given by someone who worked for it if you never did. You will begin to expect others to give and give and not think much of them if they do it for you, but you expect a lot of praise if you give even a single day of your time to all the world that has helped you to arrive at this time. Why? You do not work if you do not have a plan.

If your plan this time is to work on the Earth, you will not like the way things are done, but you might not realize it until long after the dirty work is done. You might not even mind that others ruined the Earth in your time, but you will want to do something to the people who do the dirt now. Why? You are called now to regain the timeline running inside all of you and expected to call upon the inner one who is trying to always communicate with you on how well you have done.

If you never pray or meditate at all, you are totally ignorant of what we do and would never have found your nose in this book or listening to anyone reading it to you, so you have to assume you do not have anything else to do, but you do. Get your own life together now and get your own mind to follow you all the way through, but get you to work on you. You will not have time to say others are not working like you do.

When you work, you criticize those who do not. You will notice more and more of the poor character or labor of others when you are working through a problem and they are not trying to do it with you. You notice and perceive a lot more when you believe than when you just say you work, too. You will now work for you!

When you do not see why we talk or walk or work with you, you think and perceive you are the human being and in charge of what you do; but are you?

What if you had to do all your work in a chamber where others could admire you or describe you in terms you would not like to hear used about you, would you want to do work in that kind of atmosphere? You fear. You see things around you. You do not look inside you enough to see you are who is there observing you. You will find there are at least three versions of you looking down at you all day as you work. You said you wanted to be whomever while here on Earth doing the part of your work you designed for you to do in this time. Can you follow through and understand that about you?

You will find that if you dream of the same thing night after night, you are just inside one other person who is in your own line and not able to do anything about that life at this time. If you can, you zoom in and do whatever you can and leave. If you arrive at a time in this life when you cannot do or you feel you cannot survive, the other parts of you or aspects of the spirit within you will arrive and take care of you. God is the view you now have of you, but you might not believe God is in you. Why?

You have been taught over and over to believe others have power over you, but they never do. You give up when you feel fear is too great for you to move or win or do whatever you want to do. Why? You do not believe you can live or do whatever you came to do for You. You will succeed, but you first have to learn to believe.

Living and believing are two ways of being you. You live and believe in you or you die not knowing why you are here doing what you do.

When your diet is slim and your mind is full of ego and not able to do much for you, are you going to be able to win the beauty pageant again and again? Not if you do not have the means to carry on and win time after time when others will try to dismantle your ego and win.

You go after the ego if you want to win? You do that all the time when you are upset and filled with pride, and you are full of pride most of your life. You have to remember that pride is needed to keep you from doing nothing at all, but too much may take you to the grave being afraid of doing anything that another might not think is right.

You will find pride is the way to stay away from others all this life, but sloth is the means to never be hired. You have to pride yourself on working hard in order to be able to get most jobs, but it can be a case of advertising that you are. You have to hold up the work to others, though, if you want them to keep you on once you are hired. If you advertise that you can do whatever and cannot do it ever, you will not be hired again once that is found out about you. You will find that you can lie, but who will believe you the next time you do?

You will find the Ten Commandments and the Seven Deadly Sins are all about legalities of the mind. You either follow the lines that others say are the way to live today, or you will lose and not be able to do much in your own way. The work you do is not going to end up ever paying you if you never do the work given to you. If you never work on the work that the universe sends this way for you to do, who do you think is going to do this work for you?

What you do and how you perceive you are the ways you will win or lose. You can decide now what to do, but you would be better off doing whatever you have to do and then later thinking about a better way to do it, too. You put off too long what you do if you first try to streamline the work of today. Do it first. Look it over three times and forget it until the next time you are asked to redo or do it another way, then you will blend again into the way you worked today and see what is the better way. If you try to do perfect work, you shirk a great deal of work that others must do for you.

If you blame others for making mistakes and you never do, who is doing the work? Not you. Those who work and make few mistakes will arrive at a time when they will not have to work all day, but all others may.

You will find that today your mind is not on time, but on work. We want you to combine these two ways of being you at this time.

We will now let you go inside you and see what you do.
Look for you. Do the work you normally do.
Look for the new you.
When you see you, please smile and let you do the work you came to do.

Please review the work you do and why you smile if others are unable to do what you can so easily do today. If you cannot smile at you and you believe that your work can be and should be improved in anyway, please release that energy today and do it all right away.

If you try to stop a fall or you try to end it all too soon, it comes back to you in your back, but if you are able to let all go gracefully from you and not assume you will hurt at all, you can leave and be you, but it takes time to know what to do and when to leave in order to be you.

When you do leave anyone ever, be sure you are severed and not just leaving to be able to take command over those who are not going to want to see you go on into the next view of you. Take command? You leave that to others if you never ever do what you truly want to do, but if you can change you today, please do. You then take command again.

You are here and now the commander of you again—or not, but you choose every moment to do whatever you can or you choose to simply let others command you to do what they do not want to do for you. You are who and we are whom; is that correct to you? Why would any writer stop work in order to look up a word or two? You decide you will not work at that time and will stop and your mind wants a reason why it cannot follow the work to the next line. You would be better to work and then go back later and redo whatever is not working for you, but it is not you or the work that stops you over and over if you are not willing to be you. It is You. You will stop you from accelerating into the wrong corridor or stop you from hurting you or deny you the way to harm you, but if you continue over and over, the mind will help you to do it all to you. It never really minds hurting you.

When you begin a story and you see the end is near to the beginning, do you sneer and say, "I can read this in an hour today"? Or are you afraid the story is too long and you do not have that kind of time today? Are you able to see that you judged the story by the time you believed it would take to work it out today? Are you saying that any line of credit or time is too short if you can see the end today?

You all ask for future predictions everyday or two, but when you do, you are asking to look beyond you into the near future of what you intend to do. Is that wise of you? Never, but it can help you if you are totally baffled by you and do not even understand you. Why would that happen to you?

You are guided by the Spirit within you and if you never ever ask for help or never use what seems to be there for you, you are confused about who you are. You are sure someone else has the power to be able to tell you what you will do. Is that really what you believe and see inside you?

When a fortuneteller comes to see you, are you the one seeking her or him or are you telling them what you want them to tell you?

When did anyone ever come to you and tell you what to do and you assumed they were talking about you and your future, too? No, you go to them and you place your mind upon them and believe that someone sublime or even out of line is able to tell you better what you need to do this time. We regret that if you do, but some of you will be able to see in others the future, too. Do not do that if you want to be able to ascend with this crew around you.

You will find that power and decency are seldom as required as they are when war comes into the view around you. Do you see peace? What kind of war makes you abhor such disharmony around you more? You are tired of being you? What kind of person would dislike you?

Look up! See inside and wonder why you are you. Do it all for you. Do not say a word today about what you do, but when you can slip away and be inside you for a total day or two and not have to talk to anyone else at all that way, look at you. Decide why you are and why you do what you do.

When you decide to empty you of all pride, will you fall into disrespectful ways and others will make off with your pay? You may find that some will not work if they are unable to find a way to have more than others. But, normally, most work for the pay in order to live a better way today. If you do not, think about why you are not like others today. It will shed light upon you and the ways you choose to live your life today.

When you have time and you work all the time inside you to improve you, are you going to be better than anyone else today? You could do that and still not ascend at the end. It depends upon whomever you gather around you. Are you really discriminating when you want no criminals around you?

When you are unable to seize the day and fully occupy you with work that pays you to do it for you, are you prideful and willful to not want to do such work to you? Think of pay and why you all think it is not why you work today.

You will want money if you never ever feel that you work really hard to do whatever you have to do for you. If you work very hard and feel good about what you do to others, you will generally not be upset to spend a few dollars on you and others who are just like you, but if you are not able to, you must remember that it is God who is providing for you. You desire work for money? You do if you never ever see the responsibilities within you to others who are also working with you. You will not have time to do over and over anything you do wrong against another who works for you.

You must not take over the lives of those who report to you. Why? It will become you in time and you will be so tied up over the lies they tell you about what they do that you will not be able to survive in that atmosphere longer than the time it takes you to die and not realize you took over others' lives in order to have whatever they had. You despised them and they will always repay you by despising you in some way, too. You need to adjust you when you are in a position of trust, but if you do, and they still do not recognize that you do, you will never be unjustifiably upset if they fire you. You will have to do that, too.

If you are upset with the view you have of you, you are who is doing that to you. You are who lowers the light around you so you cannot clearly define what you do. You do that at times in order to release envy and jealousy of others who are now able to do what they came to Earth to do, but that is a kind of envy that will end you. You must not ever judge anyone who is working for you in spirit and not able to talk to you? You talk to you in questions all day and you are unknown to you in a spiritual way if you never pray, so stop and think and advise you today, to pray.

When you have two or more who are totally dependent upon you today, will that day ever come when you will rise and the sun will announce that you have no such responsibilities left to pay? Yes, if your child or parent is able to do their own work and do it well, you are who is not going to help them at all by depending upon them to stay with you or do whatever you tell them to do. You are who is dependent upon them if you are trying today to make them stay. You are an adult if you have a child—they say, but some today are children long beyond the time of day when a child should be at play.

You never today seem to want children to play. You force them to work and you tell them it is okay to do the work they have all day. You never see them shirk later in life the work they had to do then? Of course, you do. You may see adolescents today at the age of 41 and still not recognize them as not being able to play. Why? You are here and there and everywhere, but the young are strong and need to learn to rest and relax today.

You will find that the child is not an adult at play, but some seem to want them to be that way. Whoever harms a child is not going to just be asked to repay that debt one day, but be retarded in social and physical ways if the society is wise today. You must stop the work upon the child that is hurting you in so many ways that most of you cannot know you. You are the child that is abused at home or not given the time of day in which to be able to talk about childish ways. You may decide they need to grow up today, but why?

When you are you and you review all the things you have let be done to you, you cannot really complain about the times when you were young. Why? You selected that family and you were given a way to get around them, but you may not have discovered it yet. All people have charm and ability to be able to live with most anyone who is fit enough to breed them today, but some are not fit today to breed with anyone. Why? You know why. You created them.

When you are young and are disabled in anyway, you make a promise to be good to the one who is trying to take care of you everyday, but some do not today. Why? The time is running out and many are not here to be good or to try to do over whatever they were sent back to do in another view of the personality they are today. You will know who is here because they asked to return or they asked to visit Earth or they want to help you to rebirth and be you. You will know them right away if you are wise and you do pray.

When an angel of the Lord is here with you, are you able to see the wings fluttering, too. We see wings that are not wings at all, but remind human beings of the birds who hover always around you. You are not able to recognize today that you have disturbed the pattern of the birds, but we do. We watch you. You do not seem to think about anyone at all most of your day. Why?

When you criticize the society you are a part of today, are you wise? You could be, but you might also be criticizing that part of you that needs to be redone by you. We would first look inside our own eyes and wonder why we do not do more before we would suggest that another do what we cannot do.

When you elect a President over you, why do you then attack that one and insist that he or she is no good? You are not willing to accept that you are not able to be ruled by anyone if you cannot do that for you. We would not mind, but you are then detailed enough to say what you would do and you never do. That then becomes you and your mind reminds you over and over again that you would have to be president if you were to do anything worthwhile again. That defeats you and the rest of the people who are like you. We want you to just do!

When you see a man or woman rise and you do not, are you suspicious of them because you do not work at all for you and suggest that they do? You would not rise to the top of any ladder if you just leaped up and grabbed and hung on? You might be able to get a head start on many around you, but it would still require that you stop and get into the next step or two before you can rise higher. You all are prone to want to leap over some others who are working there before you, but go to the old channeled work and see what they have spoken for you.

You are not to do anything at all? You can channel for you and you can learn to do whatever you think others do, but what good is it to you if you never follow through?

When you go inside the world and hide, are you sure you know what you do? You do? Well, then go in and do the work over. You are not going to be able to fly away from you until God says it is time. If you are done with all you came to do and still cannot find enough to do, do your own life over and make it better and more complete and sweeter than ever. We cannot do that for you.

If you begin to redo anything about you, make sure you are wise enough not to interfere in the lives of others who are not like you and will not like you. You seem to believe that each personality should love you or at least respect what you do, but why? You do not respect all others or you would not have to do over anything about you.

When you do not see anyone at all gathering beyond the valley or the mountain you are in or on, are you sure you are alone? Never. You have one or two of you along. You do. You take you into each avenue with you, too. If you want to redo you this time on Earth, remember they will want you to stay as you were or they will help you to do more for You. Decide today and live that way!!

We will close this work with a bit of a joke, but we want no one to say we were not serious about you. We are all ways in this work and you will find that all you ever have to do is pray to God and someone is there right away, but it might not be a Saint or two like today. You might not have a Teacher of the Higher Planes explain to you the basic work you have to do, too, but you will be assisted by someone who is able to do the work for you—but will not.

You see? You do or you do not. You are helped by a tutor at the level you are at today and will be, but if you achieve a lot more than a bachelor's degree in metaphysics from this work scribed by Ruth Lee, you will arrive at a time when you must teach if you are to learn more about you and why you are here on Earth and what you will be.

If you cannot learn more and more, what do you need to be you and return to the other work that You has in store for you to be? You have to work. There is no alternative class for Earth.

You will find that Earth is a timeline and it is not the same as another planet or solar system that you might have redone, but it is a life you now have and exists within you. You cannot imagine the entire universe? You are only then learning to know you.

You will converse with those who are higher than you or you will teach those under you to know about the level you have inside you, but you cannot leap up if you never begin to teach you enough about the next work you are to do. You have to be able to see into the next view of you, or you will never leap when this work is done by you and you are to thrive on the tide of energy coursing through this life and taking you to the other side. You will be carried away, but not by anyone else in this life. You may find an angel waiting to help you fly, but you still have to have achieved enough in this time to make the angel want to help you again.

What day do you have? You have a calendar inside. Why not look up the Mayan Calendar at this time and search for the time when you will breach the work of the other side. It will show up as a time on Earth when you are able to tide your work over until the time comes over you. You will find time is in the work you do, but you are the work, so you are time and the work you do; but what do you do? Confusing? You are not thinking then enough inside you.

The work you do in spirit is not ever going to harm you physically or mentally or sit in you, but it will move you to the next level of experience and help you. Why not work now to rise inside you spiritually so at the end of time you can fly?

We will finish this work with you—now or later—but it is entirely up to you. You have the time, but you may decide to be bored the rest of your time on Earth. It is your choice, but you will sit at the end with nothing to do if you have no time to be you. Your mind will refuse to learn what you must know to cross over into the next world, but the spirit will always be there hoping you will try to do whatever work you have left to do. Go now and seek the work. We will now finish this time with you. Will you?

Addendum

We wish to thank all of you. No matter what you do, you came to the finish and you worked within you. We will help you regardless of what you think we might like to do with you. We never think, but you do.

When you fear, and most of you do that too much now to be you, you float never inside you. We want you to float and feel like a raft upon the river, too. What kind of float can you make for you?

Now that you are here and done with this work, please review the pieces of you that do not work. You know who you are? You do. Go inside you and begin to seize upon the work you must do first and then go back and do over whatever is not really hurting you. If you do, and you will find that is about the only time we will ever use the word should, you will find you—regardless of what you may believe is true.

When the time comes to end work with a fearless crew who worked so hard for you, you have to feel so upset within you that there is no more time to say adieux, but there is always time for you.

When you feel sublime and can feel the line of time running inside you, do you want to run away with you? We do!

We want you to be all you ever wanted to be, but we remain the same. We are your friends and confidantes and we will remain the same. We never talk about you. We will never speak of you to anyone on the street, but if you do, remember it could be repeated and not correctly by others who are not like you. We will help all who want to work with you, but you have to decide what it is you work for and why you want to be you.

When you decided to return to Earth or to come for the first time to see what they believe and do that makes them so upset all the time that the universe has to work overtime, we will tell you. When you are not alive and you have all the time to be you, your life is never as easy as when you are being in a line and proceeding to the other side, so step on it. Get in line. Get your mind to mind the time. Get your own line for you to do all the way through so you can practice a lot being you.

When the time comes to say farewell to all the Saints who dwell on Earth with you, will you be in that line? When it comes time to say hello to you, we are going to want to be there working for you, too. We will help you if you need help to go, but if you know the way, go slow today and watch the birds play. They all work much harder than you do to eat everyday, so they always deserve to play, but do you? We know.

When you have time, and you do today, you will recline too many times on your work of yesterday and not work enough for tomorrow, but play and it will all come to you and you will have time to renew you in time to be you and do it over before you have to do the work of judging you.

You will judge you. No one else can know exactly who you were this time, so you have to fall in line and judge for yourself if you deserve to have the best time of all in that line or you must return again before the Earth falls from you.

You will be able to sell the book at the back of any class and you might even take orders for you. If you do, you obviously are extending the work beyond you and will be blessed and some cash will be extended to you. Two dollars a book is not the way they pay today, but we do.

We want you to refresh your mind a bit, so Ruth will pursue the first week or two and next time you all meet, please repeat.

You were blessed to be a part of this group and if you need to do more work on you to assess this work and be able to get inside the work of the work you had to do to reach this level, you will do that, but you have no reason ever to redo our work. We do not take you to court, but you may be taken to court if you do not work inside you and say you do. We would never ever expect anyone to do our work, and your mind may know what God intends for Earth, but inside you is the pattern of you. Go find you!!

Epilogue:

The Teachers of the Higher Planes were always there to watch over the work as it was channeled, and they interjected thoughts and comments whenever necessary to maintain a safe energy environment for the Scribe. Ruth Lee has channeled the Teachers for many years and needed no help from this group of individuals to maintain the electromagnetic energy field necessary to work with them. However, she was not able until then to let the gathered forces of so many teachers use her to scribe in this way—and has not attempted it since that time.

When we first participated in the channeled sessions that became the book, "Can You Pray"?—there was a period of adjustment for all the spiritual energies that were meeting to teach as a group for the first time within the room at Ruth's home. The unseen saints and other teachers were unfamiliar with working in this way with Ruth Lee. As a result, the first sessions were unlike the work that followed and we felt the pressure of trying to understand what they were talking about and what they planned to do with us during this inter-dimensional encounter. It was also apparent the entities wanted to reduce the size of the group of those who would be able to sit and be able to hold the energy in this way. To assist you to better understand how this work evolved, we will include the initial four sessions immediately following this epilogue.

First Session

The Work

The work. The work is going to be done tonight and you will sit there and just watch, but it will go and move and take on its own life. Tonight you will not be asked to do anything. You will assume you are here to bloom, but you will be told nothing and asked to assume nothing, but you will. You will assume this is a class and you are asked to be here, but you are not. You came to see and you will believe or not, but the work goes on.

The work will come and go and the computer is going to be used, but Ruth is not going to have to talk as much as usual. You will sit for longer periods now and not move and you will not do much. If you are bored or unable to sit long, you will not return. You cannot do this work. You will not do much with it if you cannot be disciplined enough to sit and ask your own life to be there. You will be watched as never in this life by those in another life, but you will not see them at all.

Are you aware? Are you very open to the air around you? What do you want to do? Are you truly in love with the being you? Are you tired of being in the old personality you have used for so long, or do you want to do what you do now?

The work of your life is now. Are you able to see? Tonight is a special day and you will arrive at another stage, but not until you are able to meditate tonight to a different level and you are not going to be able to see it now, but you will.

The work you do is free and easy if you are able to do more in your inside, but it is difficult and not easy if you are artificially deep and not able to do much work inside.

You will not speak and so it is difficult for most of you to go very deep? Yes, you talk a lot about your experiences and have nothing but praise for it, but who is talking of it? You are not allowed to talk of your own spirituality again. You have been told before that some of you are prone to pride and conceit, and you will not be allowed to harm yourself so deep, so beware. Do not sit and say you do something that is not there. Work for your own being. See who is there.

Now we will go into the work. You will see there is nothing that you cannot be, but you are and will be exactly who you believe and see and will be. You are the only one who is going to know who you are, but others will ask you more and more to talk to them about spirituality, and if you are vain and proud, you will talk to them and tell them how to do this, but you better not if you intend to ascend. You cannot do what you never do and you cannot talk about what you know not. You do not know meditation. You do not practice to any depth now, so do not say much or it will be seen that you are not in this group but in another room. Please do not move.

The real way to be today is relaxed and aware that you are here and not able to do anything now, but in a way are moving the universe to be here and not leave.

We will leave this page and go to the end of the work and see what you will have to say when the day is over and the group is able to leave.

There is nothing. You are disturbed? You are not inside then. You are not outside of the world yet.

There is a time to be and a time to succeed but you are here to be and to learn and not to see, but you will. You will see and be and then if you work harder than now, you will believe and be able to come to the point of it all. You are not upset at all, but your work is going to end the day and you will not be swayed. You will ignore or you will not be able to do this today.

The work is here and you have to see that your work is not going to be upset by the work of anyone else who is not knowing and is unable to know that you know. You will find that there is power of two men in this room now.

The first and foremost is the man who is in this area of the Earth for a better view of you and what you all do. But this is not the day or the week or the time to be aware of anyone who is not here. You are not to pay attention to anyone who is so disturbed that they would come into this room and try to upset one of you. You will find there is nothing on the line, but if you can hold it for a moment more there will be silence and it will not be told. You are now to object to no one else ever.

The time is here now and I have had a long time to prepare for this time, but how many of you are even prepared to be you? I doubt it very, very much that you are sincere and that even one or two of you is really near to being able to appear at the end of this tribunal year and be able to state with clarity and grace why you are here. Is that the reason you cheer all others into doing things that are so disagreeable to the work of the Lord? Are you aware of the evil that abounds and is near and far and never as much disliked by you, as it should be if you were truly working here?

You have to see that I'm not afraid of this day, but I have a friend who is also on the way, but today we met and there appeared that yet two more would be on the way and then two more would be delayed. Do not fret my dear you are here and we know you asked us not to go on without you, but we are here today as a troop of souls who are unable to say what you would like us to. We are instead enraged today at the pay you demand of others for work that is not in a very superior way. You have to see that so much greed is in the blood and you are all bloody this day, so do not ask for pay until your work in spirit is so great that gifts are given and you do not have to ask for pay in the form of extended spirituality.

Your own Saint and your own belief in another is not what you have to pray to today, but the Saint is here and he is not upset in anyway that you are not clever enough to know right away who is here and who is going to be here for a day. You will see that Francis of Assisi is not here, but the greater and he is here to see what is wrong in this pretty neighborhood today.

You see? No, but Ruth Lee is a friend of the friend of the man who came to be seen as Francis Xavier today. You are shocked? You know not. You are not aware he is a primary teacher of the atmosphere and he is always around you when this group is called today, but are you aware of the facts of his life and what he has done to be here for you all today?

You do not even care. You have no ability to do anything but spout nonsense about your own lack of ability to compare to the Godly as Leslie is among you and she is so ready to be here and has nothing that she has to achieve here, she is the only one totally ready. She is ready and is very close to ascending to the next level of her own ability, but it is not to be until she is free of the negativity at the time of her activities. She is to be free to talk to anyone of you, but you do not have enough inside you to be able to talk, too. You will find once you can unwind and go inside and deliberate for an hour or two, Leslie is able to talk with you, but how many can?

You will find today there are the talented in everyway, and they are the worst offenders today. You have to see that if you are particularly gifted and able to do more and do not, you are who is holding up your own work for you not to do today.

You will find that healing is in the line, and Lily you are to be healed in a most particular way. We offer this to you, study from the long work of the Saint who is talking to you and what I did while on Earth and what it is you want to do first and then we will talk again, but now you have to help within and gain a center of health within. You will be okay in a few days of life, but do not ever, ever worry about ending anything twice. You will be okay—or whatever it is that you all say today.

As a teacher and the director of an order of teachers who knew better and then distorted the work of God in a terrible interrogation of others, I am not the only one who is afraid for the ones who are still on Earth paying for the Inquisition today, but you must release any part of your being that is still in the aura of that time. You must not ever again ask anyone what they believe in. If you ever do, we will certainly punish you.

You will not say to God of All on any day what you want from God for anything at all, but you can beg for relief of your ego and such and see that there is someone who is so great and so pure who wants to be among you and to help you, but only you can teach you.

Your life is a passion, or so one of you loves to tell others about, and seems to believe that there is among you a lot of love and strife and others really look up to you. Is that right? Note that you believe it and not that others speak of you as being so great and right. You will not do that after tonight. There seems to be a breeze and we will help you to go inside the heart and see.

HE IS RIGHT. YOU ARE ALL CONCEITED AND DEVEL-OPED IN THE EGO FURTHER THAN IT IS RIGHT, BUT YOU ALL HAVE HAD NO TEACHERS AND YOU HAVE HAD NO LEADERS TO POINT OUT THE RIGHT, SO TONIGHT LOOK UP AND INSIDE THE BROW OF YOU AND OTHERS HERE BESIDE YOU, LOOK UP AND SEE CHRIST IS HERE AND YOU ARE ONLY TO FEAR THAT GOD IS NOT IN THE LIGHT. YOUR LIFE IS FULL OF WIFELY AND DEDICATED IDEALS, BUT YOU HAVE TO CONCEAL THAT YOUR LIFE IS NOT REAL WHEN YOU SAY YOU LOVE SOMEONE SO VERY MUCH. YOU CANNOT. YOU CANNOT BE AND LOVE AND SEE ANYONE IF YOU CANNOT LOVE GOD TONIGHT.

THE VIEW OF THE PLANET IS NOT AS BRIGHT AS IT MIGHT BE, BUT TONIGHT THE GOD OF ALL IS IN THE WORK OF A SMALL IDEAL AND IT IS HERE FOR ALL.

YOU SEE? NO, YOU WILL GROW AND THEN BE ABLE TO MODEL HOW MUCH YOU KNOW, BUT YOU CANNOT TALK ABOUT WHAT YOU DO NOT KNOW. YOU ARE TO SHOW AND TELL NO ONE WHAT YOU ARE AND LIVE SO THEY WILL KNOW.

CHRIST WAS MY TEACHER AND I WAS THERE AT THE END, BUT YOU WERE THERE, TOO, MY FRIEND AND YOU KNOW, TOO, WHAT CAME TO BE. YOU ALSO GRASPED AT HIS SLEEVE AND YOU ALSO CRIED IN ENVY WHEN ANOTHER WAS BY HIS SIDE, BUT YOU WILL NOT BE UPSET NOW. YOU CAN SEE THAT CHRIST NEVER DIED, BUT THESE FOLKS NOW ARE UPSET INSIDE AND NEVER KNOW WHY. THEY STILL BELIEVE THAT YOU CAN DIE.

YOU WILL FIND THAT THERE IS THREE WHO WOULD HAVE BEEN HERE TONIGHT, BUT YOU ALL ARE NOT DEEP INTO THE WORK AND YOU CANNOT GENERATE A DEEP LEVEL INSIDE. IF YOU OPERATE AT SUCH A LEVEL AS THIS MOST OF THE TIME, WE COULD RELIEVE THE SCRIBE WHO IS ABOUT TO BE SO OVERTAKEN WITH ENERGY INSIDE, BUT IS KEEPING UP. YOU MUST DO MORE TO TAKE ON THE FIELD OF MAGNETIC ENERGY IF SHE IS TO BE ABLE TO SCRIBE AND READ AND BELIEVE AND FEEL THAT HER WORK IS INDEED HER WORK AND NOT THE WORK OF A WOMAN WHO IS NOT ABLE TO BE.

YOUR WORK IS YOUR TIME AND YOU WILL EXIST AND BE, BUT ARE YOU NOW? ARE YOU FREE OF THE BELIEF SYSTEM THAT THERE IS A TIME FOR EVERYTHING AND YOU HAVE NO TIME LEFT TO BE? ARE YOU AWARE THAT THE SEASONS ARE IN THE AIR? ARE YOU FREE OF THE FEAR OF DEATH OR DO YOU PLAN TO DECEIVE YOU FOR A LONGER TIME YET?

YOU ARE HERE AND FRANCES OF ASSISI IS NOT, BUT YOU COULD BELIEVE AND HE COULD BE WITH THEE

AND YOU WOULD KNOW IT OR NOT, BUT DO YOU GO SLOW OR NOT? ARE YOU AWARE THAT SAINTS CARE AND DO RELIEVE THE SOULS OF THOSE LEFT ON EARTH IN ORDER TO PAY FOR THE TIME THEY ARE AWAY? YOU SEE?

NO, BUT WHEN THIS DAY IS OVER, YOUR DREAMS WILL TAKE YOU OVER AND YOU WILL BE ABLE TO SEE THAT THERE IS NOTHING AND YOU ARE NOTHING AND YOU WILL BE NOTHING IF YOU CANNOT BE AS YOU ARE. YOU WILL RELEASE AND RELIEVE AND CENTER BETTER THAN NOW.

THE TIME TO RELAPSE INTO THE MIND IS NOT NOW. YOU ALL HAVE TO BREATHE, BUT BREATHE IN TIME. DO THE WORK AND PRACTICE AND IF YOU CAN DO IT, FINE, WE WILL IN TIME BE ABLE TO TALK DIRECTLY IN A LINE ALL THE TIME AS A GROUP AND YOU WILL BE ABLE TO FEEL IT IS IN THE ROOM, BUT TONIGHT YOU ARE NOT A GROUP AND YOU ARE NOT IN A LINE OF THE SPINE AND THERE IS A COMMOTION AND A MOTION THAT IS NOT GOOD AT THIS TIME.

LESLIE IS NOT IN THE NEXT ROOM AND SHE IS NOT AT HOME NOW, BUT SHE IS TO SIT DOWN AND NOTICE THAT THERE IS SOMEONE IN THE ROOM NOW AND THAT MAN IS GOING TO HELP HER SOON. YOU WILL FIND THAT THERE IS A BALLOON AND IT IS FULL OF AIR AND YOU CAN BREATHE INTO IT AND IT WILL BE OR IT WILL NOT. BUT YOU, LESLIE, WILL BE AND WILL KNOW WHAT ENERGY IS NEEDED TO BE AND HOW TO GROW. WE WILL NOT BE UPSET WITH YOU AT ALL, BUT OTHERS WHO ARE ABLE TO DO WILL NOT NOTICE YOU.

YOU ARE HAPPY AND WE AGREE THAT THIS IS THE GREATEST NIGHT FOR THE LEE FAMILY, BUT IT WILL NOT BE IF THERE IS NOT HONESTY.

WE WILL ALSO BE AWARE OF THE CARE OF THE FAMILY IN TIGHT ROOMS TO NOT NOTICE THE WAYS OF OTHERS WHO ARE NOT AT HOME. WE WANT THEM TO BE ABLE TO SEE THAT THERE IS NOTHING IN THE HOME THAT IS NOT THEIRS AND BY RIGHT IS THERE BECAUSE THEY CHOOSE TO BE THERE AND HAVE IT RESIDE THERE.

YOU ALL WILL GO HOME AND YOU ALL WILL FIND A BETTER SPOT TO ALIGN AND ALIGHT AT NIGHT IF THE ONE YOU NOW USE IS NOT DOING ENOUGH TO HELP YOU.

THE DAY IS OVER FOR ME, BUT I RETURN THIS TV TO MY FRIEND AND YOUR FAMILY.

The work is over for Francis and his best friend on Earth, but you will find there is a sublime fear of death that must disappear. It is in the room and it is soon to be expelled so you can bloom. Something woeful is in the family that is unable to grow out of the past and into the next century. You have to agree. You have to see that any family grows and expels those who are not able to age gracefully among them, but there is not such a need if love is among the family.

You will find that there is a kind man, who is going to teach and refine the work of the rest of us over time, but he is not known by anyone of you from the past and his work is not there on Earth, so he is not as "famous" as we are. You are to see that we laugh at your conceit and the way you try to feel today as though you alone are special in some way, but all can learn at the Master's feet and they do most every day.

You will see that some of you want a degree in spirituality and you want to be able to say to others that you can do whatever and make them envy you, but that is past. You will use whatever you have and that is that and never again say you are better in a spiritual way or it will be taken away.

TODAY THE ROSE IS IN THE GARDEN OF GETHESEME AND SHE IS ABLE TO PLAY AND DO THINGS THAT HER YOUTH TOOK AWAY WITH THE EARLY DEATH ON THAT CHILLY DAY, BUT SHE IS SWEET AND ALL THE THERESAS IN THE STREET BELIEVE THAT SHE IS A PART OF THEM TODAY, BUT SHE IS NOT. SHE IS HER OWN SOUL AND CHOOSES TO BE HERE TODAY BECAUSE THREE OF YOU ARE CLOSE TO HER AND YOU PRAY MANY TIMES A DAY TO HER. SHE IS NOT THE WAY, BUT SHE DOES LISTEN AND SHE IS AWARE OF THE WAY, BUT YOU WILL LAUGH NEVER AT ANYONE AFTER TODAY WHO SAYS A SAINT IS GREAT OR NOT OR WHATEVER SINCE YOU MAY HAVE BEEN ONE IN ANOTHER DAY.

I AM NOT HERE TO TALK OF SAINTS AND BROTHERS AND NUNS AND SISTERS AND MOTHERS AND WHOMEVER, BUT I AM HERE TO CONTINUE THE WORK OF THE FATHERS OF THE HOLY GRAIL AND I AM HERE TO ANSWER FOR THE REST OF THE WORLD THAT YOU ARE ALL HERE TO SEEK FOR THE GRAIL AND NOT BE UPSET OVER TRIVIALITIES AND SUCH HERE, BUT JACK YOU ARE NOT HERE. YOU CAN'T SEEM TO STRAIGHTEN UP THE SEAM, SO DISAPPEAR INTO THE AIR AND YOU WILL SEE THAT GOD IS TO BE A FLEEING WORK OF ART IF THIS NIGHT IS NOT ABLE TO SET YOU APART MORE AT WORK.

You all are not going to be lectured or dismayed by anyone today, but you all are here and now not to be here if there is anything that you would rather do anywhere else. If you appear only to be here, you will hear nothing you can use and it will not help you.

The Teachers of the universe are a tribal collection of intellectual beings who are able to now work with the Scribe in a list of books that come alive with each reading, but you will find there are five not being read at this time. We will not be alive. We are not alive, but you are. You are to scribe the other five in time and do it with the life of your own insides, but you have to do more for your own life if you want to be alive to the life that is flowering in your own inside.

Now Julie is here this evening and is going to grieve that she is leaving? No, she is going to know what to do and who to talk to, to find out what is going on, but do you know? Are you able to talk to her and talk about what you know?

Leslie knows a lot, but she is not talking and she is collecting a lot of her energy to talk tonight, but she is not able to know enough tonight to lecture or to comment so we will talk for her now.

The day is over and I have had a long day in this work and I am excited that there are several teachers here in this room who know me, and what I do and who you all are. I am proud of that, but not pride filled, as that is not a good thing to be. I will not be upset if you never talk to me. I am able to see. I see all of you glimmer or not, but you cannot see that I glow. I am here to be a missionary and I am free. You are not. I have all day to meditate and pray and all of you have to work for pay. I am here to live and be, but you all are upset over me. I get upset only if you cannot do what you came to do. I love you Ruth Lee.

The day is not over and you all have to see that our own presence is upsetting one or two souls more than intended to be, but we will get you to the next level if that is what you wish to do and we will proceed with you if that is what you want to do.

You will not be unhappy, but you cannot do this work. You are not writing to us or anyone off the face of the Earth, but if you are writing and not collecting a good note, you are not centered, and your belief in the God of All is not going to the right source, so be sure you pray more than you do today.

You all can do this? Not a single soul here is able to take away a tool or give what is given in such generosity and complexity of understanding, as this machine, we asked for it and the message was received and it is a gift as much as anything that Ruth Lee has been given by us or others to use in this work. Thank you, Kathy.

You will find that all the people who say they cannot unwind and meditate do most of the time, but those who are inclined to brag about the depth of their meditations and revelations are not on time.

You are to study and know why you are, but time is not studied enough and none of you is yet aware that this time is enough. The day is over. We will all talk it over and go home and then we will feel good? No, we will accept that we are not here to do anything now, but will feel more and more as each day goes on or we will not come here and sit here and do work. We will either do the work of the world better than we could or we are not working here for our own good. You are all able to sit and stare or you can do whatever you wish and not do anything that you want to do now.

We will show you the right way to be or you will find it yourself. You are not going to say a word about who you are, but you can talk now about the fear of being left out of life or being moved away, but do not say a word about how you will be. You do not know. You are to do nothing now, but you will go inside your own mind and clear out the scum and the smut and whatever you have let accumulate in order to be base and dishonest and not your own purest self. If you let it accumulate and are in this work, you will be singed and smoked within as each piece is burnt out of you, so better be able to know now where to begin and what to do about the smoke. You will not be able to say you had a stroke, but you will definitely not work as well as if you had no dross there.

Your day is to be over when you get home and do your own prayer to be blessed by the God of All above, but if you never pray—love and that will be enough for today.

The day is now ended. We will not talk about the work. We are not even aware of the work and what we are doing, so how can we say more?

I am grateful to all of you, but if you feel cheated by the way you are asked to do nothing and sit there, please do not say a word and just not return. We will not miss the time you are not here. We will be doing nothing any different, but the time is short when you will be allowed to sit there and do nothing for you and not care.

What you are going to do now is sit. Please feel the room, come back into your chair if you are still out there somewhere. You are the only one who is not able to be in this chair? You are the only one there. Now open your mind and close your air in your mouth and make sure that you do not shout about what you know nothing about. We will go.

THE GUIDES OF RUTH LEE WILL NOT BE THERE TO TALK TO ANYONE OF THEM AGAIN. YOUR WORK IS NOT GOING TO BE TO END THEIR IGNORANCE AGAIN. YOU WILL NOT TALK OR DO ANYTHING WITH THEM OF AN INSTRUCTIONAL WAY AGAIN. THERE IS NOTHING AND YOU ARE NOT TO FEEL BAD IF THEY CANNOT ACCEPT THE WORK YET.

Second Session

The World

The wars of the world are over and all are here to be rebirthed and then to rise higher, but how many will be able to go beyond this room and help another? Only if you are able to rise will you be able to ascend and be you, so why do you try to rise and then tell others when you know it will offend them that you are going higher than they are?

Are you aware of the time? Are you aware, the work you did last week, has been used by us to help many others? Are you using the work, too? No? You have not heard about what anyone else did, so you are not sure the work of last week was here or not. You are very tired of being told not to do work for you and then you go home and continue to never do a thing for you. Are you weary? Or are you very confused about you?

When a woman is married and has family and is very pretty and has not problems at all, what do you think will happen to her? She will be bored before the end of the tenth year anniversary ceremony if she is to be like the ones who are all around you. You are not here to decide why and what and who and whatever, but you do. When you look to see why one is unhappy and another nervous, who are you judging? You are not at all sitting inside them, so you must be judging you.

You will not say a word to anyone again. That is not the way to be today, you will say, but we pretend that it is in order to see if you can follow orders. You can, but generally you will not do anything you do not truly believe or want to do. We will help you do this work for you, but you have to run in circles in order to find the teacher who is going to help you if you never ever decide why you are as you are and will be.

When the day is over and all of the work you do is full of work for you to be and live and see, are you doing enough to do it today, too?

You are free of disease and pain and sorrow and then you decide you need to be someone who is not like you are. You ache to be someone else or have what another has or you boast and try to become someone who has the most—whatever, but are you being?

You are as you are? You will be as is until you decide to die or hide you or look inside and try to be another way or see another side of you. You cannot try to hide and see at the same time, but you can look and not do anything and that is about as good a way to hide as any today.

When we work in this group, you will feel a certain kind of stress in the knee or the back or wherever you are pressing down on the leg and the seat, but you will not notice until the day is done. You will then rub it a bit and settle down, but do not pretend that you felt nothing from all the electricity in this group running through you now.

You will feel there is a time and place for you to learn to do more, but this group is what you make of it. Most of you do nothing to be in this group from week to week, so we will ask all of you to do nothing again and again when you join this group. You will in time be relieved of whatever is preventing you from believing in you and in others now and then, but you will have to frown at others. What? You are frowning now at many who are very much aware of it, but you do not care. You walk around without a smile now and then you smile at one or two and the rest get the frown. We want you to smile all the time and frown at one or two and get the message across to them that you do not like them or what they do to you. Be honest. Do more to get the message across or stay indoors and never go about in the city with others.

You will find that there is a house and a time and both are here and there and then may be gone, but what do you know? You are not here all the time you sit in that chair, so how do you know about the house and this air and the others gathered here? You will find the work of God and others is not so worthwhile to you if you never say a word about it to others. You will find there are very few people who gathered here last week who thought enough of the work we did with their work to thank another for what they had done to help do that work for everyone.

The week was a tragic week to no one, but still none of you is upset enough with you to say what you have done today. You are not going to be used by another or abused by anyone, but if you are, you do that to you and let it be done. If you are ever attacked and do nothing, you did that to you and will not love you. You must begin to see that your mind is what makes you feel beliefs or not, but the spirit is in line with the spine and can realign you all the time, but you are going to be upset and nervous if you try to do that to you inside.

You will find that tonight the Spirit of God is inside you or you are not going to be able to sit here and stay in this group much longer. You will either feel something grip you or you will sit there and not say a word. If you talk and it is about you, who are you to anyone who is gathered here to talk with us about you?

You see?

No, you do not see if you believe. You are going to know you have to go slow if you want to learn to leap and bound with energy. Why? You have not done enough of the work to build your own frame strong enough to work this long in another time or place or domain.

You will find there are a lot of people who are in a group tonight sitting and talking and feeling okay, but some are at home and blue and upset that they are not able to find a group that will admit them into a room to do this for them, too. You will be okay and you will find the way only if you pray. You cannot really know what to do and who you know until you can trust the view of you that comes to you from God of All inside the small of your back and sticks to you inside.

You can view you. You can rise above anything that comes to you, but you have to practice daily more and more never being upset or bored with you. You have to upset you if you are bored or are boring another and that is possibly why you do that to you, but if you are upsetting others simply to be able to say you are better or more able or whatever, you will be upset to find you will not be in line to the other side. You will have to do this work over.

You are going to find that people who are here all the time are going to be able to see more and feel more and do better than those who are not able to do this and do not wish to continue to be in this work, but if you continue and never do anything within you, you will not be able to do more than you do now or before. You must practice and decide within you what to do—be like you or go with the world and do whatever you do and continue to believe in your own belief system that you grew within you.

You will find your belief system is challenged if it is not good and is not going to be able to conform to the beliefs of others around you, but if you conform to everyone who comes to you, you will be bent and unable to continue. Your life must be one of strength and help within you to do better than you do or it will not be able to help you cross into the next view of you. You will be bored, too.

If you keep making the same moral mistake and you try to undo it later, are you really making a mistake?

Are you using another in order to be able to teach you a lesson about moral behavior and what it must be if it is hurting you or another to do this?
Are you moral or not?
Are you able to spot those who are not?
Are you able to sit at a table and sense who is there and who is not?

You will find at this time we will take over, but you will not be able to sit and stand and remain stable if you are not doing moral and worthwhile work. Why? You are who is in this tribe and you decided to live in this life, so you follow the messages of your own tribe and time and do whatever, or you will be chastised and unable to fly with them when they all decide to go forward. You cannot sit and do nothing and win.

There is going to be a silence and then a new beginning and then you will learn what you need to do, but please remove the conceit within you. You are not perfect or unique and you are not even discreet and you are very neat if you have not foolishness inside, but we work with whomever and wish you all to be clever, but you all need to be here week after week and not seek to be so upset as you are when you are at home. You will learn by listening and not doing much, but you will learn what you need to feed you and be within you and seek what you have inside you that makes you see you.

You will now breathe deeper and deeper and deeper and see if you can be.

When you are ready, the room will disappear and you will sit here and do nothing but stare into your own air. Please do not think of anyone who is not here.

When you are able to continue, please remove the air from your room inside you. You will exhale out all the frost and stale air now, but do not spout it out. Keep your breathe inside the aura until the aura is able to clear it for others to breathe and not be upset or diseased.

You will find now that there is a time in your life when you must sit in a chair, and tonight you have arrived here and been told you cannot walk about or talk out loud or move into another who is not here. You will leave all others outside tonight.

When the mind wanders or you wonder what another is all about, it makes waves and it can shout. You think you are able to confuse others, but never are you aware of the time you are in the air. You are not able to see that you channel to all who are around you what you do and what you believe. You may believe it or not.

You will now sit and stare inside your own work. Now we will begin.

LET THE ROOM COMPLETELY EMPTY OF THE WORK AND THEN WE WILL SEEK OUT THE TEACHERS WHO ARE TO BE THERE. WE WILL NOT SAY NOW. YOU WILL FIND THAT THERE IS SOMEONE HERE NOW WHO IS GOING TO SPEAK TO YOU AND TALK THROUGH YOU, BUT WANTS TO SEE WHAT YOU ARE DOING WITH THESE KEYS. YOUR LIFE IS FULL OF LIFE AND EVERYONE IS GOING TO NOTICE THAT YOU ARE NOT GOING TO CARE OR DO ANYTHING TO UNDO YOU. YOU WILL SHARE, BUT NOT CARE AS YOU ONCE DID FOR EVERYONE. YOU ARE NOW GOING TO BE INDIFFERENT TO MOST OF THE WORLD. YOU WILL LEARN TO DO MORE AND MORE AND NOT CARE IF THEY DO NOT DARE TALK TO YOU OR WORK FOR THE WORK YOU PREPARE. YOU WILL NOT CARE. YOU WILL DO YOUR OWN WORK AND DO IT AS BEST YOU CAN, BUT NOT TODAY.

I am the devil of the life you once prophesied that you would have and then did nothing at all to make it happen within. I am the one who comes to you and talks to you and reminds you of what you might have been. I concern myself with others. I try to find out where they have been and who their mother and father and such small things about them in order to make them feel inferior or upset within, but I am not of you, I begin in your mind. I am here all the time waiting to begin. Are you able to shed me at this time?

I see there are several people absent again and I have news for them. I want no part of them. I will not increase the people who are to be a part of this women's and men's association that is a part of the work of art I have been instructed to begin.

I am not a Saint within. I feel, without revealing who I have been, that I often was too virile to be a Saint or anyone who was able to inspire others, but I was a Saint to some when I revealed that God had stepped inside me and taken over and guided me to help others. I am not here to teach you, but I am here to preach. I preach because I have the right. I have learned through a life to be me and to succeed and to be able to learn what I did not want to do and what was right. I tried to do a lot of things that others said were right for me, but that was wrong. I tried to blame a brother and then I tried to blame the Pope of all others that he was wrong to chastise me for being a Saint when I was dead and could not defend me, but I was put straight. I cannot blame you and those who raised you, but you do. You seem to believe that others are always to be blamed first and then you will answer to no one, but what do you personally believe is you?

Are you there? I was here and I talked with you, but Leslie is here, too. You know that she is a foolish woman at times, but do you see that inside you? You are aware that a childish familiar is able to be inside you until you cross over into the next vision of you, but why do you let the child within you preside when you should be the one who is the adult now?

I FEEL CERTAIN THAT THERE IS ROOM FOR GREAT IMPROVEMENT IN THIS ROOM, BUT WHO DOES THAT BOOMING AND THAT SHOUTING AND THAT CONSUMING WHEN THIS ROOM IS NOT IN USE? I FEEL SOME OF YOU ARE REVEALING TOO MUCH TO OTHERS AND SOME OF YOU REVEAL TO YOU TOO MUCH OF THEM, TOO. I WOULD ASK YOU TO FIRST VIEW YOU. ARE YOU? NOW, THAT IS HARD TO DO WHEN YOU ARE SO HUMAN AND WE SEE THAT THEY DO BELIEVE THEY ARE SO HUMAN TODAY THAT THEY WILL DIE SOMEDAY. ARE YOU SURE? AM I SURE OF WHAT?

I MEAN ARE YOU SURE THAT THESE PEOPLE ARE NOT HERE AND PURE? I AM NOT SURE OF ANYONE. I HAVE ONLY MY OWN LIFE BEGUN IN THIS WORK AND I FEEL THERE IS ROOM FOR IMPROVEMENT IN EVERYONE—ESPECIALLY IN ME. I WAS TO TEACH AND NOT PREACH, BUT FRANCIS IS SO SURE THAT ALL HERE ARE PURE BECAUSE HE WAS HERE ONCE. I THINK FRANCIS IS NOT HERE FOR US. THAT IS ENOUGH.

YOU HAVE HURT THE FRANCISCAN AMONG US. WE ARE NOT HERE TO CHEER OR TO CONGRATULATE ALL THE SAINTS WHO ARE ARRAYED AMONG US, BUT WE HAVE ASKED THAT THREE PEOPLE OF THIS CLASS BE ASKED QUESTIONS AND THEY WILL ASK THEM EVERY WEEK UNTIL WE FIND WHAT IT IS ABOUT THEM THAT NEEDS RELEASED.

WE WANT A QUESTION.

NOW THEY ARE CONFUSED. YOU HAVE SAID IT TOO BRIEFLY FOR THEM TO BE ABLE TO SEE. I WOULD SUGGEST, BUT I WAS NEVER TAUGHT MUCH. I WAS NEVER TOLD I WAS BRILLIANT, SO I'M NOT BOLD.

I LIVED IN A TOWN THAT NO PEOPLE COULD SEE WHEN THEY WERE THERE AND ABOUT UNTIL THEY STOPPED AND LOOKED AND THERE THE CHAPEL STOOD, BUT I WAS AT EASE AND I DIED AT A VERY YOUNG AGE AND I DISAGREE. I FEAR THAT YOU HAVE TAKEN TOO MUCH FOR GRANTED AND THAT THEY ARE NOT READY TODAY.

I SEE AND I WILL OBSERVE THAT YOU AND THE PAST ARE HERE AND NOW ABLE TO SERVE AS A LESSON TODAY, BUT LET US PRAY.

Humbly we beseech thee and the mercy of God and that this is a time when all can align and preach and teach and serve to make this a way for others on Earth to find their way. We want this book to be about a person who is not able to go further than they are today and when they learned to criticize their own life, they moved straight away. I am humbly beseeching all today to hear us as we pray. Thank God for all, and all we say is in the way of a blessing today. Amen.

There is some concern there are too many today who are not able to pray and in some way contribute, but we are here and we are around every day, so we know each of you continues to grow, but not to pray. You will now know. You have to grow or decay.

This room of people is not that deep in misery or in spirituality that it can continue, but it will in some mysterious way continue long after today.

I will find there are several different kinds of people who are here today and they pray and they seem to believe it when they say words that they say, but are they inside really moving themselves to be better in all ways? I will begin.

I have a lot of experience and I have not had any mysterious means of communication with anyone on Earth until today, but I will help all who pray to God of All in anyway. I will not let you call my name, and I will not profess to anything you say to me about the way you wish to be. I will help if I may be able to pray for you and your family and what you do, but do not call upon me ever. I will not call upon you.

You are conceited and you are very naive to believe that anyone of these people today is going to pray directly to you today.

I was not conceited when I said I would not permit anyone to call upon my name or to ask profanely that I help them to be whatever they can be if they will work all day. I am of God and not going to be profane in any way. I will not be beloved as so many want today.

I see. You are here to teach the teachers, and we are confessing that your message is right for us today. We are pleased. We have agreed to meet this way, but you all are not here to talk to us, but to teach these mortals how to be.

You will see. We have to teach them to be? Why? You just are. You either see that your own life is moving forward and you are either in this life, or you are passing over it and not going to be in it.

What is it that makes you so busy? Are you sure these people are unable to know for sure what they are to be?

I feel that when you are born and you have a degree of knowledge inside you and know what you definitely want to do, you are going to do it. You could be tried and held up for a time, but you will do it. You will. You will fully explore what others may not want you to do, but if you came to do it, I think you will.

That is a bit naive and you should agree that all of the words that Philip is talking about are not for us, but for those who agree that God is the only one to see.

Yes, but we are philosophers if we begin to discuss what God is or does or sees, and that is not to be. We are teachers and we will now ask the students what it is that they cannot see and why they are here and what kind of work they want to be.

WHAT QUESTION DO YOU WANT ANSWERED? WE WILL ENTERTAIN A QUESTION FOR US, BUT DO NOT ASK THE SAME QUESTION EVER AGAIN. THIS IS NOT A TEST OF US, BUT WHAT YOU NEED TO BE ABLE TO BE.

Group questions:

Q. **(What do you ask of us?)**

A. WHY WOULD YOU ALL COME TO US AND NOT HAVE ANY IDEA OF WHY? YOU CAN ASK ANYTHING AND IT NEED NOT BE WISE, BUT IF YOU HAD THIS NIGHT TO LIVE OVER AND OVER, YOU WILL ALWAYS REMEMBER THAT YOU COULD HAVE KNOWN WHY.

Q. **(How soon will we be teaching others?)**

A. THAT IS A GOOD QUESTION. YOU HAVE TO LEARN AND YOU HAVE TO ADMIT TO OTHERS THAT YOU HAVE STUDIED AND WISH TO PROFESS TO THEM WHAT YOU WISH TO BE, BUT ONCE YOU DECIDE TO TEACH, YOU BEGIN THAT DAY AND ARE ADMITTED TO THE WAY, BUT YOU MAY NOT BE AWARE OF IT YET. YOU WILL LEARN MORE FROM TEACHING THAN YOU WILL EVER LEARN BY SITTING THIS WAY.

I feel that if you want to teach and you may be allowed to do it wherever others teach, you can reveal so much that you do not seem to know about your own special touch. I think, Robert, that you are going to be able to sit and stand and feel relaxed enough to do it, but do you?

There is a bit of pride in anyone who has to ask another. I feel that if Robert were really in search of a job and wanted to learn more about others, he would seek out a position where he is and teach. I feel that the fishermen and the laborer are more empowered to teach than anyone. Why? I was a fisherman and I caught enough fish to feed everyone and I never ever said to anyone, I am a fisherman of men, but it was said that it was me who inspired God to make a fisherman of other men. I am not a fisherman now, but I was a teacher who became a preacher because I spoke to everyone.

That is a sermon, and you are supposed to be teaching.

I see. I guess that Robert is going to be confused and if that is the way to teach, we can surely do that today. Is that the right way to teach?

The sermon is a homily and it teaches and it serves to show the way. I find that Robert is the means and the end of a perfect day. I want him and everyone to pray.

TODAY IS MY LIFE AND I FEAR NOTHING. I AM FREE OF ALL STRIFE AND I WILL FIND A WAY TO TAKE CARE OF MYSELF, MY CHILD AND MY WIFE AND STILL BE ABLE TO TEACH EVERYDAY.

This prayer is now in bas-relief and all of you will pray it today so that Robert may be relieved of some things that now block his energy so much he cannot see that he teaches every day.

Now Robert, you are okay. I can tell. I was in the well and I was put down there to teach others that if you make others envious of you in anyway, you will be put down and put away, but someone came and showed me the way. I feel that you need to reveal to others that you pray and you do believe and you feel that you could do better, but you want to relieve others who are drinking themselves into the gutter today. You will be able to stop only one man from drinking again, but Robert, that man is you in a way, so do not ever look for a class of men, just look about you every day.

Is there another question?

Q. **(How can I best help Leslie?)**

A. YOU ARE RIGHT, AND WRONG, BUT LESLIE IS NOT PHYSICALLY STRONG AND SHE IS WEAK IN THE FEET AND SHE HAS TO DO THINGS THAT SHE FINDS NOT PLEASING TO BE, BUT SHE ASKED FOR THIS LIFE AND SHE IS NOT CONFINED AT ALL. YOU ARE.

You will see that he meant no unkindness to you at all, but Peter is indiscreet and very prone to speak too long about others who are not strong. I feel that the weak of the physical being are stronger than you and others who are able to move along, but do not.

When all of this is said and done, she wants to know what to do to help Leslie speak through her to everyone, so why ask so many morally laden—I guess I mean why stress so many morally laden ideas in this lady's way?

Now, the morality of being able to help someone and not doing a thing is one thing, but to say that you want to help another when your life is lying in the way, that is not enough for us to say one way or the other, but you are learning more from Leslie and learning faster this way than ever before this day, so you are a teacher of her and you are going to teach others this way, but what is Leslie teaching you?

Leslie is not going to perform and bounce around today in order to conform and she is not going to sit and do tricks and say words so others might be able to say she is brilliant in some way. She is. She is not here on Earth to be anyone but who she is and she is. She is the most evolved of you all today, but she certainly still has room to improve her own work, too. We will help you all to learn what to do, but Leslie is not going to be here tonight and she is still working with you. Do you do that when you are not in this room, Marlene?

You have to see that you are seeing yourself as strong and she as weak and all along, it is she who is moving you to be. You are now further along than ever in your entire being and you are strong and you have it all wrong, but we love you as is.

That was truly sweet. I think that teachers should not be sweet, but if all of you are going to talk as though humans have to be coaxed along, maybe we of the Higher Planes were not the right ones all along. We never saw that Marlene or anyone on Earth was that strong that another human being could tag along and learn from them, but you all were on Earth and all of you seem to be so sweet to them tonight. You are inhuman and you never ever knew it? Now that is not nice. Oh, well, let's get back to the room again. Is there anyone here who is filled with cheer? Is anyone here? Is there nothing going on in that room? We hear nothing. Oh, so now we are awake? Are you cheered by us?

Group response:

(Yes!)

WHO IS IN CHARGE? NOT A VOICE CAN BE HEARD, BUT ALL OF YOU THINK YOU ARE.

Now who is this Ruth and why is she in this room so long? What a nerd. You would think that anyone who had come to this group and been here for a day or two would know what we do. That Ruth is not here for her at this time but for another work that is going to be done over time. What? What is going on? You should have attended the meeting.

Well, since we were out of the world doing work in another frame of reference, would you tell us what it is you want from us and we will do our part? We want this group to unite and not to fill with delight if that is going to stop their flight. You are all here and you all disappear when we teach, but we are here tonight to help you help them to find a way to speak to others who are blind.

What a relief! I was so sure I was going to be told what to do, too, so I'm aware that your teaching in the universe is so rare that only a few beings on Earth at this time are aware of the sun and the moon and Saturn and the stars that consume so much energy from the air. I will learn to control my pride and the idea that I was a great teacher of Earth. I will compare my methods to yours, but you will find that universities are aligned in the way that I prescribed and that today many are aware of God and all that is because we prepared our people so specifically to beware of those not of God, but we failed. We failed to teach them to preach to others. "Thy will be done" became the battle cry of everyone who refused to work for themselves and decide what to do with their own lives. We failed. We were not secure in our own lives, so we were so sure to idolize another and another so that they would idolize us no matter what. That was not right, but it was human and we were not aware of the fight that would happen to others who would not stop and think and understand what was right.

Your life was full of excitement, Francis, and you were never upset by people who ran up to you and demanded of you indignities and such and never liked you. You were a miracle worker and they loved you. But, you are not known by many who are like you. You are not known today by healers and many who say they heal others, but we are able to see that you are remembered as the greatest teacher among us forever.

NOT ME. I WAS NEVER A TEACHER, I ORGANIZED AND I WORKED AND I TRIED TO BE BETTER EVERY DAY OF MY LIFE. THAT IS WHAT IT MEANS TO BE. THAT IS ABOUT ALL THERE IS.

What about the students? Are they not to have a chance tonight?

Oh, yes, our little rose of the rose garden and her remembrance of everyone who is nice.

You are mean. I was just reminding you that they do think of you and wish to know something for themselves. Can we not teach them as we were taught by others?

You are here to remind us of the time in life when a child is unable to leave the parent and cannot learn much, but we have to make up for lost time.

You preach time too much. There is no time and the illusion of it is what is confusing them. You have to learn to think that time is not there and time will not take care of them. That is why we are here.

We came to this planet in order to help them learn more about themselves in the shortest amount of time or whatever you wish to compare it to, but some of them are so selfish and foolish as to think that only they need to be prepared. Are you aware of the things these people are doing everywhere?

I see books and I see people and I hear that there is a message going out of there and that many are attracted to their air, but some are not there. Some are not able to see into the air, but we will help those who can to teach.

Robert and his wife and Marlene and her husband are both there and believe they are able to teach someone who is there to teach them both how to love one another. Is that a joke or is it a job, or what?

You ask questions when there are humans who need to be taught what to believe and you are going to ask us?

If no one there cares to ask questions of us, I think it fair that we ask them questions and find out what it is that they believe about us.

You are not in this air to compare. You are all of you here and there and everywhere and this woman at this machine is unable to be clean of her own air if you do not let up on the work you are trying to knit together. You must use the air and not her energy so much.

We can see it is useless to try to combine and teach as a group unless there is a group to teach.

We have not prepared them to seek deep enough. We have not prepared them to be deep enough. They are mysterious to themselves and we have not opened them enough. Who is to do that? Not us.

We are here on Earth to teach and to help and then move the lot of them off Earth, but if none of them learns and they are unwilling to help others, we are not burned.

You are harmed if anyone does not do enough. Yes, that is true of all of you, but the universe is huge and can do without too many things being moved. You are in the universe and you will be moved, too.

Yes, but this is a dialogue of fools who are not above talking over the heads of others. We will not continue to talk like this with the students sitting with nothing to do.

You see. You all get so in earnest and disagree and it seems to not be working, but we are getting into a seam and it will work, but not until this group is taught to know what to do when it meets. Thank you.

> What to do with a group that has little energy and very few ideas? What to do?
>
> You just let them sit and dream and meditate and see what it seems to be.
>
> We will let them all talk and then let them decide what to be.

The day is over for only those of you who are not able to work inside for the rest of your life, but you will find that grief and sorrow are two emotions you will want to keep. Why? They remind you that you are treading upon ground that others have also worn out with you before. You are not going to feel good if you hurt anyone who is kind to you, but grief is not the kind of emotion you will feel if you do that over time. You will be unkind and that will then be repaid to you by the God of All and many others who are all around you now. Be true and fail never to talk about what you do within you that is good, and try once more to remove the grief of the work you do that is beneath you. If you cannot elevate you, who will?

If your mind is unable to forgive you, will you love anyone? No, but you might believe that another can help you forgive and forget you. It never works, but some of you try over and over to learn each year the same old errors do not take you higher than you were before this year. Why? You are conceited and you are evil within and not going to win. You will end your life in the poorest of people who are within thee. Why not prepare to live in the humblest way now so that later in life you can live as you are now and not worse off? You see? You will over time.

Your work is not going to just fade and die, but you may. We will help all of you, but today we will sit and let the Scribe rest until another day. You will all teach what you do for you.

You will now talk. You will now watch what you want and what you do to get it for you. What do you want and how do you think everyone will work? Are you able to go forward? Not if you never know where you are, who you are, what you want, and if you are in love with another and unable to feel the power of love within you and then able to share it with all others who are good to you.

You will now go out of the line and say goodnight or just say you are fine, but some of you will find it is best to work and not hide. What did you find inside you tonight and what are you going to say to others if you have to talk to them about what you did inside you tonight? Are you able to speak or do you boast and then not speak of you and what you do? Think and then speak and see if you can teach others.

Third Session

This is the way to be:
Fully erect.
Not upset.
Content.
Not able to see anyone, including Ruth Lee.

We do not see you looking inside you enough. Please pretend you are unable to bend. Look inside and if you cannot, leave.

When you can do all you are told, please remove the pride you hold inside. We want the three who are here just to see, to move and be unable to see. We will not let you upset this room and we will not let you boldly go home and talk over things that you have no knowledge of and do not want to be involved with much, but want to see. You will not come back. We want this group to shrink.

We will arrange the people to be even in number and meet within this room twice a week, but only when we can be taped easily. We will not take as long as today, but we will take enough time to tape.

You will not be upset by the equipment and Ray. Ray is able to pray and move around at the same time, but can you pray and concentrate today? One of you is gone to the day, but most of you are still in the outer room trying to consume too much energy. You have to do more and more to conserve the work you did before, so now sit and do your own work. Make a wave.

You will find we have time each time we meet to get you off the street and into the group and then to get out again, but you cannot be uptight and nervous and some of you are today. Please leave your emotional self out of the day.

You will not be bothered by us or LeeWay, but we want this work to talk to others of the day, so your questions today will reflect the degree of work you are doing and how you will proceed. If you know not what to say, then do not say a thing. You do not know anything. You do not know Ruth Lee and she is not going to be around to be told by anyone who is known to you what she is to do, so stop holding her to the ground. You will not be invited to attend any large assemblage or be around when the group ascends if you do not know what to do and just pretend. You are all aware of the room. Do not blend into the furniture and the area, but be you in the purest essence of what you are and will become.

You are not blending into the work. You are not even bending into the flow, so go inside you and know that your work is not going to be able to help you if you never do what you are told to do. You are not obedient to the one who is over you? You are then upsetting your own view of being you. Do not ever again come to be in this group if you cannot see into you.

What do you need? Are you able to see that Ruth Lee is free? Are you able to free yourself to be like a being that resembles the being now known to be Ruth Lee? Are you free? Who is the being that is being? Who are you?

Who is this woman they call into you when you are not being you? Are you the only man who is being you? Are you all being you or trying to play around and be all others who are close to being like thee?

When you settle down, please refrain from being upset.
Now, please look inside.
Are you able to see?
Who is there?
Look into the third eye and see.
Are you able to be?

We will now ask the Guides of all to perform the impossible today and take you away from the center of your ego enough to let you understand a bit more about what it is to be like a human being who is much altered in their attentive state to just being.

Will all of you be?
What are you going to do now?
Are you free of the time?
Who is now watching to see what is happening?
Please leave if you are.

When you are asked to leave and refuse, you must be held in this room until we are all through. You will endanger Ruth Lee if you move and try to get out of the line. You must be able to do your own breathing and let the seam of your energy merge with the rest of the folks who are in this room until there is a seamless flow. Are you being yourself?

Who is this woman who is refusing to do this now?

You are not to return. We feel the bad vibration at this time, but we will in time remove it and take you all the way through to the bottom of you if you do not stop looking to see who is in the room and who is to be. Curiosity is not curiosity when you are in your spiritual work. It is disbelief and will lead you into the density of nervous exhaustion and not able to work. Please release your energy and just be if you cannot join the work. That is the command from everyone who is around you, but you will find tomorrow that Ruth Lee will not be upset, but you will not be able to work and do what you want if you are just here and care not for the work she is about to be.

The time has come to welcome and accept the work that has begun. You will now be able to ask a question, but Ruth Lee has already listed several that she is in need of having done. You will never question Ruth Lee once the session is begun. You can ask questions when they leave, but not now. You are all to acknowledge the presence of others, but not be upset by anyone.

The Scribe:

(I have a question to ask the assemblage about what has begun. I would like to know if we need to do something more to welcome you and keep us as a group working together long enough to get the work done. Are we working now as a group in a way that will help you come to this place?)

We have the means and the ability to compensate for those who refuse to be in the way of God and prefer to remain as human, but today you are okay. Please refrain from believing in anything, suspend your day. Be aware of nothing and let your mind not slip into this day. Make your mind go away.

As a group you can do better and better as you learn this is no play and it is not even worship in the usual way. It is work. You all have asked for it and been even prepared a bit to do it, but you have to slip into you. You have to be able to see you. Are you fit? Are you feeling good? Are you able to sit? If not, this is not the group you are to fit into.

(I would like to ask if it is proper to talk to you at night?)

There is nothing wrong in talking to anyone ever, but if you just talk, that is an effort of ego that is depleting you and not doing anything good, so why just talk if you have nothing within that needs to be said to another? You are too much in ego to know who is good and who is not, so stop trying to be clever. We, however, are not here to just talk and then stop and never care or whatever. That is the human element. You do whatever and then try to blame another if it does not weather well at this time, but tonight, you will be fine. All of you are beginning to come into line.

(Is it okay to talk to you as though you are alive?)

No. We are discarnate and we are not alive in the usual way of today and our energy is also deprived if you are too negative or too positive and you are not willing to be grounded enough to go inside. If you need a friend and you sometimes do, first seek one on your own side and if none is around, then go inside and seek your own line. If there is one on this side of the line that speaks to you deep within you and you connect with very little problems most of the time, you can establish a line, but be sure that line is with a very, very fine saint of your own time or one who is great in the established way of measuring men and women today. You cannot afford to pick out a strange being who might be there waiting to come into the air and be. You cannot afford to open any door and not care. It will in time make things less than sublime.

(Is it all right to just sit and not talk, or do you expect some of us to ask questions?)

We expect respect. There seems nothing else need be done, but if you are overcome with a question you want to hear and will help you and your own line to ascend at the end of time, then feel free to be and ask and see, but you must not ask Ruth Lee.

She is human and not attempting to be anyone who is not like thee. You are only asking someone to do your work for you if you ask Ruth Lee to think for you and answer you.

(What is the protocol of working into the work once the group is not as a group? What are we allowed to repeat?)

Nothing. You are not here to be amused or educated or used, but to look inside you and take away with you what is good today and not be bothered by anyone who is not able to be like you. You are okay? Are you?

(I would like to be able to repeat what is going on to people, but is that not right since they are not invited?)

That is right. No one is invited anyway to any day and so it is created by the God of All and decided what will conspire and transpire and be invited today, so all are very welcome now. You all see and sense that only those who can deeply evolve are going to be able to be and to see and to rise in this company.

(If someone comes to the group who is uninvited, what is to be done?)

We will help in that regard, but from now on, no further invitations will be issued and all must call. We will not accept anyone who is not in this room as they are not a member of the clan, but if they call and they truly are a part of this group, you will be told what to do.

(What can we do to write up this meeting and use the work for others?)

We will take this under consideration and the behavior of this group will be an indication of what is required and if the work is high enough to inspire others to try to also lighten up their spines and acquire information from a higher source that normally is permitted on Earth at this time without a rebirth.

(I wish to thank all for being willing to write through me.)

You are the Scribe and you will write and write and write, but today a power is going to inscribe all that is and all that will be. We will now take over.

There seems to be something in this heat that makes me warm. I feel hot and I feel this group is going to be able to go to India before long, but what is it that you need? You all sit and stare into the air and seem to agree, but what is it you agree to see?

I feel that the way to encourage a pupil today is to meet them halfway, but you get so rabid and so outraged so easily these days. What if they don't give? Who is to stop you from doing what you did?

When there is no reason to just do nothing and you sit and do nothing—not even read and you seem to agree that whatever is on your TV is okay and it is greed, evil, negativity toward your neighbor and others, I search for the word, but I feel enough. You will know that to channel your own soul is not able to go far if the room where you are is filled with such negative views of you. How can you be sure you are any better if you sit and listen and view those who are so evil to you?

This group is now at rest and not able to see that they are like TVs, but we are. We can see there is a cable that extends to wherever your own body connects to another and another and another and you either find the connection and work to make it error and static free, or you bleed internally and never see what it is you came to be.

I think this is such a sorry way to begin the work today. I have never been in the world as a woman would be today at a young age, but why are we angry? Are we the ones who are here and there and everywhere? We are, but we are now invited every time this particular group gets in line to communicate a message of love today.

That is Theresa's line at this time, but ours is to teach and preach salvation and the delay of decay today. We are not Jesuits without a reason to meet this way. We do not meet everyday to say a few words of pleasure and hope and then move away. We are here to preach that if these people today do not move into the new wave of the future and are stopped in any way, we cannot help them ever after today.

You are right, Francis and we are here to say that this group is a part of the entire wave of life today, and as a particle of spray and water and not of decay and future work that is not used in anyway, we are here to help the animals and the people to move over into a better way of living today, but we need to pray. Preaching is not teaching.

We have begun in earnest today. I feel there is a certain amount of work that is being used between the four of us and that is okay, if that is a proper way to say okay or whatever they all say today, but I have to preach. I was raised that way and on Earth I revert to my old ways. You can preach, too, but if you feel that a teacher is what you are inside, you will go astray if you try to leave it to others or you stop and never do it for you. I will teach you to teach you to be you and find a better way to be you today. I am the Francis who is in the flower fields of today, but you may see a butterfly and always say there goes Assisi on the fly. You will not be viewed again as you are as men and women. However, if you feel the need to confirm each and every one of us, we will be okay. We see the need for you to always identify each of you everyday or two, so if you need to be informed of who we are and who you can be, if you wish, go inside and join with us on the other side.

That takes time Francis, and you and Theresa are two of a kind and we are all here to work a miracle at this time. We are here to align a group of mankind large enough to make the world want to also decline the work of the world for all time. We are here to help them discover the positive train of mind that makes you want to create and divide your time with here and the other side of your own life.

You all are going to meditate. You will find that it goes deeper each time. You will all decline to be questioned by others. After all, only braggarts would be aware of what they are doing here at this time and anything you say or do is held up as you, so do not talk or boast of the time. You are all chosen to be here at this time, so accept that mantle and accept this time, but you do not have to be here all the time.

The work is going to go forward and be there all the time, but someone has to sacrifice the effort of learning better and better how to remove time in order to subside inside and go into the tide and let the work begin at this time.

You are all sure I have to preach and that I have to be in charge, but truly I was never of God and I was so sure that God was not just clever but a figure of imagination and that some were able to manipulate others by using that emotional chord that exists and play on the minds of the dumb and nervous all the time until they could not resist, but then I was overcome with pain and sorrow and the work of my mind refused to comfort me over time. I learned and I was sorry the delay of my own life was caused by me everyday, but now I have the right to preach because I learned late in life what it was that had to be done and why.

Yes, you are a very holy man of the cloth and you were there when they crucified the Lord of the world, but you are not the only one who learned later in life why they existed and what was expected on the other side. You will be remembered, but I have stated over and over that I refuse to be called anything but Xavier and I feel that is why you must remove the mantle of pride and stop letting others pray to you and ask you for favors when they have a life that is in their own hands and able to be rewarded and healed and given power if they will just ask for it.

There is nothing in your demeanor at all that seems to say you lack pride Xavier and yet I believe you do see things that only a saint could see and thus when a wholesome woman or man calls upon you on the other side, I believe you could do more. You have the entire work of your life, but you still have to work all the time you are alive wherever you are and so you work to be as clever as ever.

I resent that statement in a very unusual way. I work everyday to help my soul to grow beyond the pride that had it taken off of Earth before its day. I was so sure that I could heal the lame and sick and never die, but I was taken in my prime to prove to the others who work on this side that I had no pride. I was there when my Lord and Savior died, but I was also there when they hit the square and the Cossacks caused all to die. I was there, but I spared no one that day.

You are wise. You could not interfere again in the lives of people when miracles never ever seem to work miracles among the spirit of men. Most do not believe their own eyes. You proved to others beyond all circumstances and lies that miracles can happen over and over and still many will not become changed by the experience of others. You have found out what I never did. You? You are so great among us.

Heavens! If that is permitted to say, I am not a saint today. I live. I have never ascended you would seem to say if you tell them that I am not living among the peasants today. I help all who are here to be with you today, but I also play and seize the day and say to animals, "What are you being today"? I love the animals more and more than ever because they are so faded away. You can hardly see them today.

I was truly sorry that you were so wronged in your day, but when you come into the room and you seem to bloom, it is hard not to be awed and I am aware there is air that is stronger for humans than it is for others, but what can we do for Ray?

We will clear that bronchial tube and see what else is there for you to do. We see that Ruth has a bit of a cold on its way, too, but not after today. We will also see that you all believe. That is what ails you all today. What can this group call ourselves?

I think that this group is embarrassed to say we are Saints and many have always said none of them were saints until they were dead, so why would they call us saints today? We know only those who live in the most spiritual way on Earth are saints and not anyone ascended again to the next or higher planes. All who ascend are better than they were while on Earth, but what about these mentors of those folks who never ever came to live on Earth?

There is an entrance into the universe and it opens every so many months or so and we come through that gate and flow and grow and communicate and then go, but we are on Earth to show them that we can grow men and women into the most spiritual beings they can be while on Earth, but you were on Earth and you never ever spared your own senses long enough to call upon God of All to teach you and not have to learn from your own experiences. There seems to be a rift among men, but you are not men and we are not living among them, so lets not get upset and let's not go into the atmosphere at all.

Leslie we will excuse you now.

The room is now open to anyone who has a question today.

What do you say? We will restate that in another way.

You have been into this world and you have lived within you for more than a few days and yet if you pray and go inside and go deep enough and away from all pride you will find that your own life is assimilated inside and goes away and you still sit and you still look as if you are human in every way. But you are in spirit and able to just melt away. You then decide. I have reached the other side, so I wish to return today. You may. You then move inside you and you blend into the being who was you on the other side and become one with the being whom you are now. That transformation is not obvious to others, but you can watch it when you are in another view of you or in another plane above this one. You will not view you as this at this time, but when you absorb your own mind and can control your mind all the time; you are able to do stage one.

The second stage is the most obvious one, but it is not easy. It requires a state of animated exclusion of your body and what you consume and where you are and what you do. It requires total seclusion and is a dreaming state in which you do not seem to hesitate to leave your mind and life for days at a time, but those in this room are not nearly at that time in this state of mind.

The third state of exclusion of the mind and the body and the spirit totally evolving into the next view of you comes at times when you totally give up on being you. It is a moral combat to overcome the ego of you and only a very select few are allowed to do this and you are not one.

You will find that there is a time to be human and this is such a time for you. You are to see inside you and work to review all the work you do and find out what it is you should or should not do to be you all the way through. If you find that there is a line of emotion that is rotting within you, you should then take that line and begin to rewind until you get to the portion of the line where you went off the beam of you and find out what to do at this time. If you let it alone, it goes home, but if you do the work now, you can cross over the line and be on the other side earlier this time.

Now there is such a degree of animosity in some of you who are not able to see you as you are and it crosses into your own view of you over and over and somehow dismisses that you have the power to blend into you and You and YOU and still never be absorbed by anyone other than you. Do not ever let another take over you.

Group question:

(Are we at a point in history that Spirit has chosen to reach out to us?)

WE COME AS A TEAM! WE SEE YOU ARE WISE TO THE DAY AND THE HOUR, BUT YOUR LIFE IS STILL A MYSTERY KATHLEEN. YOU WILL FIND THAT THE HOUR OF THE DAY AND THE MYSTERY OF YOUR LIFE ARE JUST SWEPT AWAY, BUT TODAY WE ARE AS A TEAM OF TEACHERS TRYING TO BE AND HELP ALL OF YOU SEE THAT LIFE DOES NOT HAVE TO BE AS IT SEEMS. IT CAN BE WHATEVER.

There is a figure of speech that seems to say that people are who they are and what they believe, but you are and then you see and then you believe whatever you see is a better way to explain Earth today. Why has it gone that way? We are all here to discover what went astray.

When a being and another and another choose to do whatever is wrong for them on a given day, no one cares what it is they say, but when an entire clan or an entire city or a nation goes astray, we are called to help you all and this nation is about to explode in a racial way that is not being prepared for today. We teach you to tolerate all, but you do not see that there is such a terrible toll now from what went on and was prepared by the established world up until today.

The Earth is old and the Earth is not going away, but you all are more afraid of it leaving you than the men and women of today going astray and not believing in God in any way. We see that as the problem, so time is a way of calling all of you into the fold in a way that questions not the past ways of your own believing and just seem to prepare you all for the next way.

You will find three of the people who meet today are totally without deceit and conceit and have never said much to stop others from tormenting the folks who are not being treated right on Earth today, but most do not notice.

You will find that animals are fine and not going to be extinct until the day they are taken away, but you are upset over them more than human beings being extinct from countries where they are not permitted to pray. We want the Tibetan monks to return and be able to say whatever they wish on any prayer day, but do you?

Are you aware of the Red Chinese or whatever killing the tides of people at this time and they are doing it this time to themselves and normally it is they being undone by others in the Orient today. Why?

You will find we are not here just for this group and the message of time, but whatever you can all do to help the world be sublime and to tow the line can help. You can help or do your own work, but if you are holier than they, you better do more than you do today. If you say I am humble and do not fear others, you can stay and never ever fear you will be slain by others, but if you do not care at all what others have to pay to live today, you will be as much to blame as the evil of others who do not ever care to pray.

The prayer is:

I am the holy one of my own being. I live on Earth and I fear that Earth is living its last days and I feel that I can do much to save this day, but what is this work and when is it to begin? I want to work for the faith of God and all man to be one. Amen

Francis is so obvious and honest and totally in the work of his own clan, but if you are a man or woman and you do not feel any stirrings within you when you see a butterfly fly among you, you need not fear. He is a man to you. He appears and he comes to you and flows right into you and then goes, but he is no ghost to you. You are who is alive to only you. All others survive and today we will help you who are afraid to die. We will also teach you what the difference between a channel and a medium can be to you, but it is different from what exists on this side.

You are always sure of the time? Yes, if you are entirely successful in the work you do at this time. You have to abide by the rules of the committed that established time for you and what it is you are to do that makes you more successful than others, but if you change the view and decide among you that is not what you want to do, can you change the world at this time?

Yes and no. You can channel to everyone alive that you are not in the work they do and you have a plan to be more and more successful than they can be in this time and day. Your clan wherever it is will pick up that message from you and say, "Help us or we can help you." That is what you channel today. We are here as a people who are on the way over to another view of the world and the work you do and we see that some of you are refusing to conform to the work force of today, but you confuse you too. You have to see that if your family and you need money and if you do, then it will come to you in a way that will never disable you. If your family is provided in various ways with enough to cover your bills each day or two, you have enough. If the ego then says, I must have more and more to save my own day, then you have to work more than others do that day.

You can save or you can raise the standard of your pay, but it is not going to ever be a case where you are not provided for unless you let a government or a state take over for you and then they let you slip away. You have made them your God, so you pay.

Now the means to channel is the means you have today to correspond with this group and others and when you pray you should or could or would be wise to state clearly at the beginning that you wish to do good and it will not be jammed into you in any way. You have to be able to say I love you or I am of God, too, or whatever you may wish to say and then the gate opens wider and wider everyday. How do you suppose the Scribe is alive and is open to planets very far away? Are you?

You cannot open immediately and you see that when Leslie tried to open too quickly tonight, she was swept away with the tide of energy inside. You cannot do that to you. That is okay for Leslie today, but we work within her to design a better way for her to communicate with you and when that is through she is going to be able to talk to you and be able to channel with others about the work she is doing for you.

You can see that channels are not made in a day, but a medium is able to be swayed into another line over time and not notice that their line or the line of another is mixed into theirs in a very familiar way. You then can call upon a deceased party of souls or you can ask your dead mother or father to help you win the day, but are you truly doing work your own way? You are seeking help from another person—even if they are not in flesh—and not seeking God enough if you ask them for work or permission or whatever. You can be overpowered by them, so be careful of always protecting your own personality whenever you are in a room or group of people who are not like you. How can you know? You feel it inside you. If you are insensitive to all other beings, you are alone. You will not be able to open to anyone ever, but to open and open and not be careful of where or when or how you are to behave is a gradual means of deteriorating your day into a method of seeking power from another who is not able to be you.

Seek you. That is the channel within you that will never ever upset you or cause you to delay your day and have to return to Earth for another try at rebirth.

We see that Ray has a question and is trying not to intrude into the room, but Ray you are a member of the team and we want you to be able to see what you have to do. So ask what you may.

Group questions:

(I would like clarification on who is speaking to us today?)

We are the Teachers of the Higher Planes and we are discarnate and very absorbed into your way, but some are here who have lived before you and have been in the human way and some are here for the first time to teach humans the way to pray, meditate and live today. We will help you to control the volume and the cost of the tape if you will not hesitate to listen and abbreviate whatever is there that is not very clever and is not going to help you or anyone at any rate. We do appreciate this opportunity, but the group knew before today you would be working in this way. Why didn't you?

No comment.
You are wise to never advertise ignorance of the other side.

We will also do more and more work for the group, but there are two more questions we will take from you today and we will carry forward until the next day, but ask what you may

Group question:

(Leslie would like to know if the ability to be on Earth and in the next plane is possible today and if she is able to remain here always and visit for a day?)

That is a unique way to say how you pass most every day now, Leslie. You are not here so much of the day, but your energy field remains as is and you pass into the next plane and then you flit back again, but you are okay. You will be able to feel this as a short pain only if your spine is not able to remain intact better than today. Work on the spine and make sure your spine is in line. Okay?

Leslie refers her medical problems to her mother today. We will not bother her at this time in any way, but what does the mother of our oldest soul have to say?

Group question:

(When Leslie last worked with her facilitator Marlene, was she working as a medium or a channel that day?)

When it comes fast and furious and not bridled in any way, you could say you are taken away and that is a sure sign of mediumship today, but Leslie is inclined to not want to ever be in that way. She is not blind to the problems that come to others who submit themselves to the throes and pains of others and then display those throes and pains in themselves on another day, so she is not inclined to be a medium at this time. You may be one, but why? You will find you are opening to channel more and more and that is not the same line as acting for another being to talk through you or about you or inside you. You can be misled by others who are not able to be you, but you in the spirit of you cannot ever mislead you. You refuse to be used and it will never happen to you, but you can ask and be allowed to open to whomever. You have freedom this age.

Yes, in fact, Leslie was accepting the role of another that day, but no more. She is not going to do that that way. Her channeling will begin better and better after today. She was blocked in a few different ways, and Joanne has been the subject of one who has tried to act as a medium for the other side and she will let you know it almost cost her a family situation that she enjoys today, so it is not something you want to be in on if you do not know what is going on. You must be open only to God if you want to ascend, but in the end, you can have a lot more energy and fun and deliver you in record time if you do channel into the greater being known as You.

Group question:

(Any guidance on how to release ego and pride in order to go deeper inside?)

We notice you work and you diligently follow your own tide, but you become confused when you do that and do not anchor you. Please remember to set up a sort of refuge for you and if you ever become confused while working on the other view of you, you can just resurface and it will not confuse you. That is truly what you need to do, but your remark about ego is very astute, but not for you.

You do have to work on setting aside the ego of man when you wish to work inside the spirit of you again, but it is not hard to do once you settle the wars inside you. This is the plan. You will sit and breathe and deeply acknowledge that you are not a man or woman who is able to do more and more for you and that someone greater in this world and beyond is going to help you to be you and you can accept such help as long as the being is within you working for you and is of God. You can then accept whatever comes to you in meditation and not be upset when the plan is begun for you. You will know more.

Group question:

(Can you offer any guidance on controlling emotions?)

There is a time to be emotional and it is when you are wrong and when you need to consolidate and get along and when you have to fully accept that the grace of God is traveling and moving within you and making you do whatever you do, but all other emotional states are ego inflated and probably wrong for you. You have to see that an ego might not like to agree and might not like humility and might not like to be free and might not like to have anyone be like them or better than them, but that is ego, you see?

I am here today to help you personally, but you have to see you alone are here to be and I cannot enter you or take over what you are and do, but you can invite me to help you to see. I am not invited now.

Do you notice that or are you totally free of all invitations to those who are in the spirit and working beside thee? You are open to no one? No, you open and close and you are not as strong emotionally as you could be because you see nothing wrong with being emotional and not strong spiritually. You will find if you become more and more spiritual and drop the ego inspired emotionality, your life will flow from one room to another and never be upset by others. You can be whatever you wish to be as long as you are on Earth this time, but to ascend at the end means you have learned to control all the problems you came to Earth to experience and then were able to move on. Are you working on you enough? We do not know and we are not permitted to ask, but that is a rhetorical question of anyone in stress. Are you working on you enough? That is what you must do if you are unable to feel the power of God within you.

Emotions are truly very important to you and you are so in need of your own support that you are emotionally using that line too much, my dear, at this time. Please pray and find a flower every day and see what a beautiful day that flower is having by being in your power and then be free.

Group comment:

(I've been quiet for so long and now that I want to teach I have trouble being as eloquent as I would like to be.)

The words of God are felt more than listened to, and this is a room of souls who seldom ever listen to you or to themselves, so this is a group that is full of experience for you. You will find this is a group of egos and confused wits at most times, but since this is a time of confusion and lack of wit in the world about you, it is truly the way and means today of being able to teach and preach about what you never were able to say. You do not have to preach or teach if you are you everyday and succeed at whatever you believe. It is there for all to read in you.

When asked to talk, just breathe and stop and look for us in the eyes of a crowd and then say a prayer that you will lead you into the best means of teaching anyone whatever it is you might have that they need, but do not pride yourself that you can teach others. That is not possible unless they are willing to submit to you and have a need for what you teach that day or you are their own way. If you wish to align your spine and teach in the channel way, you may, but it will not be your words you say, so why worry today?

Group response:

(Teach me how to pray.)

You are a prayer and you are an angel who is on Earth to be and to accept the work of today, but all are angels in their own way? Not all are today, but most can see the work of God is what they believe, and if you strive to be alive to God in all ways, you are praying and being blessed all day. You have to breathe into you better than you do, and if you breathe and then collapse inside your mind into the belief that you are better for helping you to be, your prayer will remove the belief that you are in need of being better than you are. You cannot be hard on you, but you can decide to do better than you do.

As I see this prayer and this movie of you, I look at you and I perceive you to be fully you and that is okay and you are going to do better if you breathe into the left lung deeper than you have begun. The heart is okay, but the lung is shrinking a bit today. Your own ability to heal others is not open today, but when you are able to see you are the helper, you are, because you do pray everyday in the right way. You will be free of pain and sorrow for you everyday.

There seems to be a problem in the mainstream of society and it gets to you when you walk in the water with a few other kindred spirits, and when you do, please remove the negative issues that crowd you. You do not have to be baptized ever, but when you do wade in water to clean the Earth for you, please remove the power of anyone who is not able to see things as you do and let them zoom and not be around you. Think of the work and the world will slip away from you.

This is the end of this period and we will now slip deeper into your own work with your permission. Please let your breathing commence to be deeper and deeper and see what you may see about you today. We will work you over never, but you may use our power within you to do whatever you wish to do today.

This evening is over and there is a state of being that is being broken so we can all go back to being as we were before this evening, but will you be? Will you be as you were or will you be changed by what you are and will be?

I want to thank the power of your own mind to let you connect with our time, but your bodies will remain on line until it is time to cross into the next timeline. Please do not breathe too deeply at this time.

You will now breathe more deeply.
Are you able to feel anything in the air?
Will you despair?

If you are depressed, nervous or without air, please refrain from being in this room again. You know who you are, but several of you are not prepared and will be stifled without enough air if you continue to do this work. Ray, we will prepare you in a day or so to do the work you must do to prepare for the work there, but do not work too hard in this day, for you have been in the power in a very unusual way. The sound is in the ear and you will record what it is you pray about, but will not know if it is your way or the way of others. You will do your own work and the help you need to proceed within you will be. You are released now from the electrical state of being able to rate the rate of electrical activity in this state and not bother Ruth Lee. You can now disconnect. The room is to now come alive.

You are not connected to the individual line you have inside established to this day. You will refuse to play with the mind at home or on another day trying to remember what you did today. You cannot hold onto the time. Do not think of this day.

Move into you now. Move into your usual mood. You will remain as you were today. You are not going to take away energy or be in the room if you cannot do your own work to raise your own mood. We will refuse you that today.

Many have come to this room over and over to gain energy from someone and many times it was the hostess who had to give her home and lungs up so you could do more, but never again. You will not be energized at the expense of Ruth Lee. You will repay. You will not be asked to submit to any test, but we will not pay you or anyone to be as able to sit as you are now.

You will not come back. You will have to change and submit to the new way from now on. You will enter a state of bliss and if you fit and can feel the energy flit inside of you. Please remove all barriers that keep you from attending this group. If you feel nothing, please do not try to come here too often and sit. You will be able to try again, but do not sit so long and flit inside and then do nothing with it.

We have an egotist in the room and she is not wanted. You will be able to know who you are and if Leslie is able to point, she is going to know more and more, but she is not allowed to talk just yet. She will find that her own line of work is beginning to be refined and she is not to be upset over it. We will finely tune the energy for you, but you must not try to state too much of the time what you do in this time. It will get to you.

You are all asked to sit.

When you are able, please sit for a few minutes and remain within you and then you can go into the next room and stand around the table, but do not try to do something you cannot do. Be you and try to do whatever someone else tells you to do that is not at all you.

Your day is over. We will help you to get home and feel fit, but if you have lied to be here within this group, your heart will ache from the attack of energy that you submitted it today. Do not do that to you or your body will not be able to live as long as it should. We will talk to you, but see that you do listen as well as you think others should.

Fourth Session

The way of the work is to be yourself and stretch. If you can do more and more everyday you are on Earth, what you do will surpass you and the biggest error you will make is to be less than you were. You can decide to not work for you and help others to do whatever they want to do, but what will happen when they decide they don't want you? You will just not like them or you, but you will also have so much work to do for You that you will most likely ask to return to Earth to do it, too.

You are all here supposedly because you as a group wish to ascend at the end of this work and do the work of a group, but some of you are not here to do anything with anyone else and you only pretend to be here to help the group. We will help you, but you will either become like this room and float or you will not be able to adopt the work we do. We, is the term we use when we are all together, but you will not be a part of the group if you never do the work. The group works and works and does its own work as a group, but do you?

Seven men and seven women began with you, but you are the only one within you who is in this room. You are the rope that pulls you or you are the string that cuts into you. What do you want to be? Strong or just a piece of thread not used by anyone to hold anything together?

The night is not long, but you will see before long that you have nothing inside that is going to help you be amazed. You believe or you would not be here tonight. We want nothing inside to slide or be upright when you spin out of sight, but you might decide to keep your eyes wide open because you want to know what is going on. Is that the spiritual side of you or the ego talking about who you would be if you could only be you? We see one or more of you talk inside to you all the way through not wanting to do this work and not wanting to accept that Ruth is doing this work that you cannot do. Are you profiting from it? You are? Then you are not expected to pay for taking someone else's place in this room. If you are not, leave a lot more money than you ever thought you should and get on over into the role of being a student of Ruth. You have to do more. Your idea of being in school is the one you wanted so you did not have to work, but all of you were told this is no longer a school. You are no longer considered to be students and you will not be meeting in this room on Tuesday evenings soon in order to make sure no one else thinks this is the group they once came to.

You will know more and more what is happening to you, but not if you do not work inside you. We want the three who are prepared tonight to ignite, but if you cannot work that hard inside you, please do not seek anyone who is not within you. Ruth, you will lead with a question of what to do when you are here inside the room and no one else is here with you.

The Scribe's questions:

(I would like to know why there are so many people in the room?)

The room is now being used by the group known as 'Teachers of the Holy Writ' who no longer pray in this world, but many of this world still pray to them so fervently that they cannot move away.

(Who is now working with me as I prepare for this group?)

The group you work for is not the same as you are, and not the same as your Guides and otherwise are not as easy to know as you are to your own side of the world. You are going to find that you have to do more and more and more if you want to open any door, but Ruth is open to the work and all of you are able to talk to her about what she is doing, but none of you do. Why? You do not know her. You do not even listen if she talks to you about her work. She is only going to talk to you if you ask her, but some of you never want to know because you see her as a tool—dumb and not very smart or she would know what to do and say so. You do not respect the work now, but when another speaks of it to you, you all get upset if they know Ruth better than you do. Is this the same group? Yes, and no, but you will find that some of the pain in the group was placed upon Ruth in order that she could help you. Do you know what pain is? Are you aware of the work you can do in a group to remove pain from Earth?

(I wonder who this group is? Who are the individuals assembled in this room? Why are we all tied together? Why not people I have worked with all this life?)

You will find that the room you have within you and the work you do is a part of the people who have helped you. You have made a few people turn inside and view what they do, but most of the wise sit beside you and act like you and do not want to be you. Are you aware some of the people who are not able to be in this room are not here because they do not need to ascend at the end of this time? What do you need?

(I would like to be able to center a group with one thing and not have to talk all day to get them all to center and grow. What do we need to know?)

That is not bragging and boasting. Why? You are a teacher long before this birth and you asked to come to Earth to help those who refused to go back to the path. You asked to help those who could not know you as a youth and never would believe in you if you were not born of the best of folks, so you are here today with no one of the old days and you are not old.

That is the best way to be and you have learned so much from the old and little folks, that you do not want to spend much time with those in-between, so we asked you to help those in-between now and you agreed. We thank you for all you have had to do to get ready to be on the town and in the gown in order to be able to do what they would need to have you do before you could proceed to help them leave Earth. We will help you to proceed now with the group training you need.

(Thank you.)

The group has heard us chat just this way only one time, but now they are unable to say they do not know where you get your stuff everyday, but you study and study and grow sometimes from it, but mostly you are preparing everyday to get the rest of the work you asked to do out of the way. The publication of the wisdom of others is not the only way to share the work you scribe, but it helps them in many other ways to accept what you already know and would not be allowed to tell them about while on this side of life. You have to do more and more and more, but you will arrive before the rest of the room unless you can conduct a class to teach fusion.

(I will try.)

You will find it easy once you reach the other side, but while you are alive you will try and try and die trying, but you will not be able to teach anyone who is not already aware of what fusion is all about and why it is needed to get to the other side.

(Will all of you arrive tomorrow when the group assembles with the teachers who are teaching us more and more each week?)

We are a part of the group known simply as The Teachers and we have been working with this group for years or weeks depending upon what they seem to know best, but one of the group must run by the scale and check out a few books on how to be ultra light without losing weight. You all have to do more and more to learn how to float, but now you have one or two who are not able to zoom. Why are you all here if you are not preparing to ascend with this group? You are not to judge the room, but we are judging from the content of what you want to do that you are here to help the room and not regret that you are here, so please do not speak of anything you do not do.

Now that you are able to sit and do nothing, are you?
Are you feeling like you have enough to do now?
Are you feeling a little bored?
You are not here.
You cannot be here and a part of the group that plans to ascend at the end.

When you breathe, are you doing the work of the world or what you were taught to do by the group who channeled the breath work of a few who came to you before this group came to astound you?

Practice breathing all next week. If you cannot notice anything being opened within you, do not return. Your work will not be held up on Earth, but this room is not going to help you to learn what has already been brought to you to do.

We will not be upset and nervous, but you are if you come to this room with a lot of garbage and negative beliefs within you. Some of you want a guru to tell you what to do, but Ruth refuses that role. Do you wonder why she is unwilling to take on all of you?

She is not going to be held back. She has done that once before. You were not in her group when she had to be a guru for a large number of Hindus, who were in this work, but she was led into it and let the group determine that she had to tell them what to do—and she let them. She was a man then, but she let them lead her into the ego of a man who was eager to please and do whatever it would take to make him a man no one would ever humiliate, but she was not able to learn from that man. She was put in the back of her own class for trying to take care of them. Are you aware of the work it takes to stay back and not let others lift you up and place you forward so they do not have to work? You will all imagine yourselves now as a guru with a group of women and men trying to make you do their work for them.

Are you so human you cannot believe that you would be the guru of anyone on Earth? You are human and wise if you cannot, but if you could, are you so wise as to now see that you could rise much faster if you were not tied down to ego needs?

If you want to tell everyone what you have done, listen to them and then try to see if anyone will listen to what you have done. It is not likely to happen to anyone at this time. Why? You all do what you can and it is not anything new to you. You do not even read or study what has already been done. You think only of the way you have been and not let up on trying to watch to see if others do more and why they are going to try. You need to let your own mind work harder on understanding why you have no fun in your life at times when you are working so many hours.

What do you think the group known as LeeWay learned?

Are any LeeWay people alone and in this room? You will find that none of them is here in the room or at home doing nothing at all. All of them work so much of the time now that they have little time for fun. If they were having a lot of fun, most of this room would want to be among them and they do not want so many to run. You are not working for you or for anyone when you work in a group. You are submitting your own ego to the good of the equal in everyone and if there is no equal, you do not get anything done, thus you reduce the size of the group until it is not easy to know whom you are and what work is done. Do you see that LeeWay was a way of releasing ego and many are now done?

You are not in the work of this group or here to do the work of another, but if you are here to work in this group and achieve what you never believed, you can now work in the work of the group and not have to leave. We have filtered out the only part of the work you do not have in your heart to do, but soon you will have to work on it, too. You will have to submit to your own mind and not let it control you all the time. Are you willing to start to learn to do it now?

The time to leave the mind in the next room is now here, are you able to do it now? I am, and I will be, and I have been, do not exist to anyone who knows there is no time on Earth, but do you agree?

How many of you still do not know the basic work of the Teachers and others? Are you puzzled by the degree of health and prosperity of people who are totally unknown to thee and try to tell them how to live on Earth? You will be judged unwise if you try to help others in this room achieve. You cannot help anyone now. You are here to assist others in some small degree to achieve a bit of harmony or money to do whatever it is they have come to Earth to do, but resist taking credit for what is not needed and just added by you to please the ego of you. You are now going to be able to breeze into the next work. Are you able to do anything now that will help you ascend? You will be fine, but now the teachers are on line.

Hello! Good day, and we all want to say good-bye to the few of you who are so deep at this time that you do not have time to cry.

Thank you, you are very, very wise to not cry. Those of you who are inclined to cry all the time are not wanted by others who are not at all pained inside. You may find that this is a time when computers and people who are in a line think only of time, but you are here in this room in a sense cornered by time. You are here and I am in the same line as you are again, but I also reside in another timeline.

There is so much material and so little effort expended by those who say they are immaterial today, but who is to teach and who is to stop this infernal machine long enough so that I can put up my energy screen?

That seems pretty good to me. I feel like I have a piece of machinery attached to me, but if that is what works on Earth to help teach you to be you and do whatever you are to do. Why, am I so happy that I will let this mathematical machinery continue to work inside me so I can continue to be with you? I was sure that this machine would not be so good as to be able to beam into the energy, but you all are able and fit and will sit, so I can write away today, as you will.

What is going on? Are you sick? I find that the cold is a kind of method of shedding the time and saying to everyone at this time, I need to be at home and I am here instead of being in bed.

Is that kind to a body? We wondered about it, so we are asking the group who is so specialized in this mode of medical wisdom and is very wise, what to do for your eyes and what to do for your nose and why you are unable to cough up all the phlegm inside.

Yes, there is a spot on the right lobe that is cold and full of mucous and you are uncomfortable and you can see that the spot is not too bad, but you are not able to let the weakness get to you. You need water. Please find a spot where you can drink water, too. Please remove you now and get a drink or two. Thank you.

The room is short one soul, but others take over. You are not here to talk it over, but some of you are so sure you have the work to do and have moved further than others. We cannot offer you any privileges above others. We will work with those of you who are too young in your soul to know exactly why you are in this room and why you do not zoom.

What is going on? I find that today is not as wide and as deep as the last time. I feel a difference from this week to the last and next week will be fast, but what can we do now to zoom into your line and work with you? Are you able to connect inside to you all the time? One said yes and a few did not do anything at all at this time. Why? Are you detached from you?

If you are able to connect inside you and all can if they truly are spiritually adept, you can do writing and reading and working in your garden and never be out of tune. What makes you so sure you cannot work for others and still be inside tuned into you?

Are you able to find a stable relationship where you can be you and do exactly always what comes to you to do? Are you fit? Are you able to maintain the table where you sit? Are you able to fit inside the clothes you have inside the closet? You are to decide what is in your own room at home and then remove what does not fit you.

You might decide this is a time to relax and do nothing, but you came to this time and you asked to help time unwind and leave with a sense that many are able to know what time is and is not and why you are in this existence and what you can do for them, too.

I fear there is a change within the room. Would that lovely lady remain in the room if all of you could help her to win? Will she be able to swim this summer again? She needs to open the door more to her own relations within. I am not saying she is not fit to talk to her saints and brothers within, but she is resisting it. We will not talk of it.

Water! That is to be the issue of Earth.

You have water since you are of birth, but do you drink water of Earth? Are you sure what you get in your bottle is water that is near where you live and has the proper amount of minerals that you need to live in this climate?

You cannot drink water from a sewer or from another country and not be upset inside, so stop the water shortage now. Get your own water pure.

What is to be done when vegetables are sprayed so much that if you ate ten of them, you might be upset in the stomach and not be able to wash them out the usual way? We were asked that yesterday, but not by anyone in this group. Why are you in this group if we intend to answer questions from everyone in the work you do? You are here today to provide this living room with a platform to float Ruth away. You will find Ruth is not off line if she talks to folks, but more and more of the time, she is not happy to spend time talking over and over the same material to folks who never listen on time. You will find that there is a difference from one room to another, so why is one time after another?

Are you working on time?
Are you able to define time?
Are you free?
Do you see what is in front of you more and more of the time?
Are you in a degree of positive energy or are you upset and nervous and cannot see that you are exactly who you are going to be?
Are you going to be okay?

We will help you to devote more and more energy within you to healing you and not accepting energy from other folks who are here to use you, too, if they may. You will now protect your body this way. The woman who is not sick any longer was picking up on another who was across from her, so let us not depart today without praying for all of you to be able to withstand one another and not pick up anything you do not want from another. You will now do this:

Work your way around your mouth with your tongue now.
Think of all the poison in your day and swallow it. Are you okay, Ray?
All of you are able to swallow more and more and more readily today, but you all have to do more and more to pray everyday.
We want this to be a mantra today.

I AM FREE. I BELIEVE IN BEING THE FREE BEING.

Say it now and say it inside and really see that you can be and you can find your own ceiling of time. Look inside now.
Are you being upset by a little commotion on the time?
Are you able to connect?
Are you free of the commotion and the sense of motion?

The sense of motion is not the ocean. The ocean is not constantly moving the Earth, but the Earth is constantly moving the ocean and time is connected to it over time and it works overtime to do what you cannot know—time.

The ocean is a mess today. Why would you profess for a moment to be a wonderful person who is confessing the day is perfect in every way and yet the Earth is not growing as it did before today.

Are you all so sure you know who you are today?
Are you sure this is the way?
Are you tired of working this way?

We will help some of you and we will confuse the mind of those who are not able to understand time along with you. Why? We will ascend with you and practice to ascend with others, but you all have to do this:

You must continue to love you.
You must not forget who you are and what you have done with you.
You must sit and stare into you longer than you do.
You will submit to YOU.

YOU all capital letters are the power of you and what you do and whom you will be when you are through being the little you. You are not here to be anyone else but you, so why be anyone else and why act like you think others know more or cannot know as much? You either see you belong to you and you are a unique group within you or you do not sense that you have to be you and do what you came to Earth to do.

You are moving your own time, and if you do not find yourself in line at this time, who is going to know? We do. We see through time. You know, too. You are either ahead of your time or on time or behind your own life at this time. What is it to you?

You will find that if this is a time of sleep and you are awake and it is not frequent enough to rest for you inside, you might feel like a mess tonight. But if you do, remember you did it to you.

You might find there are several of you at this time who feel less and less nervous about the work we are doing in this time, but we regret to inform you that your lesson is not on time, but before you.

You are here to teach you what to do with a group and then ascend into the center of you time and time again so that this practice with this group will encourage you to ascend when the time is up for you.

You will lift!
Can you ascend?
Lift again.
Are you able to feel a pull of a rope or are you bending?
Again, can you ascend?
Are you lifting your mind or are you tied to time?
Look at YOU—the power is within you.
Who is God to you? Are you a god or are you YOU?
Will a future you want to know you as you are now at this time?
Are you aware you climb up one memory at a time?
Are you surviving?
Are you living in time?
Who is inside you all the time you are not alive for you?
Are you going to do what you came to do, now?
Are you going to now feel that pain is not real and you bring it to you in order to inspire you to get over it?

Most of you do not feel pain, as you once knew it. Why? Your mind is not so tied to you at this time. If you feel pain and you seldom do when you meditate within you, are you feeling it or is the body telling you it is sick? Which is it?

What kinds of things do you bring to you when you sit? Are you astonished at the questions we bring from the past to this evening and make it seem like a class? You are not in school again. You are all adults and you all have feelings within you, so let the ego know now that you want to go when the group tries to work on this life and when you are able to do the work for you, let it. Yes, work is what you are and do.

You either feel new when you work on you, or you feel like it isn't working to you. What? Yes, you are either in this work or you feel you must not jerk out of the way of work.

What our learned colleague is trying to say is, that if you work inside your own life today, tomorrow is there inside you and not a part of others, unless you teach them the way you are today. If you never teach another, are you better for it?

What if you try to possibly take over another's life and ask them to give you all their problems?

Will you absorb them?
Who is taking you to the end?
Are you going to take anyone before you?

Who is this woman who is unable to do the work she has inside her yet to do? Is that not true of every one of these women? Of course, or you would be gone from this world and not working within.

You men will find time and time again, you are unable to pretend to enjoy being a friend to women at this time. Why? Too many of them are not telling you the truth about them. You may find and you do decline to say much, but many of them are not going to mind if you never mind them. Why? They are trying new roles and are practicing among them. You might find a real estate agent among the few who do not believe in being on Earth to survive after this birth, but some of them are so practical and earnest and still will be ascending from Earth even if they never ever thought a moment to practice. Why?

Why is a Realtor so able to ascend when another man or woman may not be able to ascend and will gladly help others over at the end? You should be aware that anyone on Earth who helps others to find a place on Earth to root inside is going to help you in the end find out what you can do for you, and if this person is able to help you find a home that is good for you, the blessing is within and given to them. You give them a soul bonus to be at home there with you. It seems strange to believe that salesmen and saleswomen could be seen by us as helping you to arrive at what you are to do, but why not?

You buy what you think you want? No, but you might buy what you are told is wise to buy. By whom? You.

You are who makes all the decisions for you. You can say otherwise, but only the sick, the immature and the elderly are unable to now make their own way in this day without anyone ever saying what they may do on any given day.

You might find that if your mind is on Earth and you find time is not, you are learning today. Time does not exist outside of this timeline. You are often told to manage time, but who does it?

You are always managing you. You might try to say others tell you what to do or otherwise, but that is a lie. You do what you do and all others do the same unless they are unable to shed the body of lead or whatever is keeping them down inside.

We want everyone now to pray.

Today our glory is done. We are all here as one. We are all going to ascend to the proper level and let time end, but as a day begins and ends, so be that person who is able to ascend at the end. Amen.

You all are going to slow you down inside, but God knows when the time goes. You will know soon enough what time is, but will you use that time?
Are you going to find that time is not going to ascend with you at the end?
Time is what is not going forward after this end of time.

You all ascend? No, only those who are at their end in this time. You all can return to it—time and time again, but never ascend from it. Why not move on to something better and more challenging than whatever you do with time this minute within you.

We sense a problem is now erupting in this group. The time to share and the time to do work as you are is descending again and some of you cannot keep you in this work much longer and Ruth is unable to control some of you, so if you cannot now sit, we will now commit no more time to you. You will come forward now. Your back is to be free of fits of pain and your breathing is to remain stable as is. Please return to the room.

Are you breathing as deeply as you can? Remove the crime you see as time. Do not let time run you again.
Are you going to agree to work as a group or do we all have to move to another view of you?

We will assume you all can be here next week in this room and will not assume you have to be at home or elsewhere for an hour a week. You cannot be here and there. You will find the ego does not like to sit at home when it can be on time. You will find that your line of time is now moving forward a bit. Are you going to be late?

Not much longer.

You will find time is not a station and you are not on line, but it is a state of mind. Fit. Sit. Look in that closet and take out what does not suit you and what is in it that is not you. Work this week to breathe better than all of you do together. Look and see. Deny nothing. Seize this time to unwind, but no chatter about empty things. If you cannot talk wisely in this group, please keep silent among you.

If you have to do anything, please be careful of those who cannot see what you mean.
If you want to be clean, try energy and provide you with a life that keeps it moving inside.
If you want to be healthier this week, try to live as you wisely see yourself being at this time next week.
If you try to be someone who is not like you, we will advise you that you will find your body is not going to like you. Why? You are who is saying you do not like you by trying to be like another or a whole group.
If you want to fly, flee.

The room is to resume. Please open your mind, but keep your eyes on your own eyelids inside.

After you are able to descend again, you will find there are twelve people who are not here and will ascend at the end with you. Who do you think of when you think of the twelve who will ascend at this end with you?

When you are able to do your own work, do you? Are you through tonight trying to be you? Are you trying to talk inside to you about what you heard this evening and what others might like to say to you? Are you pretending you have enough emotion within you to decide who you are and what you do and why you can sit through all this evening's work for you and never even seem to see a thing coming into you, but you are definitely not the same being who came into this room this evening. Are you pleased to be you? Are you foolish enough to think you alone deserve to be with this group? You do not even know who you are and why you are able to see the inside of this room, but you do not see enough. You will not be able to talk enough about it soon, but you are going to be asked to change the way you talk today and you will be asked to stop sneaking away to be with us for even a day. You are either a true acceptor of your own life and what it brings to you and the joy you can give from you, or you are lost to your own ego and soul not to be here tonight.

Please remember, we want to keep the numbers slimmer than you do. We will arrange in weeks to come to meet on another night or on a day of the week with the schedule of many of you, but do not be upset if you cannot come since it means you are not here for anyone, but you were able to be here tonight.

When a friend or a lover is unable to discover who you are, is it their fault? You are who you are and if you never discuss with that friend or lover what they must not do or cannot say to you, are you the one who is thereby letting them do the abuse to you or are you expecting them to do it to you? You will have to remember that from week to week and not let it happen to you.

You are also expected to work on releasing the breath as long as you can and longer than you take in air time and time again until we meet next week.

You can eat whatever you like, but it is advised that you take a few ounces off this week in order to be able to control your desire to eat sweets.

We will all go forward and you will find there is sweetness in your work. We will help you to move forward and the world is going to know you are not here to not work, but your work will do more and more for you.

Listen to others. Stop and listen to them and then think if you really do understand them. If you do, then you can answer for them, too, but if you do not, do not let them talk themselves into returning to Earth again. If they never assume they have to do their own work, who is helping them to learn what work is to do for them? Are you if you tell them what to do? Your ego is not strong enough to fight away the blues of night if you try to fight with anyone over the way to work with you, but work for them and find out what makes them feel good when they are around you now and then and you will find sleep is so deep you cannot stay out of the way of the people who are there working and guiding you. Sleep tonight and work inside and find out what you have to do for you. Forget all others. Your work is going to help you.

Group questions:

(How best to share what we are learning with young people?)

The best test is to live and be a model of what an adult is and should be. Why would a child want to get older if the adults are all ill at ease, unconfident, insecure, hateful, neurotic, not able to leave others alone to work at home or do whatever they love to do. Why would a child want to be an adult now?

I think the educational system is truly to blame and I see that there remains to be seen a lot of explanations for the entire waste of a generation's pay on schools that no longer seem to pay anything and no longer educate the personality. If you can find a person alive who is undereducated, who would that person be? A child at this time.

None of you seem to view what we do. We are surrounded by energy and if all of you could conceive a school and do this—talk to them inside you and pray all day that the children will not be swayed by the adult influences all around them today, and then you also go to the media and demand an expulsion of all messages that are not good for the child within you or within anyone today. That will help all of you.

We want to thank you and the crew you work with for being able to save others from looking away from people who are so used to people ignoring what they do. We will pray for you today.

Group question:

(How can I tell if Leslie is ill or injured?)

The same way you can tell if your mind is unwell. You are to not worry so much and let time and nature tell her what to do and when she is unwell so that she will be able to tell you. She is now telling us that she is well and able and trusts all of us, but she is not sure of everyone in this room. Now as far as I can see, Leslie is free of any disharmony.

I feel certain there is a blockage in the bowel, but small enough that a few prunes every day or two will move that away, but do not let her swallow seeds too often. She is inclined to love the sweets too much of the time, but then she seems to be sweet all the time inside, so who can mind?

Leslie is not your burden or you are not her nurse or how ever it doesn't sound worse, but you are to be you and if you are okay, she seems to be able to do things that you would never be able to do today. So, if you feel ill, think to her—are you okay? If she says no, then let it show in your voice that you plan to run your hands over her body until you locate the place that is not okay to her that day.

You will find there is a lot of time in this day, but Leslie is trying now to unwind. She was so deep inside and the time was so long inside that she is not sure now who she is and was at that time. Let her go and let her do whatever she is able to do.

Group question:

(Will healing be a part of my life?)

Life is one long session of healing. You are never without a healing inside. You are always healing and helping you to discover the possibilities of being you. Do your work and see what you can be, but never ever again say you cannot be—whatever. Say you choose not to be—whatever.

Now as for healing and teaching and whatever there is that you are here to do, you cannot refuse if it comes to you. If you plan to study and grasp what others do, you will not be able to do anything you truly want to do. Yes this machine is able to be manhandled by Leslie and those who are trying to help her to grow, but she is restless it seems, so whatever questions you have on your beam, better ask them now. We will return to healing in a few weeks, but you will learn what it takes to get your own body through its mistakes. You will find a lot of confused ions in the blood stream, but do not work so much that you cannot be you. Bob, there is not time for you to wonder. You are behind your own timeline.

Group question:

(How can we best use our minds for good?)

Minds are like computers and never good or bad, but whatever you do comes back to you and can be removed, added to, or simply not allowed to be in you. The mind is not a computer at all times because you need time to be you. You will then perceive within you the ability to do more and more within the spirit and your ability than you wanted to be. If you grow naturally, you do use the mind all the time, but the body is free to do its own things, too, and the spirit is allowed to be free. You then are able to know what is good for you and what your mind is trying to save time for you to do. If you demand money and refuse to work for it, crime is then going to open inside and you will want to submit, but it is not the mind. It is the spirit not doing work inside you and providing you with no ability to be you.

We regret that so many of you are at unrest and there is not enough energy left. You will find you cannot think of anything and yet you are all curious about what the rest of you might have asked Ruth to do. You are now able to talk about you. We regret nothing actually, but we use those same little things you use to say—that we do not like to work this way. We will be back on another day.

Other Works by Ruth Lee:

Books in print:

WITHIN THE VEIL: An Adventure in Time
An action packed mystery set in Mayaland, Mexico. Truly a book that teaches many concepts of space and time using a thrilling adventure yarn to do it. A 'novel' experience! $14.95
prior

Audio Books:

WE ARE HERE: The Teachers of the Higher Planes
The book that announces the arrival of teachers from planes far removed from this one who are here to instruct us in the ways to save Earth and to ascend at this world's end. Educational!
4 audio cassettes—420 minutes. $26.95

NOW IS THE TIME
Fourth in the Books of Wisdom series from The Teachers of the Higher Planes. Everything you ever needed to comprehend time and your life as it exists right now. Inspiring!
4 audio cassettes—290 minutes. $22.95

Workbook:

IT'S ABOUT TIME: Work for a New You
Fifteen lessons that can change your life. A systematic way to connect with Spirit as you learn to meditate, journal, and recover all you have within you in order to become all you can be. $24.95

Audio Tapes:

A FULL CIRCLE OF MEDITATION: The Healing Breath and an Ancient Tibetan Mantra

Knowing how to breathe properly produces miracles of healing and well-being. Learn how a unique chant of the Ancient Tibetan Mantra can open new worlds.

20 minutes each side $9.95

WORK FOR THE GOOD LIFE: Winning the Game of Life, "Power Goes to the Winner"

Two meditations geared to today's life in a stress-filled, seemingly dangerous time. Discover your strengths and use them wisely as you develop your ability to visualize.

20 minutes each side $9.95

Maggie Shoemaker

As the younger of two daughters in an average working-class family living in Mid-America in the 70's, Maggie and her sister were raised in a family that embraced her grandparents' generation, and she spent much time with them. Her memories of those times are filled with hard work, trials at school, and fun times with everyone. When she was age 14, her grandfather died and left her so devastated from grief that she grew even closer than before to her grandmother.

Early on she sought out information on spirituality rather than organized religious teachings. Maggie was most impressed by a woman who introduced her to meditation and spiritualism through a six-week course covering topics that affirmed her belief in reincarnation, angels, and dreams. This still remains the basis of her works in faith and she feels a bond of spiritual kinship to that woman.

When Maggie turned 16, she met a man whom she would marry five years later, but during that time fate placed her in the path of yet another woman who would love and mentor her. This woman showed her a world that she might otherwise never have entered. She was taught how to run this woman's business and was entrusted with every aspect of it. Such commitment led to her becoming a pros-perous and independent woman at a very early age. That friendship continues to flourish and benefits both parties and contributed to her decision to join Kathy Safchick in this work.

At age 21, married, with a good career and a comfortable life style, Maggie met yet another woman whom she told others, "Changed my life forever. Ruth Lee introduced me to my Spirit Guides! Using prayer and meditation even more than before, my thoughts and beliefs created a new and better way of life for me." By age 24, Maggie was ready to sit for hours and watch Ruth Lee scribe this book without worrying about what other people might think of her-or what it might mean in terms of personal change and challenge. She sat and prayed and meditated and listened with the other members of this group to what was taught by masters of other planes. She knew nothing about the other group members but was confident of the final outcome because she trusted Kathy Safchick and Ruth Lee. Her life took her away from the group more quickly than she expected, but she never gave up believing that this book would help others one day, too.

When the manuscript was issued in a first draft for the group to edit and live by, Maggie said then, "It's great to know that this was all guided in my direction. Life has been good to me. I thank GOD every day." Years have passed since Maggie was interviewed about publishing a book written in Spirit, and many changes have come about over that time, but she knows the way to live and how to get back on track if she should ever slip.

Today Maggie is married to a man who did not exist in her mind when the book was scribed, and she recently received a baby boy, Scott Alexander. She continues to grow in her career and remains closely associated to her mentor, Kathy Safchick. Maggie's world is how she wants it now, but changes are underway to improve her life soon.

Kathleen (Kathy) Safchick

When this book was channeled through Ruth Lee as the Scribe, Kathy described herself as the mother of two, grandmother of three, and that she had owned her own hair styling salon since 1981. Summing up her entire life so humbly when she had so much that she could take credit for exemplifies the way Kathy lives every day.

On one fateful summer day, Kathy and members of her staff traveled to meet Ruth Lee who was conducting free seminars at the annual picnic she provided for her clients and students.

Eagerly waiting for Ruth Lee to tell them what to do and what needed to be done to help her, they all listened as she talked about meditation methods that could change your life, how to heal yourself through proper breathing, and how to write in Spirit. Somewhat surprised at this laid-back approach to Spiritual work, Kathy raised her hand and said, "Ms. Lee, we came today because we listened to your book on tape: "We Are Here, The Teachers of the Higher Planes." We want to know what you are going to do to clean the air and water. We want to help you." To Kathy and her crew's amazement, Ruth smiled and said very slowly, "You mean, 'What am I going to do about saving the Earth?'" Kathy nodded before realizing that Ruth had put the job back into her hands. She was confused by this but later learned that Ruth believes that her role is to deliver the message as conscientiously as possible and that others will take the work from her and do what they are called to do.

That day changed Kathy forever. Without any idea--and many doubts--about how to form a foundation dedicated to cleaning up the Earth, Kathy did whatever it took to gather a group of volunteers to clean debris from streams and dump sites, thus restoring them to a pristine state. That is how the group, "Earth Angels for Clean Water," came to be and Kathy became recognized as a pioneer in environmental action in her community.

When this group came together as strangers to help Ruth Lee produce "Can You Pray?," she was given assurance that no matter what might happened once the book left her hands that Kathy would get the book out and that it would be done right. Once she received that confirmation, Ruth never wavered in her confidence that this group would get the job done.

Today, Kathy describes herself as Kathleen Safchick, a friend of LeeWay Publishing, dedicated to the distribution and publication of books, tapes, CDs, and workbooks scribed and written by Ruth Lee that contribute to the enlightenment of the human race. Also, the owner of Uforia Salon and Spa in Monroeville, Pennsylvania.

She describes their mission as follows: "We at Uforia celebrate inner beauty as well as the illusion some call vanity." She credits her success to being in touch with her inner guidance, Ruth Lee's coaching support, and the love of her husband Larry.

Leslie Lockerman

Editor's Note: Ruth Lee was asked to recall her first meeting with this fascinating woman who worked in and around this group from the beginning. Ms. Lee agreed, provided that what Leslie channeled then would also be included here.

Without the intervention of a friend, Marlene Kubina, I possibly would not have met Leslie, even though she and I believe we were destined to meet again. We bless this woman for her help in bringing us together.

Marlene and I met at a Health And Wellness Fair at the Pittsburgh Convention Center where I was lecturing on healing through visualization, meditation techniques, as well as promoting our workbook, "IT'S ABOUT TIME! Work For A New You." She inquired about my private work channeling the Holy Spirit of others as a scribe. Satisfied, she asked if I could help a young woman whom she worked with who had been diagnosed as autistic, but showed signs of a great mind as they worked together with a small Canon computer. Marlene had read a book that followed the progress of an autistic child who was able to reach out to the world via such facilitated work and wanted to help Leslie do the same thing. Her motives were pure and her logic flawless enough for me, so we made arrangements to meet with Leslie and her mother, Barbara.

My first meeting with Leslie was in my home on a Tuesday evening while I held a weekly gathering for clients and others. The opening meditation was in progress when Leslie came into the room, and she became ecstatic! I felt the electricity immediately and knew she was, in her own way, able to pray with everyone immediately--no introduction required. When I read the material previously channeled for that evening's class, it was obvious that Leslie was expected and welcomed as a great friend of our work. That was enough for everyone present-all wanted to know Leslie better.

It is difficult to reflect back to those early days since so much has changed within the world of Leslie and everyone who knew her then.

My sessions with Leslie have always been of a very personal nature, not to be talked about by me, but I believe she has not yet hit her stride and done what she wants to do with others like you. Having said that, here is what Leslie wrote in Spirit when this book was first given to her to review:

"The work of God is now! By the time God sees you, He usually feels energy. By feeling energy, people feel God.

"This book really has good words in it. This book is good for people to read and study healing words for the soul. The people have to read.

"Yesterday is forgotten. The consciousness used will save the real work. The God of All is real to the world. The book is good. God has spoken through the channel. The conscious being is God. He has the time to heal. The book will cause some to be very free, some to be doubtful.

"I am a channel. I am God's messenger. This book is channeled by Ruth Lee. I am fortunate to have had the opportunity to work with her. This book was the opportunity of a lifetime. "Can You Pray?" is going to give a new view of the world's religions.

"I want to express the love of God for all. The work of the Spirit for all. The work of this book is for the growth of our human race. The work of the Spirit is to ascend. The race of man is going to evolve. The race of the soul is how we feel about this book.

"I feel that "Can You Pray?" will develop souls. This book is destined to further the work of many souls. "Can You Pray?" is powerful. The work of the Spirit is most important.

"The book is God's energy. I am eager for the public to read this. The reader has the duty to share what is written. I see the book as God's energy.

"God is good and we are of God. The foundation of the religious systems will be questioned. I am a faithful soul. I am a channel of the Lord. I am the faithful soul who goes to God. The very fact that I am able to do this is a sign that I am doing easy work.

"I am going to give God's energy to each of you as you read this work. The God of All is glad the book attracted you. The book is the church. The book is the gift of God. Read this book and share the Spirits. The Spirits are the Saints. Give thanks to God and the Saints.

"The Teachers of the Higher Planes are thankful that the book is done. So much energy was needed to channel "Can You Pray?." I do God's work and energy sends the message.

"I am a channel of Mary. God uses me to send energy to all. The doubts so many have of doing the work are natural. The work must do the special work. The work is so very good for the spirit. The doing of the work is done for you. The fool is the first to seem to be the wise one. I am a channel of the Lord. Read the book."

Today, Leslie reaches out through a group of devoted friends to others through the internet and private consultations relative to living a life often described as limited by those who are ignorant of the great spiritual gifts each and every soul can give to each of us to use today.

Bruce Weddell

Editor's Note: Due to the press of business and the need to watch their children while his wife, Lynn, participated in this group project, Bruce did attend as many sessions as he wished to do then. His involvement in LeeWay Publishing preceded this book by several years. He was appointed Chief Financial Officer of the company when it was first organized by Ruth Lee and continues even today to give financial advice and assistance as needed. Ruth Lee acknowledged his contributions to the publication of her first workbook: "IT'S ABOUT TIME! Work For A New You." It has been recounted many times and in many places, but in his words, Bruce will tell you what happened then.

"As I recall, Christmas 1994 I bought my wife, Lynn, a color printer and scanner.

This left us with a HP DeskJet printer we had no use for. I awoke one morning with the thought that Ruth Lee needed it and that I should call her immediately. I felt a bit embarrassed when I called and asked if she would like to have the printer to use in her work. She cried out that she had been praying about how she would print out a new workbook when all she had was a dot matrix printer at her disposal. I was stunned that she had been working for about a month editing a complex workbook when she had no formal training in computer design and was exactly at the place where she needed a printer to publish it. She said her Guides had assured her that the book would be out to the public by mid-January--only a few weeks away. Arrangements were made for me to drop the printer off right after Christmas and install it for her. I also decided to make an appointment to have a private session with her then.

"When I had my reading, one of the things I asked about was how to advance at work since I was in a dead-end position that provided no further opportunities. I had been on staff for more than ten years with very little advancement. I was guided to take the very next opportunity to get noticed within the organization. Determined to do whatever it might take, when a job was posted two days later for someone to setup and install computers throughout the organization, I jumped at the chance and have never looked back.

"Shortly after taking that job, I was promoted to Project Manager and named Employee of the Month. When we merged with another hospital, I got another raise and within weeks I transferred to the Finance Department and received yet another pay increase. All of this happened within six months! At work we joked that after ten years with the hospital I was an overnight success; and it didn't stop there. Eight months later I was promoted to Manager in the Finance Department, and ten months after that I accepted a position as Controller at another hospital.

"My career did not stop there, either. It's three and a half years later and I have accepted the position of Chief Financial Officer at yet another hospital--with a large pay increase. In fact, I will be making almost three times what I made only four years ago. That is six promotions--all because I was willing to give a little bit of myself to this work.

"Yet another dimension to my story is that there has been a lot of personal and spiritual growth all along the path I chose back then. I was not ready to be a CFO in 1995, but with the help of my Guides, and God always in my mind, I found myself able to go through the maze to get to this point. How? I followed the lessons given to the public then in Ruth Lee's first workbook and learned how to journal and talk to my spiritual source daily.

"There are lessons to be learned every step of the way, if you open your eyes and recognize them for what they are--opportunities. I am sure I will be able to add more to this testimony as time goes on, but for now this is enough for me and my family."

As this book heads to the printers, Bruce and his wife, Lynn, and their three children are relocating to Tulsa, Oklahoma--ready for whatever life holds in store for them there. Can life really be so easy? Can you really expect to get back ten times what you give in spirit? According to Bruce, that is all he did.

Jack Kaine

Each person originally joined this group to witness Ruth Lee channel this book and add energy to the project to help her reach higher levels than she had ever before reached. They all come from different backgrounds and their work with her was even more diverse. Such is certainly the case with Jack. When Ruth Lee completed her work on "Can You Pray?" and turned over the manuscript to this group to publish and profit from all proceeds derived from it, he described himself as follows:

"English was one of my worst subjects in school, as were the others, come to think of it, so when we were asked to help edit this book, my jaw hit the floor. A paragraph in Chapter Nine was, like the rest, causing me concern. I crossed out a word I thought was a typo--enmity. I brought it to Ruth's attention during one of our group meetings and she asked me to find it in the manuscript to show her. It is quite a large book, but when I flipped it open, it fell to the exact page that I needed. After reading the paragraph, Ruth explained that this was a real word containing the deeper meaning of enemy and should be left as is. I knew then that I was being watched and the work was being watched over and that every word in this beautiful manuscript was important and should not be overlooked.

The last few years working with this group have been a great experience for me. I have learned so much about myself. This book has helped me to break out of my cocoon, and I am looking forward to flying as high as I can. I hope it does the same for you."

When asked for an update to include with the book as it goes to press, Jack abstained. We honor his input and work with this group and wish him the best of life now and in the future.

Barbara Lockerman

Barbara, a very private person who prefers to work behind the scenes rather than in front of the footlights, and has been instrumental in getting the work of The Scribe published as well as helping her daughter, Leslie, create a life in writing. Perhaps her modesty and hard work are best described by the simple lines she prepared to explain her presence in this work:

"My childhood and youth were spent in Philadelphia, within the very strong presence of the Protestant church. In adulthood, I continually asked to be used as an instrument of God's work. However, it wasn't until I was introduced to the writings of the Teachers of the Higher Planes scribed by Ruth Lee that I knew where to look for that work and how to put it to use in my daily life."

It is not possible to describe, without much input from her, the life of a gifted woman and mother who has worked diligently for others, but we can imagine that it has been a long, arduous journey of self discovery. We salute you, Barbara, for what you do for Leslie and your family as well as what you now do for this group. Thank you.

Robert "Bob" Kubina

"I grew up in a large Christian family of three girls and seven boys. I was the eighth child. My parents endured most of the problems of child rearing through the older children so they had mellowed when it came to raising me. My older siblings taught me many of life's do's and don'ts. Although my mother was the disciplinarian, both parents were exceptional examples to follow. We all went to church on Sundays and Bible study on Wednesdays. I regret that I did not do much Bible study then, but it is never too late. I now read the Bible almost daily.

"My school years were memorable with few problems remembered except that of shyness, but it seems that being shy and quiet kept me out of trouble.

"I was drafted into the Army in December 1965 and was trained as a Radio Teletype Operator. Because of procedural delays following my training, I was shipped to Germany instead of Viet Nam. I now wonder if my Guides had a hand in that.

"In December 1967-- I was discharged from the service and by the spring of 1968 I was married. The marriage ended in divorce after producing two children--a boy and a girl. My son, Kevin, is the best worker I know and demonstrates patience and great skill. He is a great and caring son. Marcie's ways and ideals are, on the other hand, far from my views. It came to pass that Marcie came back into my life after I asked my Guides for help with her. Marcie and I now talk and have lunch occasionally. Our future together as father and daughter looks bright now.

"In 1981, I married Marlene and we have one daughter, Francine. We are both dominant in this high-spirited girl. She takes after Marlene with her bright quickness and skills, but has just enough of my patience and calmness to not be over the edge of the fine line of 'normal' with too much brain activity for one child to handle. Marlene has shown many people the right path to take in life, including me. I would not know Ruth Lee, the "Tuesday Gatherings," or my purpose in life without her intervention.

"I have worked at the United States Steel Clairton Works as a Utility Analyst for over 30 years and plan to stay until my retirement. My job is a rewarding one and my Guides are ever present in it.

"Many of the world's woes reflect what man has done to Mother Earth by polluting our waters, contaminating the air, destroying the rain forests and depleting the ozone layer. Some say that one day the air will be too thin to support life. Others say there will be major earthquakes and our planet will be unrecognizable as we know it today. We have the ability to change this outcome or at least slow it down for future generations. We must do our part, and with the help of our spiritual teachers we can help mankind to help themselves and their neighbors. We can show the way, and with God's help make an impact.

"Each night in my evening prayer I thank God for another beautiful day, for the rain, the heat, the cold, the air to breathe, water to drink, loved ones within my grasp, for friends and sunny days, cool breezes, food to eat, and most of all, God."

Lynn Weddell

Many people may believe that Lynn has little to say or is very shy. Neither is true. She is very careful of what she says and does, and speaks out only after careful consideration of what she holds to be true and wants to do.

The second of three daughters, Lynn's parents divorced when she was very young. As a result, she was raised primarily by her grandmother, who recently passed away. As a child, Lynn attended only Catholic schools and is an alumna of Duquesne University. She credits her spiritual development, however, to two other main influences--her maternal grandmother who raised her and Ruth Lee who introduced her to the work of The Teachers. Ruth Lee has been a friend and spiritual mentor to Lynn for many years. Lynn describes their very special relationship as follows:

"Ms. Lee and I have worked on other projects together, and I studied with her for several years privately prior to this work. As a result of the work of The Teachers of the Higher Planes, Ms. Lee helped me conquer severe depression. I believe it has all been responsible for other healings that I have experienced, as well. I am grateful to The Teachers and Saints for allowing me to participate in this life changing work called "Can You Pray?."

Lynn describes her life, since getting involved with this book and this group, as follows: "I try to live my life as directed by the book. I left a 'stay at home Mom' job when we moved to Bradford in order to get back into the world, to interact more with people, to try to understand how others live, what they believe in and where they are coming from, so to speak. I've met some very wonderful people and feel that I have grown as a person since the book was written. I never talk about my beliefs with others unless asked, but hope that people can see what I believe by how I live and my daily interactions with others."

With all her responsibilities, many wonder how this woman does so much for so many--but now you know. Lynn currently resides in Bradford, Pennsylvania, with her husband of 22 years, Bruce, their 3 children, and three dogs. She is a Medical Technologist by trade and enjoys boating, golf, reading, gardening, and spending time

with her extended family. Born and raised in Pittsburgh, Pennsylvania, the family is in the process of moving to a new life in Tulsa, Oklahoma. In addition to all of these obvious major life rearrangements, Lynn is enrolled in an alternative college study program and a participating member of the LeeWay staff.

Joanne Hollstein

Ruth Lee would not have been able to function as well as a channel at times if not for the help of women and men who volunteered to help out when members of the group could not attend. Joanne was one of those who filled in when needed, and she stayed on to work closely with a study group that developed over the years in the home of Leslie and Barbara Lockerman. Joanne describes herself simply as:

"I was the oldest of three children. I was born on February 10, 1966, in the small town of Gibsonia, Pennsylvania. I have come full circle since then and presently reside with my husband in Gibsonia. From early childhood, I have known that there are many aspects of life, the Universe, and myself to be explored. In the search for answers to my questions, I found Ruth Lee. While studying with Ruth, I have learned much and I continue to grow with the passing of each day. I am honored to be a part of this group."

When asked for an update on her life since she wrote the above, Joanne said, "That description does not reflect the new person that I have become."

Raymond "Ray" Hasinger

When this group began this work, Ray described himself as: "The youngest of the old folks on this project and perhaps the most questioning." Ray questions not the source of this material nor the method by which it is given, but the reason for each statement. For example, he asks: "Why me? Why a picnic? What is the purpose of this?" The Teachers requested during the book's dictation that he hold a picnic for the group, which he did not do because it made no sense to him. While his questions may indicate a lack of faith to some readers of this text, his spiritual growth and development serve as a model for all doubters.

Today, years after asking those questions and others, Ray describes how these teachings affected him. "I am much more tolerant of others, that is, behavior that would have driven me crazy to witness back then, I am now able to observe and find the joy in their diversity. I work with people who may be described as difficult to be around, yet I just watch and learn and smile. I do not worry about anything; at least not that I am aware of. I have learned that what happens, happens. I subscribe to, 'Trust in wise protection but lock your car.' In other words, have a strong belief in good results, but take sensible precautions to avoid being a victim. Be ready for joyous opportunities. I now find it easy to find goodness and beauty in everything and everyone; however, some take a bit longer than others."

In his personal life, Ray continues to be a dedicated family man and a foster parent when needed. Raising children who also question authority and continue to ask 'why,' takes up much of his mind's time, but not so much that he does not get involved in working hard away from home and in the community now and again.

Professionally, Ray is a renaissance man. His education in electronics as well as years as a "fixer" have enabled him to repair almost anything broken.

His dedication to music has led to the preservation of the sound of this book as it was channeled by Ruth Lee, as well as other works from The Teachers.

His commitment to "getting the work out" has enabled many spiritual lessons from many sources to be published.

For the love of wife and family, Ray moved away from the Pittsburgh Area soon after this book was recorded. He left his position on the local school board for a life in New Mexico which is definitely not boring, but looks forward to the time when his wife graduates from an acupuncture and Chinese medicine school there so they can all move to a more hospitable climate.

Julie Hart Powell

Julie is an artist, writer, and certified polarity therapy practitioner. With a background in yoga, a degree in Fine Arts from Washington University, and a desire for spiritual growth, Julie became a regular student and private client of Ruth Lee in 1994, shortly after she and her then-husband relocated to the Pittsburgh Area. She participated in weekly meditation and study groups, as well as frequent seminars, and assisted with the early work of LeeWay Publishing.

Through her work with Ruth, Julie was able to realize many personal dreams as she nurtured her longtime interests in yoga, polarity therapy, working in clay, in-depth Mayan calendar study, as well as writing. She credits the influence and example of her mother, numerous spiritual teachers including her Guides, as well as her work with Ruth Lee, Scribe, as enabling her to tap into her own inner sources of wisdom and artistry to produce a life that grows ever better for her.

Along the way Julie founded Heartsong Center in New Haven, Connecticut, where she taught yoga, art, meditation, and holistic health practices. She created the cover art for "Within the Veil: An Adventure in Time" and helped edit several other novels by Ruth Lee, as well as contributing student commentary to "The Maya Word," which Ruth channeled from the Ancient Maya Timekeepers. Annually she produces Mayan calendars inspired by teachings of the Maya Timekeepers and beautifully enhanced with her art. As if all that was not enough, Julie lectured, taught, and practiced polarity therapy in each city she lived in during a time of transition from busy wife and mother to singular star.

Today Julie lives in Asheville, North Carolina, where she is an executive marketing assistant at the Grove Park Inn Resort & Spa. Outside her office, she offers polarity therapy, yoga, and group study in her home as she continues to write and pursue her most recent creative art in the medium of clay. Julie is now happily married to renowned glass artist, Carl Powell, who specializes in large public art commissions, stained designs for residential settings, and contemporary glass sculpture.

Sharon Wilson

"When I first heard about the work of Ruth Lee, I was totally confused and frustrated with my career, with no idea what work might fulfill my soul while providing a comfortable life. She helped me open to the many possibilities that were within me and could be used when I finally trusted myself enough.

"Our first private session was truly divine intervention after a year that I frequently describe as the dark night of my soul. When that session was over, Ruth talked to me at length because I was very troubled and deep in debt. She invited me to attend the Tuesday Gatherings she offered the world.

Setting my fears aside, I went to the meeting and found myself overcome with the Spirit of God almost immediately. It was through these weekly meetings that I learned how to meditate and connect with Spirit--and to trust my own spiritual guidance more and more in my daily life.

"Since I had never before in my life seen life transformations such as I frequently witnessed at Ruth's home, I came to truly believe that people can turn their lives around by inviting the higher energy of Spirit into their day-to-day life events. I learned various processes and methods for clearing out lower level energies while absorbing Ruth's wonderful workbooks and tapes, thus attaining peace after my long, dark journey. That is when I began to live with Spirit.

"Old fears and doubts melted away so my true light could shine through to me and my work! I was affected at the cellular level! Something was activated in me as I witnessed the birthing process of this book. It created a new calling within me. My life's purpose and life's desire ever since then has been to help others awaken to the Spirit within us.

"Flash forward to today--- I am living my ideal life. I work as a certified spiritual counselor and manage "Coaching From Spirit," which I founded. Similar programs and practitioners exist in the world today, but my coaching work is based on training individuals to enhance their lives with the help of Spirit as they create better careers. My company has trained hundreds of people to use the principles found in this book, and I work as a Master Coach enabling others to release whatever is blocking their success while attracting to themselves whatever they need and want. This work also includes guiding successful corporate managers and visionary entrepreneurs along new paths as they recreate or create companies rooted in spiritual principles and laws of Universe that are well grounded and practical.

"My practice now extends to mentoring other successful coaches on ways to integrate Spirit into their mentoring work, too. As co-founder of "Explode Your Business and Income," we produce phone-based seminars aimed at helping entrepreneurs manage the energy of their thoughts, feelings, words, and actions while building spiritually-based organizations. We strive to awaken the connection between mind and Spirit within them and their business ventures. Once they experience the extraordinary results from making that connection, my job then changes from coach to cheerleader.

"So much has changed since I first met the other participants in this grand experiment that turned into a life-altering experience. The power within me was released then! The result brought me my daughter, Joy, as well as much happiness in my marriage! All of this came to be because of this book, "Can You Pray?," and Ruth Lee, whom God sent to me. I am having the time of my life and I am so grateful to Spirit for all I have and will be and am eternally grateful to my friend and mentor, Ruth Lee, for her guidance, support, and love. "I believe this book will touch millions of lives and activate their inner power, too, and it will act as a catalyst for positive change throughout the world. It is my hope that just reading this book will change students at a cellular level. However, it is all in your hands now--the choice is yours."

Sharon lives north of Pittsburgh, Pennsylvania, with her miracle daughter, Joy, and loving husband. You can reach her on the internet through her web sites: Coaching from Spirit-www.coachingfrom-spirit.com

Explode Your Business and Income–
www.explodeyourbusinessandincome.com
Or e-mail Sharon directly at: sharon@coachingfromspriit.com

Sharon Wilson co-authored: “Intentional Change and Living an Extraordinary Life,” and co-authored another book which is to be released later this year: “Coaching With Spirit.” Also later this year, she plans to launch a new program, “Living From Spirit,” and introduce her specially trained coaches to the public in communities across the world.

A Final Word about ‘The Group’

Nowhere on Earth in this time, or the next ten, will you ever again find a group of people who would change as much as these men and women changed since their first meeting with Ruth Lee, but the change is not complete. Their lives are forever in motion and will lead them to great things or fretful dreams as they learn to pray. Hopefully the spirit of The Teachers of the Higher Planes and The Saints will come through to help them again and again as it will any reader of this book who aspires to help self.

More Books By Ruth Lee

Other Books of Wisdom From
The Teachers of the Higher Planes

The Work Begins
The Art of Life - Living Together in Harmony
Now is The Time
The World of Tomorrow
Bliss is It!

The Word of The Maya
The Making of a Scribe ~ How to Achieve a Life
You Can Write About

Novels by Ruth Lee

Angel of The Maya
Within The Veil: An Adventure In Time
Writing In Spirit ~ Jeanne's Story
Writing In Spirit Workbook
Writing In Spirit Notebook

About the Author

What is an author? Is the author the person whose hand produces the words on paper or the mind that delivers the information from unknown places we cannot even imagine or perhaps they combine in time?

This work was conceived in the spiritual realm in an attempt to bring wisdom to all humans about living and dying on the Earth plane. The Teachers of the Higher Planes joined forces with known saints of this world whose names are easily recognized, in addition to others who refused to be named.

So who then is the true author of *Can You Pray?*

Ruth Lee is a spiritual channel and author of various published works. She is the only known channel who works with groups of entities who bring information to our world from planes far removed in an effort to help us live successfully here on Earth now. Ms. Lee taught classes, seminars, and workshops, as well as hosting a radio talk show dealing with issues of the spirit, in addition to channeling the Spirit Guides of thousands of individuals before she scribed this book.

Ms. Lee resides in Florida, but is a native of Pittsburgh, Pennsylvania, where this work in spirit was achieved. For more information on the works of Ruth Lee, Scribe, visit https://leewaypublishing.com/

Recovery counselors and life adjustment coaches use her books and tapes as part of their therapy work, but the majority of her clients, readers, and audiences use the work on their own at home to enhance self-development.

www.ingramcontent.com/pod-product-compliance
Lightning Source LLC
Chambersburg PA
CBHW060236100426
42742CB00011B/1547
* 9 7 8 1 9 3 4 5 0 9 9 5 1 *